RICHARD F. YOUNG

RESISTANT HINDUISM

PUBLICATIONS
OF THE DE NOBILI RESEARCH LIBRARY

EDITED BY

GERHARD OBERHAMMER
INDOLOGICAL INSTITUTE
UNIVERSITY OF VIENNA

VOLUME VIII

COMMISSION AGENTS: E. J. BRILL, LEIDEN
GEROLD & CO., VIENNA–MOTILAL BANARSIDASS, DELHI

RESISTANT HINDUISM

SANSKRIT SOURCES ON ANTI-CHRISTIAN APOLOGETICS IN EARLY NINETEENTH-CENTURY INDIA

BY

RICHARD FOX YOUNG

VIENNA 1981

The publication of this work was made possible by the financial support granted by the Bundesministerium für Wissenschaft und Forschung, the De Nobili Research Foundation, the Missionswissenschaftliches Institut Missio, Aachen, and the Department of South Asia Regional Studies of the University of Pennsylvania

—ISBN 3 900271 09 7

Druck: Ernst Becvar, A-1150 Wien

CONTENTS

To Bror Tiliander

ACKNOWLEDGMENTS

Throughout the course of this research, I have benefited from the wise counsel of numerous authorities of various nationalities. To them, and not only to the subject itself, must I attribute the considerable pleasure that I have derived from this project. Especially to be credited are my professors in the Department of Oriental Studies at the University of Pennsylvania, whose patient and skillful teaching whetted my interest in Indology and enabled me to undertake research in that field. To Professor Ludo Rocher I owe thanks for making the intricacies of Sanskrit intelligible to me; to Professor Peter Gaeffke for doing the same with Hindi; and to Professor Wilhelm Halbfass for leading me artfully through the labyrinths of Indian philosophy. Despite their demanding schedules and my often importunate requests, all three never stinted either on time or attention. Each read with me in the principal texts constituting this study, giving me bearings I needed in order to find my way.

To my advisor, Professor Halbfass, my debt is immense. He brought to my attention Nīlakaṇṭha Goreh's Ṣaḍdarśanadarpaṇa, the final product in the series of treatises comprising what I call the Mataparīkṣā Controversy. Without this original clue, I would never have discovered the other parts to this literary puzzle, nor would I have been able to make of them a coherent interpretation without his guidance. At the initial stage he convinced me that this topic rightly belongs to Indology rather than theology; and to the end, through much consultation and many letters, he constantly widened my horizon with respect to the implications of my materials.

Enroute to India for a year of research, generously provided by a grant from the American Institute for Indian Studies, I was able to spend five months in Great Britain, utilizing the libraries and archival resources there. That my time was productively spent was due in part to the cooperative staffs of the British Library's Department of Oriental Manuscripts and Printed Books and the India Office Library and Records. Especially helpful were the archivists of the Church Missionary Society, the Baptist Missionary Society and the United Society for the Propagation of the Gospel, all of which must be credited with sparing no cost to preserve materials invaluable for this study. Also to be thanked is the University of Edinburgh for granting permission to reproduce the John Muir portrait.

While in Europe I also had the privelege of consulting in Lund with Reverend Bror Fredrik Tiliander, who served the Church of Sweden for many years in Andhra Pradesh. The example he set for me is not adequately measured by citations in the notes referring to his pioneering doctoral dissertation, Christian and Hindu Terminology. If my research is subsequently applied to interreligious hermeneutics, I would hope it follows methods already established by this outstanding missionary-scholar.

I am also grateful to Professor Dr. Gerhard Oberhammer, Director of the Indological Institute of the University of Vienna, for impressing upon me the principle that good theology cannot ignore the results of Indological scholarship — a conclusion that I hope Christian readers of this study will reach independently. A newcomer to scholarship always hopes that the significance of his research will be recognized by scholars whom he respects and admires. It has been my good fortune to receive from Professor Oberhammer not only expert guidance and constant encouragement but also a generous offer to include the present volume as the eighth in the De Nobili Research Library Series.

The ease with which I was able to conduct my research in India, 1977—78, was in large measure due to the assistance of Tarun Mitra, Calcutta representative for the American Institute for Indian Studies; and to the Reverend Pritam Santram and the Reverend Michael Westall of Bishop's College, Calcutta, with which I was temporarily affiliated. Living in that institution brought me into contact with the heritage of Indian Christian hermeneutics, particularly with respect to Church Sanskrit, which was given momentum by the first college principal, William Hodge Mill, in the early nineteenth century. The staff of the Carey Library of Serampore College deserves recognition for help in locating many of the journal articles cited in the bibliography. To Fr. Pierre Fallon, SJ, my dissertation advisor while in India, I am grateful for many hours of conversation in his North Calcutta flat, acquainting me with his observations on terminological obstacles impeding interreligious dialogue today, just as they did during the Mataparīkṣā Controversy — observations informed by his immersion in the life of Bengali Hindus.

Bringing the writing of this dissertation to a close while teaching in Japan has made necessary the utilization of resources in the Sanskrit library of the University of Tokyo. Through the good offices of Professor Sengaku Mayeda, I have had access to everything I needed. Thanks to Professor Dr. Minoru Hara, I have been able to solve several Sanskrit conundrums. Without contact with these Indologists, Tokyo would indeed have been an incongrous place in which to prepare for publication a dissertation bearing on India.

Despite my debt to the above-named scholars, whatever mistakes I may have made must not be attributed to them.

I am especially grateful to my wife for her patience, encouragement, and careful typing of the original drafts and final copy during the last four years.

Tokyo, March 15, 1981 *Richard Fox Young*

ABBREVIATIONS

ABORI	Annals of the Bhandarkar Oriental Research Institute
AJ	Asiatic Journal
AR	Asiatik Researches
ĀSS	Ānandāśrama Sanskrit Series
BI	Bibliotheca Indica
BM	Benares Magazine
BMS	Baptist Missionary Society (London)
BPP	Bengal: Past and Present
CCO	Calcutta Christian Observer
CI	Christian Intelligencer (Calcutta)
CMS	Church Missionary Society (London)
CR	Calcutta Review
EIC	East India Company
FI	Friend of India
Hara.	Haracandra Tarkapañcānana
IA	Indian Antiquary
ICHR	Indian Church History Review
ICQR	Indian Church Quarterly Review (Calcutta)
IOLR	India Office Library and Records (London)
JAOS	Journal of the American Oriental Society
JASB	Journal of the Asiatic Society of Bengal
JES	Journal of Ecumenical Studies
LGPGD	Lieutenant Governor's Proceedings in the General Department, North-Western Provinces (IOLR, London)
LṬ	Laghutaṃka; Subājī Bāpu, 1839
MP	Mataparīkṣā; Muir 1839, 1840, 1852—54, 1910
MPO	Mataparīkṣottara; Hara., 1840
MPŚ	Mataparīkṣāśikṣā; Soma., 1839
MS	Morning Star (Jaffna)
NEB	New English Bible, 1971
Nīla.	Nīlakaṇṭha Goreh
NWP	North Western Provinces
OCS	Oriental Christian Spectator (Bombay)
PEW	Philosophy East and West
PPMGM	Prajña Pāṭhshālā Maṇḍala Grantha Mālā
RS	Religion and Society
SBE	Sacred Books of the East
SBH	Sacred Books of the Hindus
SJS	Singhi Jain Series

ŚKhS	Śrīkhṛṣṭasaṃgītā; Mill, 1831—37, 1842
Soma.	Somanātha
SPG	Society for the Propagation of the Gospel (London)
SSJE	Society of St. John the Evangelist (Oxford)
SŚP	Siddhāntaśiromaṇiprakāśa; Subājī Bāpu, 1836
ŚTV	Śāstratattvavinirṇaya: Nīla., 1844, 1950
TM	The Missionary (Calcutta)
WZKS	Wiener Zeitschrift für die Kunde Südasiens
ZMR	Zeitschrift für Missionswissenschaft und Religionswissenschaft

I. INTRODUCTION

This is a study in Hindu apologetics. In the history of this subject, there are a number of lacunae, many of which concern Christianity. The objective here is to fill in one of those gaps by drawing attention to apologetical efforts undertaken by pandits writing in Sanskrit against Christianity during the first half of the nineteenth century, a time of religious, philosophical, and social ferment in India.

One may ask why such a study as this is attempted, especially when apologetics is a term generally associated with that branch of systematic theology responsible for defending Christianity vis-à-vis its adversaries by scriptural argumentation or otherwise. Although seldom called by this name, there is in Hinduism a similar type of intellectual activity definitely falling into this category. Hindu apologists did not defend Hinduism as such, but proponents of the great *darśanas*, philosophical views or systems, endeavored to brace their own ideas or doctrines by exposing the fallacies in others. To cite only one instance, Śaṅkara's commentary on the Brahmasūtras refuted, in turn, each of the major theories, cosmological, metaphysical, soteriological, etc., to which other Hindu thinkers, Buddhists, Jains, and materialists subscribed. Apologetics was so much a part of classical works on religion and philosophy that a text without at least an adumbration of the standard criticisms of its rivals would surely seem incomplete. Hindus may have neglected interreligious apologetics, but they had ample practice in the field of intrareligious argumentation to prepare for readjusting their perspective to include religions of non-Indian origin.

Scholars have made many theoretical and comparative studies of the relationship between Christianity and Hinduism, but have given scant attention to the history of interreligious dialogue in India. Partly this is due to the paucity and obscurity of sources available in the pandits' own words; partly to a suspicion that the Christian records are slanted in their own favor; and partly to an unfounded assumption that Christianity did not excite in pandits much interest that could properly be called religious or philosophic. Whereas the factor mentioned first requires no explanation, the third, even more than the second, needs reconsideration, particularly in view of the important role played by apologetics in classical Sanskrit literature. One would hardly expect traditionally educated Hindus, imbued with the perspective of classical apologists, to have ignored Christianity's understanding of God, man, the world, and salvation, while evincing a sudden preoccupation with its social dimensions. It is true that, in comparison with the volume of material referring to their own schools of thought and other religions of Indian origin, Hindu pandits wrote extremely little about

Christianity. However, this contrast has led some writers to unduly emphasize social rather than explicitly religious and philosophic interaction between India and the West. To correct this misperception, literature in Indian languages bearing on the Hindu-Christian encounter must be brought to light.

The lack of documentation relating to interreligious encounter is more than merely a problem of the unlikely survival into the modern period of relatively obscure treatises. It is also a reflection of the insularity into which many Hindu thinkers had withdrawn, perhaps starting with the disappearance of the great philosophers and the rise of scholasticism. One finds that pandits wrote virtually nothing about foreign religious influences in India, restricting themselves to repetition of standard arguments against ancient rivals. Why this devitalization of a once vigorous apologetical tradition occurred, especially in view of the advent of Islam and aggressively propagandistic Christianity, is a question of central importance. One can see that, with so little written material referring to these religions in existence, there is some justification for the idea that pandits simply were not impressed with their doctrinal content. The late V. Raghavan attributed this absence of anti-Islamic and anti-Christian apologetical texts to another factor as well: dissipation in scholarly circles, bred by intrareligious jealousies.

"When Hinduism had to be safeguarded against the Buddhist and Jain faiths, Sanskrit philosophers studied thoroughly the metaphysics of the rival schools and kept up a continuous philosophical contest in the works they produced. Later, unfortunately, the Pandit dissipated himself with his internecine disputes, the pluralists and the monists, the realists and the idealists, the theists and the absolutists, and the different theistic sects fighting with one another. While the earlier Sanskritist forced the opponent to read his language, his literature and school and met him in debate in the pages of his works, the later Pandit failed to play this role when Hinduism was faced with Islam first and Christianity later; ... and to that extent Indian philosophical literature failed to keep itself abreast of the need of the times" (Raghavan, 1957: 215).

But this diagnosis involves a moral judgment; it shows traces of disappointment, stemming perhaps from nationalistic feelings. A more accurate understanding of this shortage of documents commenting on Christianity must take into account the theoretical background governing Hindu perceptions of themselves, their land, and religion. Therefore, an explanation of those factors inhibiting their encounter with non-Indian religions is as pertinent to this study as their apologetics itself.

In point of fact, the kind of apologetical material that Raghavan thinks the dissipation of nineteenth-century pandits precluded does exist. The first materials of this sort in Sanskrit appeared in response to an acerbic but sophisticated Christian treatise, also in Sanskrit, by John Muir, a Scottish civil servant and Orientalist. His Mataparīkṣā (An Examination of Religions), written in 1839 and revised twice, aroused the interest and indignation of three pandits, who were conservative in varying degrees. What resulted was nothing less than a full-scale controversy. The treatises written in criticism of Muir were the following: in 1839 the Mataparīkṣāśikṣā (A Lesson for the [Author of the] Mataparīkṣā), written by Somanātha, an apparent pseudonym for a pandit by the name of Subājī Bāpu living in Central India; in 1840 the Mataparīkṣottara (An Answer to the Mataparīkṣā), written by Haracandra Tarkapañcānana, a Calcutta pandit; during 1844 and 1845 the Śāstratattvavinirṇaya (A Verdict on the Truth of the Śāstra), composed by a Benares pandit, Nīlakaṇṭha Goreh (or Gore). Belated though they may have been, these texts are definite proof that Christianity did evoke from Hindu pandits an intelligent response to its philosophic and theological content, and that they had emerged demonstrably from the isolation to which it seems they had become accustomed.

However, what is referred to in this study as the Mataparīkṣā (hereafter MP) Controversy was not the first occurrence of its kind in India. More precisely, it was the earliest conflict to which there is access through an Indian language. An earlier debate and tract-battle was waged in the previous decade, the 1830s, in the Bombay area. Eighteenth-century correspondence between a missionary in South India and his brahmin partners-in-dialogue provides more information on the Hindu-Christian encounter, which can be reconstructed only sketchily during this period. But with these available points of reference, chapter two places the MP Controversy in its historical relationship with previously recorded dialogues. It provides excerpts from these documents, no longer available except in English or German, in order also to trace the lineaments of Hindu apologetics from as early a period as possible into the first half of the nineteenth century.

At about the same time that Hindu pandits were recovering from their reluctance to counteract the threat posed by an alien and increasingly powerful religion in their midst, scholarly Christian evangelists were engaged in developing specialized terminology in Sanskrit for propagating their message more effectively than had theretofore been possible. It was not fortuitous that the MP Controversy occurred when it did. Discovering that Christianity could be expressed in their own words and sacred cadences helped pandits to face that religion more openly. With reference to the present subject, real dialogue was possible because of the clarity and precision of Muir's MP, which was due, in turn, to the contribution of European predecessors. They had supplied him with a largely ready-made theological vocabulary, the result of diligent hermeneutical experimentation. Moreover, they had composed treatises of their own, which served as models for the MP. A thorough understanding of that text, therefore, is enhanced by an appreciation of the efforts of colleagues upon whom Muir relied. This subject is discussed in the third chapter.

It may be wondered at that chapter four probes deeply into what can be known of the participants in the MP Controversy. This information has been included because this event was more an encounter between a single Christian and three individual Hindus than between Christianity and Hinduism in the sense of abstract bodies of doctrine to which believers invariably adhere. Each disputant brought to the fray his own specific viewpoint; even the pandits were incapable of unanimity. Present-day Hindu or Christian readers are not likely, therefore, to recognize in either the Mataparīkṣāśikṣā (hereafter cited as MPŚ), the Mataparīkṣottara (MPO), Śāstratattvavinirṇaya (ŚTV), or MP those tenets or perspectives now prevailing. The latter text, for example, is completely comprehensible only to readers informed about a variety of Christian apologetics (basically Paleyan) that was fashionable in Europe before the mid-nineteenth century. Muir and the Hindu apologists must, therefore, be viewed in the light of their personal backgrounds.

The subject of chapter five is strictly apologetics. Extracts from the MPŚ of Somanātha (hereafter cited as Soma.), the MPO of Haracandra (Hara.) and the ŚTV of Nīlakaṇṭa (Nīla.) are translated selectively in order to avoid repetition, a fault to which each pandit was susceptible. The chief concern is to demonstrate, insofar as possible, the linkages between their apologetics and the classical tradition. It is probable that the three treatises largely followed defensive strategies previously mapped out within Hinduism itself in answer to the dissident viewpoints that have been expressed in each phase of its development. Due to the long-standing apologetical interest of classical Hindu authorities, to which allusion has already been made, it would hardly be likely that the arguments in the MP Controversy emerged from a void.

In addition to concern for historical connections, there is the need to assess to what extent the pandits resisted or accommodated Christianity. Any encounter between religions may involve a continuum of postures, ranging from extreme hostility to liberal attempts at coming to terms with mutual co-existence by means of syncretism, inclusivism, some form of the idea of the equality of religions, etc. These stances emerge as religions are processed through apologetical frameworks. "Resistance," then, means intellectual opposition to presuppositions at variance with one's own, whether religious, philosophical, or cultic. "Accommodation" means an attempt to adapt to or reconcile the content of Hinduism with Christianity, whether or not this is done in such a way as to preserve continuity with tradition. Naturally, accommodation of the opposite variety, bending Christianity to fit Hinduism, is also pertinent. These matters, too, are dealt with in the fifth chapter.

The sixth and final chapter concentrates on the matter of religious plurality. The pandits had not only to combat Christianity but also to explain why it exists and what function it has in an overall scheme of religion. While not theologians of religion *per se*, they nonetheless constructed schemes for assessing Christianity's purpose and salvific potential vis-à-vis a fixed point of reference, which was, of course, their respective forms of Hinduism. With regard to this, too, the pandits were not without precedents afforded by their own religion, which had, at times past, to deal with pluralism in itself. Hindus have not conformed to only one way of explaining why other religions exist, and the pandits involved in the MP Controversy were not an exception to this rule. Yet, as diverse as their schemes of religion undoubtedly are, this chapter provides a basis for extrapolating some general principles about the attitudes of Hindus toward other religions. A matter also taken up in this context is whether these schemes of religion generated tolerance or intolerance.

In keeping with the emphasis upon individuals involved in the MP Controversy, the epilogue traces, where information allows, the aftereffects of the confrontation in the lives of each disputant.

II. RESISTANT HINDUISM: AN OVERVIEW

Christianity's progress in India has always been gradual, and the factors inhibiting its increase have been manifold and notoriously difficult to pinpoint. It spread slowly, partly because the country's size and enormous population strained missionary resources. No doubt most people living outside of European centers of influence had never even heard about Christianity. With contact between the populace and itinerant evangelists intermittent at best, it is not surprising that this religion never elicited a widespread reaction from nineteenth-century Hindus. Aside from natural causes inhibiting its propagation, one must take note of intellectual resistance to Christianity, for on occasion it reached audiences that opposed the theological and philosophical content of its message.

The present chapter attempts to throw light onto anti-Christian argumentation conducted by pandits prior to the MP Controversy, but only insofar as Christianity's doctrinal content is concerned. This restriction is necessary because the subject at hand is Hindu apologetics, not the Hindu response to Christianity's social structure. Before moving into this subject, some preliminary remarks regarding attitudes that have inhibited recognition of resistant Hinduism are in order.

First of all, one must contend with the faulty but prevalent assumption that Hindus have reacted to Christianity in a uniformly positive manner. Perhaps this impression has become current because of the great quantity of paper and ink expended in writing about renascent, instead of resistant, Hinduism. A steady stream of monographs has brought to prominence Rammohun Roy and a host of successors, who, as P. HACKER pointed out, "received their ideas of religious, ethical, social and political values not from their native religion but from the outside, from Western philosophies or from Christianity" (1978: 607). Less well-known than these forerunners of Neo-Hinduism were guardedly conservative pandits,[1] suspicious of everything espoused by Christianity. For them the sole standard of reference in all matters pertaining to truth and value was Hinduism as expressed in the Vedas, the Purāṇas, the Dharmaśāstras and other texts believed to be divinely revealed or authoritative. These were individuals to whom even Christianity's ethical spirit was unattractive, if not decidedly repellent, in contrast to Roy and others who admired Jesus Christ as a moral teacher, even if not as the third person of the Trinity.

---

[1] Because Roy did not share the commitment of his successors to nationalism, HACKER regarded him as a "forerunner" rather than a fully accredited representative of Neo-Hinduism (1978: 581—82).

One can hardly say, therefore, that early nineteenth-century pandits held to a single view of Christianity. Broadly speaking, there were two sets of mind: one accommodative, the other resistant. As influential as the former may be in the minds of a certain class of Hindus in present-day India, there can be no warrant in this for obscuring or overlooking the existence of the latter. Resisting Christianity's doctrinal content was an option open to educated pandits, and the numbers of those who elected to take it were probably not so few as the monographs on Neo-Hinduism might lead one to expect.

Another factor interfering with recognition of the multifariousness of the Hindu intellectual response to Christianity is a reluctance to admit that there was interaction of any sort — positive or negative — with Christian ideas. S. K. DAS, for example, is not only reluctant to concede this but adamant that Bengalis "never" listened seriously to William Carey, the Baptist missionary at Serampore (1973: 12). Even writers who recognize that Hindus were not always favorably disposed to Christianity overestimate the degree to which Neo-Hindus were responsible for curtailing the success of the missionaries, as if the only way to overpower their religion was to absorb it. E. POTTS, for instance, argues that without Roy "Christianity very probably would have made much more formal progress than it did" (1967: 227). The same author says, without mentioning the efforts undertaken by others, that Roy was "foremost in presenting an adequate Hindu answer to the Christian attacks on India's major religion" (POTTS, 1967: 230). These assessments not only gloss over the tenuous links between Neo-Hinduism and "India's major religion" but also ignore the contributions to anti-Christian apologetics made by pandits who did not share Roy's belief that, among other deplorable religious practices, image worship was the worst, a corruption of an originally pristine Hinduism. One might find only a stray conservative (e. g., Rādhākant Deb) in the intellectual circles associated with Calcutta's Hindu College, or College of Fort William, or the Brahmo Samāj, but they were active even in that pace-setting metropolis, where, it might seem, reformed ideas had eclipsed all others. Widely read in their own religious literature and in that of their adversaries, traditionally minded pandits made their presence known by composing popular anti-Christian chapbooks and sophisticated treatises for public consumption.[2]

Clearly, one's personal orientation will determine whether or not one regards Roy's approach to Christianity as more "adequate," to use POTTS's term, than that of conservative pandits, but an informed understanding of the early nineteenth-century Hindu-Christian encounter cannot afford to overlook resistant Hinduism just because, in comparison with Neo-Hinduism, it was incorrigably obdurate.

---

[2] Even a casual perusal of the British Library's catalogues of printed books in regional Indian languages will lead to numerous anti-Christian publications. Most of these date from 1850, and many were not disseminated by Hindu organizations concerned with religious and social reform.

Just as some writers have a marked preference for the urbane discussions of Christianity found in books and lectures by Roy, Keshub Chandra Sen, Vivekananda, Aurobindo Ghose, M. K. Gandhi, and others, so do some authors underrate the Christian missionaries' sophistication in the art of interreligious dialogue in the period under review. No doubt a great many blustering Europeans and North Americans, insensitive to India's religious heritage, who acquired only enough of the local dialect to suffice in castigating "idols," were numbered among these evangelists. But this stereotype is so widespread that sophisticated dialogue between Hindus and Christians would now be said by some to have first taken place between C. F. Andrews and M. K. Gandhi in the present century.[3] E. SHARPE has sensibly written that, "It is simply useless to criticize the early Evangelical missionaries for not seeing what they could not have seen, and for not reading what few Hindus, and only a handful of Western scholars, even knew existed — the scriptures of the 'Higher Hinduism.' Nor is it very helpful to look upon men and women of the early nineteenth century and to pour scorn on them for not having the moral standards of a century and a half later (1977: 9)." Such negative sentiment as this would seem even more out of place had SHARPE added that, even at that early time, some of the most professional Indologists were missionaries, about which more will be said later in this and other chapters.

The pandits and evangelists involved in early Hindu-Christian dialogues may not have foreknown the methodology of S. Radhakrishnan, or B. Kristensen, or G. van der Leeuw, but they were professionals who paid attention to the religious ideas of those whom they wished to confute. One must not be misled by the intensity of their conservatism.

Resistant Hinduism grew in strength after the MP Controversy, that is, in the post-1850 period (*vide* note two). Before that time reference materials are admittedly scarce and none remain in their original languages, as far as is now known. Some reflection on the reasons for this scarcity will enhance one's appreciation for the materials that have been preserved.

The connection between missionary bodies and temporal powers has sometimes been close. The policy of the latter toward freedom of religion governs the operations of the former. Portuguese policy toward Hinduism, for instance, was to uproot it rather than have dialogue with it. King John III issued a directive in 1545 to the effect that brahmins and every vestige of their religion were to be banished from his territories in Goa, Daman, and Diu (LACH, 1965: 238—40), a move hardly designed to foster harmonious relations between the pandits and Roman Catholic religious orders. Because of this and many other severe disabilities imposed upon their subjects by crown authorities, the Portuguese were probably unmatched for the amount of enmity they provoked. D. LACH records only one instance of public debate

---

[3] One can see this inclination throughout K. L. S. RAO's Mahatma Gandhi and C. F. ANDREWS: A Study in Hindu-Christian Dialogue (1969).

in sixteenth-century Goa, when Jesuits, aided by a convert, disputed with pandits, forty of whom, proving obstinate, were banished (1965: 253).

Not only was the Portuguese government ill-disposed to tolerating Hinduism; the religious orders themselves, particularly the Society of Jesus, had a low opinion of Indians, and, being more impressed with the Chinese and Japanese, concentrated their efforts in East Asia (LACH, 1965: 262—64; BOXER, 1951: 78—91, 94, 167—68). Exceptional instances, of course, are not unknown. Chief of these would be Roberto de Nobili, a sixteenth-century Italian Jesuit noted for his emulation of brahmins and recognized as a sophisticated writer in Tamil, Telegu, and Sanskrit. His literary work and public disputations presumably attracted widespread notice; but none of the pandits' written retorts — if there were any — have yet surfaced. De Nobili himself faced opposition from his superiors, and Portuguese territory was not, generally speaking, an hospitable setting for dialogue.

Tranquebar, the Danish enclave on the South Indian coast, was perhaps the earliest ambience conducive to interreligious encounter. The authorities there seem only to have been concerned with trade. They were even annoyed with and unhelpful to the first Lutheran missionary to arrive in the early eighteenth century, Bartolomaeus Ziegenbalg (1682—1719). Without official interference in matters of religion, he was able to mingle freely with pandits, preach to them, and, more importantly for the subject at hand, gather their impressions, recorded in their own words, of Christianity.[4] "I was visited by a grave and learned Brahman," an entry in his diary begins, "and asking him what he proposed by his friendly visit, he replied that he desired to confer with me amicably about the great things and matters of religion" (Ziegenbalg, 1719: 214). The ensuing conversation, supplemented by many others, was a generally sedate but firm expression of resistance. Taken together, they constitute the earliest point of reference for placing the MP Controversy into relation with earlier efforts in anti-Christian apologetics.

The second point of reference, the 1830s, occurs after a gap of more than a century, during which time relations between the two religions became radicalized. The ambience this time was Bombay, the scene of bitter confrontation instead of amicable dialogue. The participants, a Scottish missionary-educator, John Wilson, and several Maharashtrian pandits, clashed head-on over the "great things and matters of religion," leaving several notable apologetical tracts in their wake.

Between these two points of reference, one can find in various Indian languages additional Christian treatises intended to provoke comment from pandits, but evidently without much success. Reaction, which surely occurred, must have been largely restricted to oral retorts. Bengal, for instance, produced several works of this type, the outstanding example of which is Dom Antonio's Dialogo, written in 1743. This author, a convert whose

---

[4] Not only an expert dialogist but a masterful polemicist as well, Ziegenbalg wrote an acerbic tract in Tamil bearing the German title Verdammliches Heidentum, which, until recently, was believed lost (see GENSICHEN, 1967: 29ff.).

Hindu name is unknown, composed his treatise in polished Bengali, aside from the title. Dom Antonio became known for his aggressive evangelistic tactics, including a probably legendary event in which, rather like Elijah and the priests of Baal, he and some pandits threw the Bible into a fire along with several Hindu scriptures. The results, with a predictable slant, were recorded by contemporary Jesuit sources (KHONDKAR, 1976: 48). Provocative though he was, it appears that this native missionary of the Mission of St. Nicholas of Tolentino (located near Dacca) never managed to elicit a literary challenge from the pandits in that region. This same pattern appears elsewhere: incitement was not often restrained, whereas the response — whether from a sense of civility or another motive — was.

One can see that the Tranquebar and Bombay documents are indispensable reference points for tracing connections between the MP Controversy and earlier Hindu apologetics.[5] In the following sections, the quotations from them are allowed to speak for themselves, largely without the benefit of analysis, which is withheld until chapter five. At that juncture it will be determined whether or not these passages tally well with arguments advanced in the MP Controversy. The present objective is simply to observe how pandits, prior to the 1840s, expressed themselves regarding Christianity.

THE ZIEGENBALG PAPERS

The following quotations come from B. Ziegenbalg's papers, written and collected during his tenure as a missionary to Tamil-speaking "Malabarian priests" during the first quarter of the eighteenth century. These extracts are

---

[5] Although organized resistance to Christianity took place in the period under review, so little is yet known about it that mention of it here must necessarily be brief. Conservative Calcutta Hindus organized the Dharma Sabhā in order to oppose government reforms impinging upon the social order during the 1830s (KOPF, 1969: 270—72). Less political were groups seeking to readmit converts into the Hindu fold, such as the Patitoddhār Sabhā, 1851, and Dacca's Hitaiṣiṇī Sabhā, 1865 (S. K. DAS, 1974: 128). As early as 1842, A̱rumuka Nāvalar founded the Saivaprakāśa Sabhā in the Jaffna District of North Ceylon. Having served as consultant and amanuensis to P̱eter Percival, a Wesleyan Methodist who translated the Bible into Tamil, A̱rumukam's inside knowledge of Christianity was formidable (KULANDRAN, 1958: 229ff.). Not less than twenty-fiv̱e scathing apologetical tracts bear his name (MUTTUCUMARASWAMY, 1965: 22—23). A̱rumukam's successors, chief of whom was Sankarapandithar, added numerous anti-Christian chapbooks to the list. Coincident with the Jaffna society were two groups organized for the purpose of obstructing missionary activities in Tinnevelly District on the subcontinent: the Vibhūti Saṅgam ("Sacred Ashes Society") and the Sādur Vedạ Siddhānta Sabhā (FRYKENBERG, 1976: 207—08). Although interaction between A̱rumukam and his continental counterparts is probable, it remains unclear when and from precisely which direction the influence mainly flowed. A partial bibliography of tracts published by the Sacred A̱shes Society is found in MURDOCH, 1968: 134—35. Of these diverse groups, only A̱rumukam's survives. Under its twentieth-century appellation, the Saiva Paripalana Sabhai, it recently engaged Jaffna Christianity in a prolonged and bitter dispute. For details see the thorough study of N. M. SAVERIMUTTU, 1978.

from two sources. The primary source, a 1719 English version of reports originally submitted in German to the Lutheran headquarters in Halle, provides detailed summaries of conferences with thirty-four partners-in-dialogue. Ziegenbalg himself was a keen student of Hindu apologetics, and it appears that neither he nor his editor censored the more serious allegations brought against Christianity. Although these reports were not *verbatim* accounts and were transformed into a somewhat Christian mode of expression, they nonetheless bear evidence of reliability. The secondary source is a collection of ninety-nine letters on Christianity, which were written by "Malabarian priests" at Ziegenbalg's behest and translated into German.[6] Undisturbed by the exigencies of dialogue, these letters clearly indicate how Tamilian brahmins actually perceived Ziegenbalg's religion. Recently studied by H. Grafe, a portion of this correspondence is now available in his English translation. His impression was this: "We are able to sense behind [these letters] the vitality of a truly religious mind open for dialogue with other beliefs and at the same time prepared to defend its own faith and to point to the oddities and irrationalities in other religions" (Grafe, 1972: 57).

Extracts from the conference reports and correspondence are given below, under general headings.

Religious plurality:

"For as Christ in Europe was made Man, so here our God Wischtnu was born among us Malabarians; and as you hope for Salvation through Christ; so we hope for Salvation through Wischtnu; and to save you one way, and us another, is one of the Pastimes and Diversions of Almighty God" (Ziegenbalg, 1719: 14).

"We live in the Kaliujur ... when all things are very confus'd and full of Irregularities; and there are so many different Opinions about the Names and Nature of God, that a man does not know what religion he had best chuse and profess; but when this duration is at an end, all things will be put to rights again, and all the Nations of the World shall be in the same Opinion in these Matters" (1719: 182).

Hinduism and the prestige of antiquity:

"We have venerable Antiquity on our side; our Fathers professed this Religion and so do we" (1719: 90).

"For tho' the Christians call us Heathens, we are not so in Reality; but we are a very Ancient Nation, whose Religion is as Old as the World itself" (1719: 103).

---

6 Under the heading "Malabarische Korrespondenz," these letters were published serially, starting in 1718, in Der Königl. Dänischen Missionarien aus Ost-Indien eingesandter ausführlichen Berichten, a periodical of the Halle Lutheran Seminary.

Christianity's lax morality:

"I never have seen hitherto any of all you Christians taking any care for the saving of his own Soul, by doing Penance for his Sins: Whereas we Malabarians undergo many tedious and long Penances, denying ourselves all the Pleasures of this Life... But I see no such thing Practis'd among you Christians" (1719: 108).

Hindu polytheism:

"We teach the People to worship One only, and not many Gods; and the Notion of a plurality of Gods comes hence, viz. because God is variously represented under different Attributes and forms; yet he is still but One God, as Gold is but one, as to its kind, tho' wrought into a Thousand different Figures" (1719: 192).

Immoral Hindu deities:

"Such and such Actions are related of the Gods which would be criminal and sinful in any Man to do the like... Yet the Gods are subject to no Law and Precepts, whether Negative or Affirmative, and we are no more allow'd to withdraw from them the useful Religious Worship paid to them for so many Ages by our Forefathers, than we are to deny our Allegiance to our Lawful King" (1719: 292).

Salvific opportunities for nonhuman life:

"[It is] firmly believed among us, that not only all mankind but all Birds, and Beasts of the Fields, shall be Eternally Happy after many repeated Nativities or Regenerations, qualifying them for the Enjoyment of God" (1719: 214).

Remedial versus retributive justice:

"Seeing that we live in this World but a few Years, and our sinful Actions are, as to their Duration, transitory; why then should the Punishment be Eternal? The necessary proportion attending distributive Justice, is not observ'd here" (1719: 98).

Jesus Christ:

"Does it not seem the height of Unreasonableness to suppose him to be the Saviour of the World, who was of mean Parentage, had but as mean an Education, persecuted by his Country-men, and at last was hang'd by public Authority upon an infamous Cross" (1719: 251).

"To our reason it does not appear very sensible that they believe in a God who was tortured and killed by his own people" (Grafe, 1972: 56).

"Why did he not travel throughout the World in order to enable all men to listen to his teachings?" (Grafe, 1972: 57).

Christian sacraments and worship:

"Both men and women sit promiscuously in your Churches" (Ziegenbalg, 1719: 286; *vide* GRAFE, 1972: 53).

"We assure you, the whole Nation would have nothing to say against your Discipline, except your giving out that you eat the Body of Christ, and drink his Blood in the Sacrament; which I humbly conceive, none of us will ever be able to comprehend" (1719: 324; *vide* GRAFE, 1972: 55).

Social impediments to Christianity's increase:

"Because you Europeans drink strong liquors, and kill and eat your Fellow-creatures, endued with Five Senses as well as yourselves, I confess, we have an inbred Aversion for you, and all that belongs to you" (1719: 276).

"The Law of the Christians is true and holy... But this we mightily dislike in your Religion, as abominable, that you spit... in your own and other Men's Presence; that you converse with your Wives in the time of their Uncleanness; and that you make no distinction between families" (1719: 312).

"I'll tell you what hinders the Progress of your Doctrine, and renders it unacceptable to us Malabarians; 'tis because you are none of us, but a White European. If you were a Native, we would hear you cheerfully'" (1719: 239—40).

THE BOMBAY DEBATES

The 1830s in Bombay, the second point of reference for the MP Controversy, was a time when tension between Hindu pandits and Christian evangelists was palpable. Largely responsible for this tense situation was John Wilson (1804—1875), a leading Scottish Presbyterian missionary, an Indologist noted for contributions to epigraphy, and an able educator (Wilson College in Bombay was named after him). Wilson's knowledge of Hindu literature was first-rate, but he did not hesitate to subject what he had read to withering ridicule from his perspective as a Christian. Inconsistencies in Purāṇas were among his favorite targets. During his lifetime Wilson managed to debate not only with Hindus but with Zoroastrians and Muslims as well, but the former proved to be his most dogged opponents.

The first public encounter between Wilson and irate pandits was to take place on May 21, 1830. The debate occurred as scheduled, but with a surrogate, a convert named Rām Candra, standing in for the Scotsman. An extract gives an adequate glimpse into the oratory's unsystematic progression.

"Second Brahmin: Of what God is Jesus Christ the son?
Christian [Rām Candra]: I mentioned before that there is only one God... In that Divine Spirit there are three subsistencies... The second of these, namely the Son, took a human birth to save men, and died for the world.
First Brahmin: Died! don't use that expression; God does not die.

Christian: Did not your Ram, Krishnu etc. die?
Brahmin: No: they only laid aside their bodies.
First Brahmin: Jesus Christ was some Philosopher (Sadhoo) among you, I perceive: we have a thousand Philosophers and Saints like Jesus Christ (Dyanoba and Tookaba, etc.).
Christian: Pray did any one of these give his life for you?
First Brahmin: Why should they give their lives when they could save us many other ways?
Christian: No, none of them had so much compassion on you as to give his life for you... Without the shedding of blood there is no remission [of sin].
First Brahmin: We are not allowed to take the life of any animal.
Brahmin: But Ram suffered a great deal for us.
Christian: All that Ram suffered he suffered for his wife, not for you.
First Brahmin: By no means: Ram pretended grief for his wife, only as a cover before the people; but in reality, he went to Lunka to free the gods.
Christian: Before Ram's wife was ravished from him, the gods had been in bondage many years in Lunka. Why then did he not go previously to their deliverance?
First Brahmin: As long as Rawun had the least particle of merit left, so long Ram had no power to slay him. As soon as his merit was exhausted Ram went to Lunka.
Christian: Where did Rawun procure merit?
First Brahmin: In a former birth, when for the sake of sovereignty he performed austerities.
Christian: Then he performed austerities with the lust (lobh) of procuring a kingdom. Well, according to the Hindoo Shastras austerities performed with such a covetous desire are inconsistent with true piety; and, of course, all Rawun's merit falls to the ground, together with all the defense of Ram you attempted to build on it" (J. Wilson, 1830: 359—64).

This raucous encounter was only the beginning; less than a year later, in February of 1831, Wilson himself debated for six successive evenings with a pandit named Morabhaṭṭa Dāndekara, about whom nothing is known. This Hindu stalwart's objections to Christianity were afterwards summarized in a missing Marathi tract, Śrīhindudharmasthāpana (Establishment of the Venerable Hindu Religion). An English translation, from which the following has been extracted, was prefixed to Wilson's portentous — or pretentious — rejoinder, An Exposure of the Hindu Religion.

Immoral Hindu deities:

"All these deeds are so many virtuous actions in the gods that performed them. We maintain further that by hearing and speaking of them the ignorance of the imprisoned spirit, and its consequent subjection to passion are removed, and that thus they have as much power as image worship itself to create in the soul pure and holy dispositions. These deeds, when narrowly considered, are even far better than those virtuous actions of Christ's that you mention" (Wilson, 1832: 19).

"Now should you ask why [Krishna] committed theft, we answer that doing so is the glory of the Godhead, not its shame. He was the Lord of the universe; and therefore whatever He wanted he took without scruple. The inhabitants of Gokula too were so delighted with him that, on whatever pretense whatever, they would have him to come to their houses; and, in order to gratify them, he used to go and steal" (1832: 26).

The Trinity:

"Among those who hold the doctrine of Christ, one God is first set forth. Afterwards, the same God, with a view to the salvation of the creature, that is, its deliverance from all attachment to the visible world and its attainment of a state of fixed contemplation of the spiritual God, is represented under three forms... As for example the Holy Spirit purifies the hearts of men, ... He is indeed said to be without form or figure like the Father; but in reality his forms are many and various. Sometimes he becomes like a pigeon. At other times he becomes like fire. When we look to the Son, we find that he is sometimes in the form of word, and sometimes again, he assumes a mortal body, ...and the reason for this is stated to be that in his spiritual form he cannot accomplish the salvation of spirits encompassed in material bodies. Having thus assumed a body he is brought into a state inconsistent with the greatness and glory of God — a state open to reproach, and altogether incongruous. He is born in the womb of a mother; he becomes a youngling like any other creature; he experiences the good and ill of mortal existence; he suffers... the punishment of a malefactor, and dies a reproachful death: by these and other means he procures the favour of God, and thus accomplishes the salvation of men. Those who hold these doctrines maintain that... the unity of God is undestroyed... If, then, these three divinities occasion no bewilderment of mind, ...how can the worship of Rama, Krishna, and other gods, occasion an ever-growing bewilderment to us?" (1832: 15—16).

Christian soteriology:

"Your doctrine is that when men could not obtain salvation by their own merit, God commanded his Son to come into the world for the salvation of men. He came accordingly, performed works of righteousness, at last gave his own life, and thus opened the door of heaven to men... Now our doctrine is this — that Rama, Krishna, and other incarnations, have for their appropriate object the salvation of the world; but without suffering pain at all to be compared with that of Christ, and without submitting to a reproachful death like him, they sported themselves at pleasure, and by these very sports accomplished the salvation of those who took refuge in their mercy... We ask you... whether these actions of Rama, Krishna, and the rest, or those of your Jesus Christ are the better" (1832: 22).

"If you ask why Rama, Krishna, and other incarnations, accomplished the salvation of men in this or that particular manner, we ask you in return why God sent his Son into the world, and why, for the salvation of men, he brought him into a state so reproachful and so appalling. What! Had he no other way of saving the world? ... After bringing into existence principles and objects productive of sin, ... he must become a man, a pigeon, or fire — he must submit to unheard of suffering! Why, pray, should he put himself to so much ado?" (1832: 23—24).

Christian sacraments:

"Why should he tell you to meet together from time to time, to take a piece of bread, and muttering a few words to eat it up? and why should he order you to drink spirits? and why should he enjoin you to pour water on the head? Alas! the bread, the spirits, and the water, are all material things, ... and how then from these things can merit and holiness result to the creature, and how by means of them obtain those qualifications that will entitle him to a state of Nearness to God and Emancipation from matter? ... If from... things of that nature, holiness is derived, ... how can an increase of ignorance arise from the use of the pure water of the Ganges, and of water sanctified by the touch of Krishna's feet or from the contemplation of his image?" (1832: 16—17).

Conversion motives:

"The man who could idly suspect his mother of adultery, when he himself was conceived in her womb, is the only man fitted to suspect and object to his own religion... This being the case, the person, that still sees something objectionable in the religion advocated i.e., Hinduism must attribute this unhappy circumstance to the sin of this or of a former birth" (1832: 28).

Next to enter into the fray with Wilson was Nārāyaṇa Rāo, an instructor in English at a college founded by the ruler of Satara. Rāo's apologetics differed from the methods of his predecessors, who criticized Christianity largely because they failed to find corollaries between it and their own religion. Although Rāo did not neglect this strategy, his tactic was the reverse of Wilson's; he tried to demonstrate that the Bible, even on its own terms, is logically inconsistent. Accordingly, he applied a literalistic exegesis to that text, which invariably turned out — by his reading of it — nonsensical. Rāo's views, combining rationalism and traditional Hindu thinking in an uneasy alliance, were summed up in a Marathi tract, Svadeśadharmābhimānī (One Who Takes Pride in His Country's Religion), and translated — this time in piecemeal fashion — in Wilson's next broadside, A Second Exposure of the Hindu Religion. The following extracts are representative of Rāo's tract, which circulated sometime between 1832 and 1834.

The Old Testament:

"It is written in the Old Testament, that God was employed six days in the creation of heaven and earth etc.; and that having completed his work on

Sunday he took rest. And since the universe was not created at once, but by degrees, it may have happened that the infinite being may have rested times without number. The conclusion is manifest, that God must be lazy" (Wilson, 1834: 86).

"God created the first man after his own likeness, by forming an image of clay, and breathing life into it. It appears from this circumstance, that God has a figure like man" (1834: 89).

"God, after some delay and inquiry, having involved Adam in deep sleep, broke, and took out, one of his bones, and made a wife for him — a circumstance which is inconsistent with the divine omniscience, inasmuch as when Adam's image was formed, it did not occur to God that a wife ought to be given to him, and that part of the clay should be allotted to this purpose. Overlooking all this, God, after making Adam's image complete, breaks one of his bones, and deceives him, and steals his bone. He ought to have asked permission, and to have proceeded honestly. He was, however, blameable in his conduct, and was guilty of theft" (1834: 89—90).

"Though God interdicted Adam from eating of the tree of Knowledge of good and evil, a serpent endowed with the ability of breaking the commandment, intimated to Adam and Eve, that they should not die, all of which is inconsistent with the omnipotence and omniscience of God. Had God foredeclared... this, it might have been reconcilable with his word. It appears that the devil is the rival of God; and, moreover, that his declaration has more truth in it than that of God, and that the divine curse is of no avail. ... And yet God cursed both them and the serpent... As far as this is concerned he must be considered unjust, and vainly troublesome" (1834: 93—95).

The New Testament:

"Joseph, who was an upright man, found his wife, before their union, with child; and being desirous that the matter should not be publically known, he thought of dismissing her privately. When he was exercising his thoughts on this subject, an angel of the Lord, appearing to him in a dream, said, Fear not to take unto thee Mary thy wife, for that which is conceived in her is of God, and then departed. Here is the fault. It is very incongruous that God should take a righteous man's wife, for there is no sin equal to this... If God really required the woman, he ought... to have got her liberated from Joseph, and then have devoted her to himself. As he did not act in this manner, he acted by stealth... The Christian religion, instead of exalting him has dishonoured him. It appears probable, that the Christian scripture irritates God" (1834: 99—100).

"Seeing that an Incarnation of God makes his appearance to promote the happiness of all, there ought to happen in connexion with him no calamity whatever, and he ought to be distinguished from all other men in that, with him, nothing is impracticable. Notwithstanding all this, he is no sooner born than a great number of infants... are, in connexion with him, unreasonably put to death... The cause of all this... was nothing else than the flight of Jesus. If he was a real Incarnation, he ought to have feared no one, and his appearance as an Incarnation ought to have turned the hearts of all men to God. Not only was this not realized; but what might at least have been expected, that no one should have an inclination to kill him, [is expected in vain]. And, as long as Herod lived Jesus did nothing whatever toward the establishment of religion, but ran away and lived in Nazareth [sic]. It hence appears that Herod was more powerful than Jesus. It is impossible, therefore, that he, who by his flight, became a murderer of children, and was so despicable in power, can be either the Son of God, or bear any relation to God whatever" (1834: 104—105).

"A star pointed out the road to the Magi seeking to find Jesus. This is a wonderful concern. According to the description of the universe given by Christians, the stars are the suns of other worlds. If a star... move in the slightest degree from its place, it will be the occasion of a great calamity; and if the star... really came near the earth, it is impossible to see how the earth could remain unconsumed. Is it not unreasonable, that religion and astronomy should be thus opposed to one another?" (1834: 114).

"The Padre informs us, that Jesus ascended with his body to heaven. But ascension into the sky with a body, is impossible on account of the attraction of the earth. What are we really to make of this astronomical and Biblical opposition?" (1834: 117).

"If the Christian Shastra be true, ...it was necessary that Christian Teachers... should have been sent forth into all the world at the time of Christ. They are sent into Hindusthan eighteen hundred years after Christ. In consequence of this circumstance, innumerable millions of people have gone, and will continue to go, into hell... The unavoidable conclusion, consequently, is that the Christian religion is false, and that the Padres, taking advantage of the sovereignty of the people of their caste, have come to this country for the express purpose of practicing deceit, and leading the people to apostacy" (1834: 137).[7]

Space does not permit quotation from contemporary Christian tractliterature, either Ziegenbalg's or Wilson's, to which the "Malabarian priests," Morabhaṭṭa Dāndekara, and Nārāyaṇa Rāo addressed themselves. If this had been done, one would have seen that these missionaries stressed so-called miraculous evidences. They seem to have thought that Hindus, just as European skeptics and empiricists, needed to be convinced that preternatural events actually can occur. Persuading an audience that Jesus' deeds were unaccountable in terms of cause and effect, so their argument went, would be a step toward recognizing him as divine. But there is no indication whatsoever that the above-quoted apologists viewed these claims with anything

[7] Christianity's Indian and Western critics sometimes share the same point of view. The argument that Jesus Christ's ministry should not have been limited to the Jewish people was first advanced by Porphyry, the third-century Greek philosopher (GRAFE, 1972: 57).

other than complete credulity.[8] Nevertheless, Christian writers in India continued to harp on this argument, and it shall reappear in connection with Muir's MP.

This Hindu predisposition to believe in miraculous acts, often associated with *avatāras*, must have made missionary declamations on this subject tedious for Indian listeners. This may have been P. C. Mazoomdar's reason for putting recitation of Jesus' miracles at the head of a lengthy list of grievances against Christianity's emissaries. Although this quotation post-dates the MP Controversy, it accurately summarizes the mood of resistant Hinduism in the early nineteenth century.

"The missionary... continually descants on miracles, imports institutions foreign to the genius of the continent, and in the case of non-compliance with whatever he lays down condemns men to eternal darkness and death. He continually talks of blood and fire and hell. He considers innocent babes as the progeny of deadly sin: he hurls invectives at other men's faith, however truly and conscientiously held. No sacred notions are sacred to him, unless he has taught them. All self-sacrifice, which he does not understand, is delusion to him. All scriptures are false which have grown up outside his dispensation, climate and nationality. He will revolutionize, denationalize, and alienate men from their kith and kin. Wherever he goes, men learn to beware of him. He is a Mlecha to Hindus, a Kaffir to Mohammedans, a rock of offence to everybody. He is tolerated only because he carries with him the imperial prestige of a conquering race" (Mazoomdar, 1883: 42—43).

---

[8] A contemporary observer, W. H. Sleeman, noted that, "Hindoos never doubt any part of the miracles and prophecies of our scripture — they believe every word of them; and the only thing that surprises them is that they should be so much less wonderful than those of their own scriptures" (1844: 51—52). Rammohun Roy was also fond of reiterating this idea (GHOSE, 1978: 484).

III. THE NEW HERMENEUTICS

From the time that Christianity first gained a foothold in India (during the third century at the latest), Western and native evangelists experimented with Hindu terminology and thought-forms. Their intention was to find, in the diverse linguistic and religious matrix that India is, suitable precedents or starting points for communicating their new faith. Unfortunately hardly anything is known about these early attempts in cross-cultural hermeneutics. Only the sixteenth and subsequent centuries yield specimens of Christian compositions in regional Indian languages. For the most part, these treatises were written by European Roman Catholics, especially Jesuits, residing either in South India or in the vicinity of Goa.

To read these treatises is to become aware at once that the missionary approach to Indian languages was cautious, even hide-bound, due to the hegemony of Latin over ecclesiastical communication in the European Church. At their best, Roman Catholics chose words in Indian languages to convey most of the high doctrines expressed by Latin terminology, such as "incarnation," "justification," and "sanctification." But even Roberto de Nobili, the Jesuit who took such great pains to accommodate himself to the Hindu mind, believed that *Spiritus sanctus* was too precious a name to render into Tamil, and was satisfied with *Ispirīttu sāndu* instead, simply a phonetic adaptation (TILIANDER, 1974: 143).[9] At worst, Latinisms or Portuguese derivatives were introduced whenever important doctrinal, ecclesiastical, or cultic ideas needed to be expressed. This was the case with the Jesuit Thomas Stephen's Christian Purāṇa, an otherwise fine example of devotional literature written in an archaic mixture of Marathi and Konkani. "Instead of dignified Sanskrit formations to express theological and ecclesiastical technical terms he chose those more familiar to his expected readers [viz., fellow Jesuits and Hindu converts]; for example he used *bautismu* for *dhyānasān*, *trinidad* for *tritva*, *sacrament* for *devadravya*, *navā testament* for *navā granth*, *padre guru* for *shri guru*, *tempal* for *deval*, *saderdot* for *guru*, *meditação* for *dhyānajapa*, *altara* for *devāra*, *sacrificiu* for *devapujā*, *prophet* for *duradrishti*, etc." (ABBOTT, 1921—23: 680).

Only when Christian writers turned to Sanskrit did their bondage to Latin loosen; they were forced away from it because good compositions in

---

[9] However, no less a Sanskritist than the late P. HACKER argued (1980: 85) that "probably the early missionaries in India were right in retaining *espiritu santu* for 'Holy Spirit' instead of attempting misleading translations as used today (for instance *pavitra ātmā* in Hindi, which literally means 'the pure soul', 'pure' understood in a religious sense)."

Sanskrit must be free from intrusive words of foreign origin. Although European Christians in the South recognized the utility of India's sacred language in their encounter with Hindus, and were aware of the criteria for achieving a polished style in it, their treatises appeared only sporadically and ceased in the generation following de Nobili (WINDISCH, 1917—20: 6—10; CASTETS, 1931: 345ff.; SRINIVASAN, 1936: 127ff.).[10] Despite the novelty and value of these Roman Catholic efforts in South India they cannot be considered here, for they are not in the mainstream of Christian activity in Sanskrit, which began again, in North Indian Protestant circles, after three centuries in abeyance.

John Muir's MP applied to apologetics the results of experiments in hermeneutics carried out by several predecessors during a long period of trial and error. As their contributions are reconstructed and analyzed here, their attraction to Sanskrit as a medium for missionary communication will be explained; the principles governing their rejection and selection of terms considered; and the overall significance of their utilization of Sanskrit for encounter with Hindus assessed.

WILLIAM CAREY (1767—1837)

The activities of William Carey, the energetic English Baptist missionary, have been documented in two reliable monographs by E. POTTS and M. LAIRD.[11] But even these comprehensive studies must be supplemented with an account of Carey's design for a corpus of Christian literature in Sanskrit, including evangelistic tracts, didactic materials for converts, and, of course, a Bible translation. In order to understand what he wanted to do with India's sacred language, one must note that Carey had two reasons for being interested in its utilization for evangelism. First, he saw that Sanskrit acted as a stabilizing force upon the unsettled dialects amidst which he worked. Second, he was intransigently opposed to brahminical privileges, one of which was hegemony over Sanskrit.

The confusion in dialects spoken in Bengal at the beginning of the nineteenth century is well documented and requires no proof here; nor does Carey's role in the establishment of modern Bengali prose (S. K. DE, 1962: 85—143). During his time pandits still regarded discourse in the vernaculars as less than dignified. This attitude reinforced boundaries between language

---

[10] It appears that de Nobili did not write anything in Sanskrit that did not have a counterpart in Tamil. Gradually, the Tamil works superseded those in Sanskrit, and the latter have mostly been lost. Some may be preserved in Paris. For details see J. FILLIOZAT, 1941: v—xii; also Catalogus codicum manuscriptorum Bibliothecae regiae, 1739: 434—48. Among the surviving Christian texts in Sanskrit is a catechism attributed to the Jesuit Jean Calmette (d. 1740): Satyaweedasaarasangraham [*sic*], edited by J. AELEN (1931). Analysis of this text would greatly improve our knowledge of missionary hermeneutics in the period prior to the one under discussion.

[11] British Baptist Missionaries in India 1793—1837 (1967), and Missionaries and Education in Bengal 1793—1837 (1972).

regions and frustrated attempts to evangelize on a large scale. As manager of an indigo factory near Mudnabati (in present Malda District), he faced the daily problem of communicating with laborers drawn from various vicinities in Bengal. The following complaint is taken from that context: "If I say *shaiton*, i. e., the devil, they cannot understand who I mean unless I should add, he is a *burra hurram laddi*, which tho used to signify a Rascal, etc., yet in plain English is a 'Son of a Whore.' If I say, 'the Son of God,' they can scarcely one in an hundred understand the word for Son: but if I say God's Boy, this is exactly conformable to their idiom" (W. Carey, 1795: 2 Oct.). Through an exchange of ideas with Sanskritists H. T. Colebrooke and Francis Wilford, Carey realized that he could surmount these and other more serious terminological obstacles by turning to Sanskrit, which learned Hindus everywhere understood to some extent (W. Carey, 1798).

Carey's letters and diaries are replete with references to acrimonious encounters with brahmins, whom he compared to "Romish" priests hiding their sacred books behind the veil of an ecclesiastical language. As a Dissenter, he encountered discrimination from clergymen of the established church, and was therefore wary of what seemed to be high-handed exclusiveness among brahmins. Potts has aptly observed that the tradition that nurtured Carey was "particularly obsessed with the importance of the individual; his rights; his freedom to read his own scriptures and to decide for himself the path his life should take" (Potts, 1967: 244). Influenced by these values, he compared *śūdras* to medieval European peasants, for whom the Latin Bible was inaccessible. He referred to brahminical hegemony over Sanskrit as "a masterpiece of policy unequalled in the annals of ecclesiastical domination" (W. Carey, 1822: 131—32). Distressed by the apparent credulity of *śūdras*, he became convinced that "India almost mocks inquiry into her mysteries and doctrines" (W. Carey, *et. al.*, 1818: 5). Carey decided to publish his Sanskrit grammar, Rāmāyaṇa edition, and selected translations of Hindu writings in order to bring to public attention "these mysterious sacred nothings, ... which have maintained their celebrity so long merely by being kept from the inspection of all but interested Brahmans" (W. Carey, 1802). But he was not only anxious to deflate the sanctity of venerated Sanskrit texts; he also wanted to utilize the psychological advantage inherent in discourse in that language. Brahmins interfering with his preaching had demonstrated the power of the language they guarded so closely: "In many of the discussions which the dissemination of new ideas has elicited, a learned Brahmun has found little difficulty in weakening in the eyes of the people the force of the clearest truths, by placing them at issue with his own dogmas pronounced in this venerated tongue" (W. Carey, 1819: 376). Weary of being put on the defensive by Sanskrit in situations such as these, Carey took the first concrete step toward its utilization by founding Serampore College in 1818.

According to the original prospectus, the scheme of instruction in Serampore College was designed for two interrelated purposes: formation of a body of competent "Christian Pandits," who would improve upon Carey's translations; and training of apologists capable of contrasting the improved Bible translation with the prevailing systems of Hindu belief (W. Carey, *et. al.*, 1818: 3—5). Carey was keenly aware of imperfections in his Bible translations and realized that his chief contribution would be to prepare for future revisions: "From... Christian Natives trained up in the knowledge of the Scriptures from their earliest youth, we may eventually hope for a translation, which shall combine fidelity to the original with all the beauty, force, and ease of language which are so desirable" (1818: 30). His intentions were also avowedly aggressive, a direct result of conflicts with brahmins. According to his plan, Hindu literature would be placed in disadvantageous juxtaposition with the Gospel, a task which could be done effectively only by evangelists acquainted with the original sources of both religions. "To gain the ear of those who are thus deceived it is necessary for them to believe that the speaker has a superior knowledge of the subject. In these circumstances a knowledge of S̲ungskri̲t is valuable. As the person thus misled, perhaps a Brahmun, deems this a most important part of knowledge, if the advocate of truth be deficient therein, he labours against the hill: presumption is altogether against him" (W. Carey, 1822: 138). For reasons such as these, the curriculum at Serampore was designed to impart a thorough knowledge of Sanskrit; pandits would thereby be prepared for critical study of the "principles and doctrines on which the Pouranic and Boudhist systems are founded" (W. Carey, *et. al.*, 1818: 6). Carey was thoroughly optimistic about his plans: "If this College be conducted with due vigour, it may be made the Christian Benares, and the tide of S̲ungskritu̲ literature be turned completely on the side of Christianity" (1818: 20). Within a decade, however, the scheme had to be revised because the number of Christian students dwindled to zero (LAIRD, 1972: 142—50).

Carey became embroiled in controversy over the heavily Sanskritic curriculum at Serampore, which he had to defend against the allegation of perpetuating idolatry. The accusation was baseless: as a language, Carey admired Sanskrit as much as any pandit did, but his aversion for Hindu literature was intense. Two passages from the Friend of India map out the main points of his defense. In these lines Carey's rhetorical skill was superb; one finds in them a manifesto for a new Indian hermeneutics.

"The people do not venerate the language for the idolatrous ideas it contains, but the ideas for the dress they wear. What can be a more effectual mode of counteracting this influence, than that of depositing ideas of genuine science in this very language, and by dividing the attachment of the people, finally transferring all their regard to those just ideas which it is proposed to inculcate. Instead of pulling down the temple around which the worshippers are assembled, let us displace the idol, and present for the veneration of the people, a new and legitimate object of regard, arrayed in new vestments" (W. Carey, 1819: 437).

"If permitted thus to take a large and more accurate view of knowledge, the S̲ungskri̲t student should happen to find that his favorite language is a golden casket exquisitely wrought, but in reality filled with nothing but pebbles and trash, he may still regard it as a golden casket, and fill it now with riches — beyond all price" (W. Carey, 1822: 144).[12]

Carey's only contribution to literature in Sanskrit was his Bible translation, the Dharmapustaka,[13] completed with the assistance of Mṛtyuñjaya Vidyālaṅkāra, his pandit at the College of Fort William.[14] Although his Bengali Bible had already gone through one revision before the Sanskrit version appeared, the Dharmapustaka exerted considerable influence over subsequent translations into other regional Indian languages. Pandits gathered by Carey from all parts of India, who were apparently unfamiliar with biblical languages, used the Sanskrit instead of the Bengali version for drafting translations into their respective tongues.

Many Sanskritic terms originally adapted by Carey were perpetuated in later Bible translations prepared by non-Baptist missionaries. In the contemporary but anachronistic vocabulary of North Indian Christians, such terms as the following were standardized at Serampore: *īśvara* (θεός), *pavitrātman* (πνεῦμα ἅγιον), *paritrāṇa* (σωτηρία), *pratyaya* (πίστις), and *anugraha* (χάρις). For soteriological terms he vacillated between words that were part of ordinary Hindu vocabulary (e. g. *prāyaścitta*) and less familiar ones (e. g., *tuṣṭikaraṇa* for the Greek ἱλαστήριον, "propitiation"). When he decided that *mukti* — perhaps the most natural choice — would inevitably cause misunderstanding, Carey was not reluctant to coin neologisms merely on the basis of philological connotation (e. g., *utkrayaṇa* for λύτρωσις, "redemption").[15]

One can see in Carey's Bible translation that he was cautious about the utilization of Sanskrit. But letters written during his first five years in Bengal reveal a more bold approach to hermeneutics. For example, although his published translations rendered the Hebrew Tetragrammaton by *Yihua*, his initial drafts avoided this Hebraism and used *bhagavān* instead: "At first I used the term Bhogaban indiscriminately wherever the English translators had used the word God[16] — but when he was said to be the God of particular

[12] LAIRD's book elided the latter part of this sentence, and, due to this inexact quotation, never clearly brought out Carey's design for Christian literature in Sanskrit (cf. LAIRD, 1972: 56).

[13] The New Testament was published in 1808; the Pentateuch in 1811; the historical books in 1815; and the Hagiography in 1816. A revision of the entire text was attempted, but never published. The first published Bible translation in Sanskrit was a pericope of Matthew's Gospel, which appeared as a reading exercise in Carey's Sanskrit grammar of 1806.

[14] For information on Mṛtyuñjaya, see KOPF, 1969: 204—08.

[15] The Bible translation prepared chiefly by the Calcutta Baptist missionary, William Yates (1792—1845), and finished posthumously by the Swiss Baptist, John Wenger (1811—1880), did not depart significantly from Carey's terminology. It did, however, vastly improve upon his style. This version, published periodically between 1840 and 1852, is the text of the present N. T. edition published by the Bible Society of India.

[16] This is evidence that Carey did not translate directly into Indian languages from Hebrew and Greek. He appears to have been more dependent on English than his hagiographers admit.

persons or Nations ... it sounded very odd, ... and several mentioned it as a solecism saying he was every man's Bhogaban" (W. Carey, 1797). Even more surprising is that Carey thought the Tetragrammaton could be rendered by the mystical monosyllable *om*, a supposition based on a false etymology: "Perhaps the Shanscrit word *om* ... may best of all embrace the idea [of the Tetragrammaton]. The word is composed of three letters in one — perhaps it is the Hebrew word *Yahooa* " (W. Carey, 1797).

Reaction to the Dharmapustaka as a translation was largely uncomplimentary. Among the most able critics was Sanskritist H. H. Wilson, who observed that its "defects were neither incorrectness nor obscurity; but inelegance of expression and harshness of construction, ... a rigour of fidelity that cannot fail to cramp and distort the style ... The novelty of the subject also, and the necessity of employing words to designate meanings which, although admissable, were unusual and unknown, contributed to disfigure the composition; and the Sanskrit Version has accordingly never been popular with the learned natives of India" (E. Carey, 1836: 606—07). Despite these critical defects, which were indeed critical because among the meanings of *saṃskṛta* are "polished" or "sophisticated," Carey's Dharmapustaka and manifesto for the new hermeneutics inaugurated a new phase in Hindu-Christian encounter, for which an entirely original set of ground rules had to be devised.

William Hodge Mill (1792—1853)

Stylistic and terminological improvement of Christian literature in Sanskrit was undertaken not by an Indian Christian as Carey had hoped, but rather by another Englishman, the Reverend William Hodge Mill, Fellow of Trinity College, Cambridge, who subsequently was elected Regius Professor of Hebrew at Oxford. Mill was appointed by Bishop Middleton of Calcutta[17] as principal of Bishop's College, that city's first Anglican theological seminary, founded in 1820 by the Society for the Propogation of the Gospel (London).

A letter written shortly after Mill's arrival in Calcutta (1821) indicates that he had quickly and correctly assessed the importance of Sanskrit for missionaries: "My own attention has been from the beginning chiefly devoted to the Sanskrit, the ancient brahminical language, in which all the terms of Hindu religion and philosophy are contained, and by which alone we can hope to understand that singular system of opinions, to which the whole of this vast population is enslaved" (Mill, 1822a). According to Mill's viewpoint, Hinduism consisted of "sublime precepts of spiritual abstraction" overlaid with "monstrous and demoralizing legends" (Mill, 1831—37: lvi—lxi, *passim*). On the basis of this judgment, shared by Rammohun Roy and

[17] Middleton is chiefly remembered for his infamous offer of an outstanding career to Rammohun Roy on the condition that he become a Christian (Singh, 1958: 249—50).

other Indian critics of traditional Hinduism, it would be wrong to dismiss Mill as a typical iconoclastic missionary. Far from being that type, he utilized Sanskrit and its thought-forms so boldly that his writings rival and often surpass Brahmabandhav Upadhyay's Hymn to Saccidānanda, the only other Christian writing in Sanskrit that is well known in India today.[18] The influence of two men must be examined in order to properly understand Mill's contributions to the new hermeneutics: Reginald Heber, a clergyman, and H. H. Wilson, an Orientalist.

Bishop Heber's episcopate was brief, but during that time two ideas foremost in his mind were impressed upon Mill. He convinced the Principal that the confrontation between Hinduism and Christianity was sharpest on the twin issues of God's moral character and the dogma of the Trinity (Roy and J. Marshman of Serampore had already argued about the divinity of Jesus Christ for several years by this time). At Heber's behest, Mill undertook two translations intended to convey these very ideas: Sanskrit versions of the Decalogue and three Creeds (Apostles', Niceno-Constantinopolitan, and Athanasian), all of which were published by Bishop's College in 1823.

Translating the Decalogue was simple compared with selecting appropriate terminology for the complex ontological and Christological formulae of the three Creeds, identified in Sanskrit as the Pratītivākyatraya. (Below this title appeared a salutation to the Trinity, modeled after invocations of Gaṇeśa at the beginning of Hindu texts: *śrīpitre putrāya ca puṇyātmane ca namaḥ*). Mill's nomenclature must have puzzled Hindu readers: the Father (*pitṛ* or *tāta*) is a *deva* (only once modified by *eka*; *unus deus*, θεός) and he is the *sraṣṭṛ* or *nimittabhūta* (*creator*, ποιητής); the Son (*putra*, *tanaya*, *suta*) is both *īśvara* and *parameśvara* and an *avatāra* (the perfect form *avatatāra* is used for κατελθόντα καὶ σαρκωθέντα); and the Holy Spirit is the *devātman* or *īśvarātman*, whose primary characteristic is *śakti*. The scope for misinterpretation was immense. Even granting that hierarchical relationships in the Hindu pantheon are fluid, the normal ontological distinction between *parameśvara* and a *deva* is so firm that an inquisitive Hindu might have wondered whether the Son was Mill's favorite deity (*iṣṭadevatā*) or whether the Christian Trinity was topsy-turvy from the standpoint of logic. A basic purpose of the Creeds, on the other hand, was to differentiate clearly between the Persons of the Trinity. Consequently, the phraseology of verses twenty-five to twenty-six of the Athanasian Creed might offset whatever unnatural associations the terms *deva* and *parameśvara* might bring into a Christian context: *na gurur na laghus sarve kintu nityās samānakāḥ*.[19] But this helpful qualification probably did not discourage Hindu readers from

---

[18] This short hymn first appeared in the Calcutta journal Sophia (Oct., 1898). For the Sanskrit text and French translation, see LE SAUX, 1965: 265—71. An excellent exegesis can be found in GISPERT—SAUCH, 1972: 60—79.

[19] "*Nihil maius aut minus, sed totae tres personae coaeternae sibi sunt et coaequales.*"

identifying the Trinity with the Hindu Triad (Brahmā, Viṣṇu and Śiva), between which an apparent analogical correspondence exists. One of Roy's remarks is pertinent in this connection, for, although he crusaded against both the Christian Trinity and the polytheism of his brethren, many Hindus probably concurred with him in rejecting attempts to vaunt the Trinity over the Triad — though few on either side would have shared his Unitarian propensities: "If Christianity inculcated a doctrine which represents God as consisting of three persons, . . . no Hindoo, in my opinion, who searches after truth, can conscientiously profess it in preference to Hindooism; for that which renders the modern Hindoo system of religion absurd and detestable, is that it represents the divine nature, though one (*ekam brahma*), as consisting of many persons, capable of assuming different forms for the discharge of different offices" (GHOSE, 1978: 675).

Space does not allow for a thorough analysis of other problematic technical terms introduced by Mill (e. g., *tatsvarūpa* for ὁμοούσιος and *vastu* for *substantia*). *Persona*, however, merits more attention than others because Mill's periphrasis for it highlights how problematic the utilization of technical terminology could be.[20] As a theist anxious to defend the Christian understanding of God as personal, Mill was apprehensive about the term *nirguṇa* ("devoid of qualities"), which he feared — probably falsely — would suggest that his religion inculcates an impersonal monistic principle. By choosing *lakṣaṇa* and *viśeṣa* ("attribute" or "accident") instead,[21] Mill obviously wanted to insure that readers would understand that the Christian God is *saguṇa* ("possessed of qualities"), not recognizing — as some Indologists and theologians now do[22] — that *saguṇa* is the less suitable of this word-pair, indicating as it does an internally complex Being endowed with attributes which are distinct from its substance.

In all probability, Mill's nomenclature reinforced the strict Vedāntin's impression that Christianity has, as R. DE SMET has phrased it, only "symbolic and pedagogical value" (1963: 22). Mill was still feeling his way toward an authentic Indian hermeneutics, and his failure to communicate clearly at this point was not because Sanskrit is unsuitable for expressing what only Greek or Latin can. Rather, the terminology had to be borrowed from sources neither completely comprehensible nor trustworthy from the standpoint of his faith. Keenly aware that Sanskrit's potential for expressing Christian ideas was greater than his translations might lead one to think, Mill turned to another scholar for assistance.

---

[20] Verse four of the Athanasian Creed: *na trayānāṃ viśiṣṭānāñ kuryyād anyonyasambhramaṃ / na cāpi bhedanan teṣu hy ekarūpasya vastunaḥ //*. "*. . . neque confudentes personas neque substantiam separantes.*"

[21] Cf., e. g., *yasmān nijo viśeṣo 'sti pitur bhinnañ ca lakṣaṇaṃ putrasyānyo viśeṣo 'sti puṇyātmanas tathāparaḥ //*. "*Alia est enim persona Patris, alia Filii, alia Spiritus sancti*" (Athanasian Creed).

[22] For details refer to DE SMET, 1963: 20ff. and 1965: 6ff., the second of which includes valuable comments by P. HACKER, including his own Sanskrit version of the Athanasian Creed.

Sanskritist H. H. Wilson, an "associate syndic in Sanskrit" at Bishop's College, began to collaborate with Mill in 1828 (James, 1830: 100). A Proposed Version of Theological Terms, with a View to Uniformity in Translations of the Holy Scriptures, etc., into the Various Languages of India, the first product of their cooperation in refining the new hermeneutics, was published in March of that year.[23] A thorough review of this proposal, which even recommended ecclesiastical and cultic terminology (e. g., *jyāyas* for presbyter and *pratijñā* or *dharmapratiṣṭhā* for sacrament), is impractical here. An examination of several primary terms is sufficient to reveal a few principles governing the development of the new hermeneutics.

Struck by the existence of a cognate term in Indian languages for the Greek ϑεὸς and Latin *deus*, and believing uniformity in Bible translations into Indian languages to be essential, Mill urged all Christians to utilize the corresponding Sanskrit word, *deva*: "The word expressing this [ϑεὸς, *el*, *elohim*] should be such as in enunciating the proposition 'God is One' — *Deus Unus* — [it] should convey a marked denial of the polytheistic proposition *Dii plures sunt*... Therefore in the languages of every heathen country, the word for the only living and true GOD, should be the same universally that idolaters affix to their gods... To avoid this... is at once to divest the proposition 'There is but one God,' of all the opposition to false worship which the Scripture everywhere intends by it: for no follower of the Vedas, and no Vedantic philosopher (whatever Rammohun Roy has alleged), regards the proposition that 'There is One Supreme' or even 'One all-pervading mind' as at all incompatible with the system of popular idolatry ... It is no sufficient objection to *devah* that it is not generally applied to this the highest scale in their mythology: the greater rather... is the necessity of vindicating to this word ... its proper meaning of Godhead in the highest sense" (emphasis added; Mill, 1828: 1). Wilson concurred with Mill, citing as evidence a supposed reference to the supreme God in this line from Bhartṛhari: *eko devaḥ keśavo vā śivo vā*. *Īśvara*, an alternative to *deva*, "involves a notion of Supremacy which would render it a solecism to say *īśvarā bahavaḥ*" (1828: 25—26), and would not convey an opposition between one true God and many false ones.

For the Hebrew Tetragrammaton Mill suggested either *īśvara* and *parameśvara*, or *śambhu* and *svayambhu*, preferring the latter pair because they convey more naturally the connotation of self-existence (1828: 2). Wilson warned against them in view of their popular association with Śiva. The first pair of terms was preferable to him because "the *Iswara* recognized by one division [of Sāṅkhya] is something different from any of the mythological persons, and by the Vaishnavas the world is said to be triform

[23] The publication date, which does not appear on the title page, can be verified in "The Boden Professorship of Sanscrit at Oxford," 1832: 246. H. H. Wilson appealed to his work on "the rendering of Scripture Terms into the Sanskrit language" when he was a candidate for the Boden Chair in 1832 (Monier—Williams, 1976: ix, n. 4).

or *cidacidīśvaraḥ*, 'Spirit, matter, and a governing Power'" (1828: 26). Whatever the final choice of translators might be, Mill pleaded, Carey's practice of transcribing *Yahweh* into Devanāgarī characters must be abandoned. "The Serampore translators... withhold from, instead of imparting to the heathen reader, the real knowledge of the name, ... at the same time tending to confirm him in his favourite notion of local religion and worship (varying for different nations of mankind as well for the object as the mode of it), attributing an unintelligible Proper Name to the foreign God of Israel" (1828: 2).

Despite the risk of initial misunderstanding, Mill was willing to utilize terminology appropriated by Hindu philosophy and religion in the hope of gradually grafting new connotations onto it. For instance, he favored expressing κτίσις by *sṛṣṭi*. "It is no objection... that the Hindus do not attach to this word at present the idea of creation from nothing. The same might be said of κτίζειν and *creare*, in the language of Pagan Greece and Rome: which are nevertheless in Christian writings always employed in the scriptural sense. The knowledge of the Scriptures will do the same for the language of the converted Hindu" (1828: 5). In reference to utilizing *mukti*, his defense was as follows: "It is no objection to the use of this word, that the Mukti or Salvation which the Hindu devotees profess to seek, consists in the absorption of individual existence in the One Eternal Essence of the Deity and is expressly distinguished by them from what they deem the lower (and perishable) reward of individual happiness in the heaven of Indra. The circumstance of this being the proper word for salvation — and the only one for Eternal salvation decides us to take this: and the right idea of it will follow to the converted Hindu" (1828: 7).

Wilson's chief contribution to the new hermeneutics was selection of soteriological terminology. As an equivalent for δικαιοσύνη ("justification"), which in Christian thought has come to mean a transhuman juridical act whereby legal rectitude is imputed to a believer (KITTEL, 1964—72: 192—210), Mill suggested either *yathārthīkaraṇa* or *nyāyīkaraṇa* (Mill, 1828: 8). Wilson bypassed both terms and proposed *śuddhi* instead, which Mill had suggested for ἁγιασμός ("sanctification"). "If we follow the example of the original and apply to forensic language for an equivalent, *śuddhiḥ* and *śuciḥ* are the terms there used. The latter however will be best reserved for the personal purification of the Jews; the former may be applied to Justification. Thus after a person has undergone the ordeal of taking a ring or seal out of boiling oil it is said *pradeśinīṃ ca tasyātha parīkṣeyuḥ parīkṣikāḥ / yasya vispoṭakā na syuḥ śuddho 'sav anyathāśuciḥ //* Mitakshara [2.113]. 'Let the examiners examine his finger, if no blisters appear he is innocent, otherwise he is guilty" (1828: 31). *Śuddhi* in this sense later became a keyword in the writings of John Muir.

Mill and Wilson had published their proposal in the hope of stimulating further inquiry, and the response reflected widespread interest. One reader, Rammohun Roy, perhaps slightly offended by Mill's reference to him (*vide* page 40, *supra*), was disturbed by their assessment of the term *deva*. Because of its consequences for the direction of the new hermeneutics, a hitherto unknown letter written by Roy about this issue is worthy of lengthy quotation.[24]

"I regret very much that the Revd. W. Mill and Dr. Wilson have relied so much on the occasional use of some terms as employed in ancient writings, instead of referring to the present acceptation of the word amongst the Natives of India. In proposing Deva as a substitute for the word God, these two learned gentlemen adduce two circumstances. 1st — That this Sanskrit term is similar in sound to the word Theos in Greek and Deus in Latin — Though these words might have been derived one from the other, the meaning commonly attached to one of them may be different from that of the others. Since words however closely connected by etymology often branch into widely different significations, being used sometimes in a vague and general sense as Spirit in English from the Latin Spiritus; sometimes with a limited and precise meaning as 'Balakhana' signifying the upper story of a house... Therefore no general reliance can be placed on derivation to justify the application of a derivative word in one language according to its signification of the original... The second circumstance to which they refer is that the word Deva is found in the ancient Sanscrit writings applied to the Supreme Being. I must observe that the word is very rarely so applied; and where so used is never taken substantively but adjectively and explained by the commentators to signify "Glorious," "Splendid,"... the ancient writer or writers of the Veds being very careful to preserve a distinction between the signification of the word Deva and the Supreme Being... The Hindus whether in the Lower or Upper Provinces, in Bengal or Hindusthan, never use the word Deva at all singly, but on the contrary have recourse to the word Deota... when they wish to express separately the meaning implied in the word Deva... In my humble opinion the introduction of this word Deva to signify God... would require a change in the vernacular language of this country and unintentionally tend to confirm irrevocably Polytheism among the Hindoos" (Roy, n. d.).

Roy's criticisms were taken seriously; thereafter *deva* was restricted to the idea of false gods. Other articles appeared in Indian journals, debating whether or not Mill and Wilson were too cautious or overly experimental. Orientalist Vans Kennedy, to cite only one example, urged translators to use *bhagavān* and *brahman* for *deus* (1831b: 200—07).[25] Encouraged by this response, Mill and Wilson jointly composed evangelistic tracts in Sanskrit (James, 1830: 129), none of which, regrettably, still exist.

After laboring for nearly a decade to construct a hermeneutics suitable for teaching arcane dogmas (e. g., the relations between the Three Persons of

---

[24] This letter is mentioned neither in S. D. Collet's Life and Letters of Raja Rammohun Roy (1914) nor N. Matthews' and D. Wainwright's Guide to Western Manuscripts in the British Isles Relating to South and S. E. Asia (1965).

[25] See also Kennedy, 1831a: 169ff.; J. Wilson, 1830—31: 356ff.; *idem*, 1831: 318ff.

the Trinity), Mill abruptly abandoned this cumbrous approach to dialogue. Instead, he began to announce Jesus Christ as the "great saviour" (*mahāmoktṛ*), emphasizing thereby that Christianity is a way of salvation, a *mokṣadharma* or *muktimārga*, not just another theologico-philosophical system, which was probably the impression given by the Creeds. Mill had realized long before that Hindus were more likely confounded than enlightened by an avalanche of Christian dogma, no matter how sophisticated its terminology. During a journey to Poona in 1822, he entered the following cryptic note in his diary: "Brahmans refuse [to accept copies of the] N. T.; [they] say they find it is not medicine [for *mokṣa*] but theology and morals" (Mill, n. d.: fol. 72).

Rāmacandra Vidyābhūṣaṇa, Mill's pandit, was the catalyst that made him decide to jettison excess ballast from the Christian message in order to highlight its salvific value. The pandit presented some Sanskrit verses in praise of Jesus Christ to Mill in 1828, and he hoped to expand them into a Purāṇa (Mill, 1831—37: ix). Commencing with the lament of a *śiṣya* ("student") bewildered by wise men, whose teachings conflict with each other (*budhāḥ samastāḥ parasparaṃ bhinnamatāḥ*), Rāmacandra's poem then proceeded to the response of the guru, a follower of the true scripture (*yathārthaśāstrānuyāyin*), who declared the path of salvation (*paritrāṇapatha*). Intrigued by this approach, Mill appropriated the project when Rāmacandra's zeal lagged. Completed with Wilson's assistance, the finished text, which retained the pandit's introductory canto, swelled to the massive size of more than five thousand *ślokas*. Mill called it the Śrīkhṛṣṭasaṃgītā (hereafter cited as ŚKhS),[26] thereby suggesting a contrast between his subject and the Bhagavad-Gītā's Kṛṣṇa. This composition, called the "Indian Christiad" in view of its epic proportions (Mill, 1831—37: lvi), is especially unique because no other Christian author, Indian or European, attempted anything on the same scale in Sanskrit until P. C. Devassia's *mahākāvya*, the Kristubhāgavatam, recently appeared (1977). It is practical to extract only a few verses from this vast text for analysis with regard to Mill's newly found hermeneutical freedom.

The most striking feature of the ŚKhS, in contrast to Mill's earlier work, is its incorporation of compounded philosophical terms already appropriated by classical *darśanas* (e. g., *cidrūpa*, 1.14.25, *rajastamovihīna*, 2nd ed., 1.1.12,

[26] The first volume, Yeṣūtpattiparva, was published by Bishop's College Press in 1831. Three subsequent volumes, Putrābhiṣekaparva, Satpālakacaritra, and the Moktṛmāhātmya, were published by the same press in 1837. A second, slightly revised, edition was issued in 1842 after Mill's return to England. S. RAJAMANICKAM mistakenly attributed the ŚKhS to de Nobili for two reasons. First, there are several anonymous manuscripts in South Indian libraries identical to the ŚKhS except for the title, Khṛṣṭugītā. Second, de Nobili is known to have composed some literature in Sanskrit, but none has yet been identified with much certainty. On this basis, RAJAMANICKAM speculated that de Nobili was the original author and that Mill's printed edition was only a copy. On the contrary, the anonymous manuscripts are copies of Mill's text made in the customary way for duplicating books in India at that time (*vide* RAJAMANICKAM, 1972: 86—90).

and *saccidvimba*, 2nd ed. 1.1.24), but without any qualifications whatsoever. Clearly, in the ŚKhS Mill was at ease with his hermeneutics. The reason for this seems to be his belief that the context itself, drawn from the life of Christ in the Gospels, would guard against unnatural associations. One example from the last canto of the Yeṣūtpattiparva (the "Īśvaraputrastotra") will suffice to illustrate this principle. This section imitates the "Namaskāra" portion of the Devīmāhātmya and is replete with unqualified epithets drawn from other Purāṇic texts. In one passage, Mill ethicized *māyā* by contextualizing it with Christ's victory over Satan: *yaccihnāgre dviṣāṃ devo bhumau pete nṛmatsyakaḥ/namas tasmai namas tasmai māyāprakṣepiṇe namaḥ* // ("Glory to him! Glory to him! Glory to him, the destroyer of *māyā*! Before whose sign [the cross or crucifix ?], the god of [his] foes, half-man and half-fish, plunged to earth!" 1.14.53). *Māyā* in this context, is not an inexplicable principle responsible for the cosmic illusion, but rather it suggests moral, even demonic rebellion in the universe. It is not only *ajñāna* on a magnified scale; it is also ethical chaos.

With this kind of *śloka*, the new hermeneutics entered yet another stage of development: philological exactitude was superseded by contextualization. That this transition had actually taken place is supported by the birth-narrative (Yeṣūtpattiparva), the context for eulogizing Christ as *māyāprakṣepin*. The significance of the setting is that Mill attempted there to satisfy an aspect of Hindu religious psychology, to which Nārāyaṇa Rāo made allusion (*vide* p. 29f., *supra*): the belief that the advent of an *avatāra* must be attended by great portents of future happiness. The author realized that the context of Christ's birth must be shifted from its immediate inauspicious consequence (the slaughter of children in Bethlehem) to the eventual overthrow of Satan and other eschatalogical victories.

Another verse at the end of the "Īśvaraputrastotra" (1.14.72), uttered by Jesus Christ, indicates that Mill overcame his previous inhibitions about terminology technically appropriated by Advaita Vedānta: *yohanni janyāyanaprastutaḥ sa mayy eva mārgaṃ parimṛṣṭam āpyāt / hatāsv ahaṃkṛtyagamāṭavīṣu tatsaccidānandanivārikāsu* // ("When the forests and mountains of egotism, obscuring [my] *saccidānanda* from them, are destroyed, may he, who has commenced on the path that originated with John [the Baptist], attain in Me alone, the thoroughly pure *mārga*").[27] Except for the intrusion of a non-Sanskritic name (Yohanni), there is no artificiality in this passage. From the hermeneutical point of view, however, it has both a peculiar weakness and strength. Unlike his treatment of *māyā*, Mill did not here contextualize *ahaṃkṛti* ("egotism") in such a way that it was ethicized and connoted selfishness as an offense against God. It is not improbable, therefore, that Hindus took this passage as evidence that Christians share

[27] In view of the current fascination with *saccidānanda* among Indian and Western theologians (e.g., BOYD, 1974: 82—84, 93—94), it is appropriate to point out that its first appearance in a Christian context was in the supposed seventeenth-century forgery, the so-called Pseudo-Veda (ELLIS, 1822: 9).

with them the presupposition, embedded in *ahaṃkṛti*, that conceptualizing oneself as a distinct ontological entity over against Brahman is a flaw resulting from intellectual — not moral — weakness. The strength of this verse is its identification of *saccidānanda* with Jesus Christ. Mill's belief in an interpersonal exchange with the absolute, as a possibility not doubtful but real, may thereby have been communicated more effectively than if such a bold reversal of the concept had not been attempted.

Mill's transition to a more mature, contextualized hermeneutics, unencumbered by countless pedantic qualifications, was foreshadowed by several statements in the Proposed Version of Theological Terms. To say that the "right idea of [*mukti*]," for example, "will follow to the converted Hindu," implies a series of assumptions. First, the established connotations of words cannot be subverted, except slowly. Second, from a Christian perspective, the concept of *mukti* is not entirely false; there is something true about it that leads into Christianity. Third, its dross will be extracted "after" conversion, as "Hindu Christians" (the expression for converts at that time) progress in their understanding of the new faith. And fourth, *mukti* may be safely, indeed persuasively, used by Christian translators and retained by converts as part of their spiritual heritage. Mill's hermeneutics, then, avoided emphasizing disjunctions between Hindu and Christian thought. Rather, by gradual, if not almost imperceptible, alterations of context and meaning, he rerouted his audience toward Christianity. The strategy was to bring Hindu readers to the goal by means of familiar landmarks, and to get them there before they realize where they are going, for then they might turn back.

One might ask at this point whether or not the ŚKhS accomplished this desired end at least in the case of Rāmacandra, whose apparent affection and even reverence for Jesus Christ inspired Mill in the first place. Mill learned, to his obvious disappointment, that not only his pandit but other Hindus as well were capable of something unimaginable from his exclusivistic point of view: multiple allegiance, whether to the Bible and the Bhagavad-Gītā, or to Christ and Kṛṣṇa.[28] Yet the ŚKhS performed its function well; it was a bridge to the learned Hindu community that would not otherwise have been there. "Many Brahmans have expressed a strong desire to read this work: and one heathen pandit now teaches it to his heathen pupils. In the temple of Cālighat, ... I have witnessed its eager reception by a number of priestly devotees, ... who in those precincts would have rejected even with contumely the gift of any Bengali or Hindi tract, but who read and chanted this with a full knowledge of its anti-idolatrous tendency" (Mill, 1831—37: lix).

Also important to note is that Mill himself realized his hermeneutical experiments were unprecedented, and that these tentative efforts might provoke a backlash in the missionary community. On the one hand, he was at

[28] "Though sufficiently enlightened to confess freely the moral superiority of the Gospel to the exoteric superstition to which he conforms, [Rāmacandra] declares with equal frankness, his decided preference to the mystic theology of the Bhagavad Gita to anything which he has seen in Christianity" (Mill, 1831—37: lx).

ease with his methodology in retelling the Gospels and undoubtedly believed he was on the right track. Equivocation, on the other hand, is evident in his concern that critics would accuse him of crypto-Hindu tendencies. Inertia in missionary methods, which regarded all innovation as paganizing Christianity rather than Christianizing Hinduism, threatened him. That the charge of creating a hybrid Christo-paganism was a worrisome problem can be seen in the English preface, where Mill defensively claimed that he "did not concede anything, either in taste or expression, to the Hindus," but took from them only "the material of language and measure, in which... Christian sentiments might be expressed" (1831—37: liii). Despite his assimilation of Sanskrit terminology in a way that was clearly not syncretistic, the foregoing survey of his hermeneutics is proof that his remark was an understatement.

Contrary to Mill's concern that the ŚKhS might tarnish his reputation for orthodoxy, the Society for the Propogation of the Gospel's annual report for 1831 informed its supporters hyperbolically that the book was "admitted as a standard work to be used in the most solemn offices of [brahminical] religion" (Mill, 1833). Lest someone might misunderstand this exaggerated flattery, Mill clarified his reference to the reception of the ŚKhS at Kālighāṭ. The report's assertion, he objected defensively, "was utterly destitute of foundation in fact" (Mill, 1833). His amended account, quoted at length below, is a poignant reminder of the uneasiness felt by this pioneering hermeneutist in the presence of doctrinally demanding peers. As an eyewitness account of tentative signs of approval given by Kālighāṭ Hindus for this form of interreligious encounter, the document also shows how brahminical prejudices eroded slowly. "I described... what happened on a particular occasion when I first distributed the tract at Cālighat... Many of the throng of devotees (not those who were then engaged in worship before the shrine of the goddess — but crowding the adjoining porticoes...) receiving the tract when offered to them, and finding it not to be a vernacular Bengali tract, but in their own sacred Sanscrit, — chanting its metrical sentences after their usual manner of reading, with evident pleasure and delight. Surely there is a vast interval between this and the assertion that the work was 'used in' (i.e., so as to be a part of) 'the solemn offices of their own idolatrous religion': ... Those engaged at the time in singing the praises of the goddess, asked for the book to be laid down on the floor beside them, — since it was impure for them to touch at that time, but they would read it afterwards by themselves! Such was the case with nearly all those; only one or two refusing it altogether: and I doubt not that every one who received it from my hands in the temple, had need of some ceremonial lustration before he worshipped Cāli again" (Mill, 1833).

The crucial, though seemingly insignificant, step forward at this juncture in interreligious relations was that almost everyone at Kālighāṭ accepted a copy of the ŚKhS — some with unfeigned reluctance but others with sincere appreciation. This happened in spite of the book's limitations: its *mleccha* (barbarian, non-Hindu) author; its odd subject matter; and even its leather binding.[29] In view of these disadvantages, Mill's comparatively favorable reception is puzzling. One reason for this treatment is that Mill, unlike Carey, admitted the existence of at least some jewels inside the "golden casket" as well as "pebbles and trash." Moreover, he had actually interpreted, or adorned, Jesus Christ with those very jewels (e. g., *saccidānanda*). Another underlying factor, which revolutionized Mill's presentation as well as Carey's, was Sanskrit itself. In this connection the ramifications of *mleccha* must be considered. The Viṣṇudharmasūtra (64.15) and the Vāsiṣṭhadharmasūtra (6.41), to mention only two texts, unequivocally prohibit Hindus from speaking to, or learning the languages of, non-Aryans (Kane, 1968: 290—91; *idem*, 1941: 383). No corresponding legal prohibition, however, prevents them from listening to a *mleccha* who addresses them in their own sacred speech and cherished cadences. Of course, presumption was altogether against such a contingency arising. By finding a loophole in regulations restricting contact with *mlecchas*, Mill managed to defy stereotypes. It is not improbable that the Kālīghāṭ Hindus asked themselves, even if only tentatively, whether or not this Khṛṣṭa (Christ), whose words Mill had framed in a pleasingly polished style of the *āryabhāṣā* ("Aryan language"), was more than a mere *mleccha* god unworthy of an honest hearing.

Parallels with the Apostle Paul's address to the Athenians concerning the "unknown God," in which references were made to Greek poets and Stoic philosophers, are too obvious to ignore. Both the Apostle and the Principal utilized languages and technically appropriated terminology that possessed an aura of sanctity and authority. Consequently, both men gained an attentive audience, which, in all probability, would have rejected their message outright if it had worn a less prestigious dress.[30] In point of fact, Mill's pioneering work in Christian Sanskrit literature did attain acclaim. Shortly before his departure from India in 1837, a Hindu *kavi* pronounced him a new Kālidāsa (*kālidāsaḥ punarajani bhuvi*, "Tribute of the Pandits," 1837: 710). It was not until John Muir, however, that the new Indian hermeneutics was applied self-confidently as a legitimate aspect of the Christian approach to Hindus.

When Christian hermeneutists took advantage of Sanskrit's recognized capacity for multiple signification, that language entered a new phase and its

[29] W. Yates had the same trouble as Mill a decade earlier: "When Yates, the Baptist missionary, visited [Nuddea] in 1821, the pandits would not receive even Sanscrit tracts from him near the river, but sent a person to procure them at a prescribed distance from its banks" (Weitbrecht, 1858: 148). Probably these tracts were Yates's now lost Satyadarśana, which invited native literati to study the Christian scriptures.

[30] To make an analogy with the Apostle Paul does not, of course, legitimize Mill's hermeneutics or immunize it against criticism. One might draw an analogy with a Hindu (e. g., Radhakrishnan) trying to communicate Vedānta to Western readers by means of English and thoughtforms borrowed from European philosophers, but then the correspondence with a sacred language like Sanskrit would be missing. Furthermore, Mill himself had the Apostle Paul in mind as the model for his hermeneutics (Mill, 1837: 721).

literature was enlarged. Just as was the case centuries earlier with Buddhist and Jain Sanskrit, the Dharmapustaka and ŚKhS transformed Sanskrit according to the needs of a particular religious community. Henceforth in this study, this material will be designated as Church Sanskrit. The reason for this name is not the same as that connoted by similar but contemptuous names, such as Missionary Bengali or Babu English. Nor is it meant to suggest a language like Buddhist Hybrid Sanskrit, which altered standard phonetics and spawned unusual grammatical forms. In its mature stage, Church Sanskrit was purely classical and clearly conformable to the *kāvya* style. But Sanskrit was not left unaltered by the impact of Carey and Mill; nor was Christianity unchanged by Sanskrit. Hermeneutical assimilation and dissimilation had its corollary in the Sanskritization of Christianity and the Christianization of Sanskrit. There was an assimilation because each term had established connotations of various degrees of convergence with the Christian idea to which it was fused (e. g., *deva*). There was also dissimilation because the associations of certain terms were overruled in the new atmosphere of forensic theology (e. g., *śuddhi*).

At least initially Carey and Mill only had tactical considerations in mind when they selected Sanskrit as the matrix for the new Indian hermeneutics. Primarily they wanted to deprive pandits of linguistic inferiority as a reason for dismissing Christianity out of hand. Another tangible, but unrealized, benefit was a standard liturgical, devotional and theological language, maximizing the benefits of uniform phraseology throughout India, for which the linguistic precision of Sanskrit would be necessary. Professor M. Monier-Williams, for one, was optimistic about this rich linguistic matrix at the disposal of the Indian church. "Such, indeed, is the exuberance and flexibility of this language and its power of compounding words, that when it has been, so to speak, baptized, and thoroughly penetrated with the spirit of Christianity, it will probably be found, next to Hebrew and Greek, the most expressive vehicle of Christian truth" (1861: 54). After reading the Boden Professor's remark, nothing could be more sobering than V. Raghavan's assessment of Church Sanskrit as "crude and unintelligible jargon" (1956: 5). Both men, however, stood apart from the historical context of interreligious dialogue that Church Sanskrit was meant to subserve. The most exacting test undergone by the new Indian hermeneutics was the MP Controversy, and the basis for judgment upon it must be the pandits who disputed with Muir, the successor of Carey and Mill.[31]

---

[31] See also Young, 1979: 227ff., for additional information about Church Sanskrit in the post-Muir period and a bibliography of literature based upon that terminology.

IV. THE DISPUTANTS

Few controversies entail such disastrous consequences for mutual respect as those about religion, especially when participants and spectators do not try to understand the complexity of the milieu in which the arguments are premised. This is why each contributor to what is here called the MP Controversy must be viewed individually rather than merely labeled as a Christian or Hindu. After all, this was a conflict not between religions per se, but rather between religious persons of particular persuasions. To allow labels to suffice in this study might lead contemporary Christians to disavow Muir's MP, and Hindus to reject Soma.'s MPŚ, Hara.'s MPO, and Nīla.'s ŚTV. Choices such as these are, of course, unencouraged here. Then, in order to enhance mutual understanding and keep sectarian partiality at a distance, each of the MP Controversy disputants is presented in the following pages insofar as biographical information illuminates their apologetics.

John Muir (1810—1882): The Challenger

John Muir, eldest son of a Glasgow merchant and sometime magistrate of that city, received his education in Greek and Latin at the grammar school in Irvine. Tertiary studies at the University of Glasgow were interrupted when a prominent uncle nominated him to a writership in the East India Company. As was the pattern for new appointees, Muir entered the Company's training college at Haileybury in 1826, where he was awarded prizes and medals in classics, law, and Bengali. A compulsory year of orientation at Calcutta's College of Fort William began in mid-1828, at which time, presumably, he studied under William Carey, Professor of Bengali. It may have been that Carey himself introduced Muir to Church Sanskrit.

Muir's arrival in Calcutta coincided with an important stage in the development of the new hermeneutics. Carey's manifesto in the Friend of India had appeared earlier in the decade, preceded by the Dharmapustaka. The Calcutta Baptists, W. Yates and J. Wenger, were occupied with their Sanskrit version of the Bible, several pericopes of which were soon to be issued. Mill's translations of the Decalogue and creeds were still circulating. The Proposed Version of Theological Terms, completed with H. H. Wilson's assistance, had already elicited Rammohun Roy's acerbic comments. More importantly, the ŚKhS was conceived in 1828.

Unstinting support as a layman for the propagation of Christianity and diligent research into Sanskrit literature were the two outstanding features of Muir's career in India. That he preferred these activities to his work in the EIC is confirmed in the fact that, although he established his reputation as an evangelist and Sanskritist at an early date, his name is mentioned only in footnotes to administrative studies of the North-Western Provinces where he served for a quarter century. By pursuing a career with the EIC, Muir was following the example of many other nineteenth-century Orientalists, who lived at a time when Indic studies was still not widely recognized as a legitimate field in an academic curriculum. Serving in the mofussil became an opportunity for acquiring languages and collecting materials useful for his sectarian works, such as the MP, and his major contribution to Indology, Original Sanskrit Texts.

The scope of this scholarly lay missionary's secondary career in administration will be summarized succinctly, referring only to where and when he worked for the Company in the NWP. There are two reasons for making this outline, even though Muir's career was not extraordinary. First, by linking his name to others in civil administration, it will be possible to ascertain some of the influences that shaped his theological outlook. Second, it will define more precisely the Hindu milieu that Muir knew firsthand and argued against.

Between 1830 and 1853, Muir was alternately gazetted to five of the six divisions in the NWP. His first assignment was assistant to the Collector-Magistrate of Farrukhabad (1830—1833). Later he transferred to the Sadr Board of Revenue in Allahabad, serving (1833—1837) as Assistant to the Secretary, Robert Merttins Bird. Appointed next as a Settlement Officer in the Meerut and Saharanpur Districts (1837—1842), he investigated titles to tax-exempt properties. It was in this period that the MP was written and revised for the first time. During a brief but eventful tenure, Muir went to Benares and supervised the reorganization of the Sanskrit College (1844—1845). From 1845 to 1850, he was alternately gazetted as Collector-Magistrate at Azamgahr, Gorakhpur, and Delhi. Three years before retirement, he served as Civil and Sessions Judge in Fatehpur (1850—1853).

It is relevant to determine the theological party, if any, to which Muir was aligned while serving with the EIC. Instead of his denominational affiliation as a Protestant (Episcopal Church of Scotland), the issue concerns views that would shape his attitude to missions and other religions. Any hope is ill-founded that would expect an answer to correspond to one of the labels bandied about in modern parlance. Moreover, to ascertain which form of Christianity Soma., Hara., and Nīla. encountered and rebutted, such terms as Fundamentalist, Evangelical, or Liberal will be less than useful by themselves.

Priority is assigned to issues in religion in a way that changes continuously from one century to the next and from one continent to another. Evangelical, a notorious term used below, no longer signifies what it did even in the preceding century. Its permutations have been legion, beginning (in the English speaking world) in the sixteenth century and continuing into the present. It further splits into British, American, and continental us-ages.[32] Whether Muir was an Evangelical or something else can be determined according to diverse sets of criteria. A pious devotional life, fired by a sense of urgency about bringing the Gospel to non-Christians might be one set (the British); and scrupulous regard for such doctrines as total depravity, substitutionary atonement, and biblical inerrancy another (the American). Such distinctive features of Evangelicalism as these often but not always coexisted in the early nineteenth-century Christian, just as they do today. In the following discussion, they will frequently intersect.

According to either of the above-mentioned sets of criteria, the MP's author was a quasi-Evangelical. One finds evidence of both traits in Muir's conduct and writings, but they coexisted uneasily with others not generally found in Evangelicals. Although he moved within their circles, he was gradually entering another theological universe, in which non-supernaturalistic explanations of biblical inspiration and miracles prevailed, as well as latitudinarian beliefs about the salvation of non-Christians. Muir made this transition partly because of his encounter with Hinduism, which had a profound impact on his understanding of tolerance and truth in religion. During the time that he composed and revised the MP twice, the severity of his judgment on Hindus fluctuated markedly. However much Muir's commitment to Evangelicalism was subject to vicissitudes, he was clearly indebted to that tradition, expressing himself conceptually in its terminology especially when he wrote the MP.

The way to establish Muir's theological proclivities is twofold. First, this subject is approached by utilizing P. PENNER's study of the Thomasonian school of settlement officers, the most thorough examination of the religious attitudes of administrators with whom Muir served. This is supplemented by looking into Muir's management of the Benares Sanskrit College in order to see how he put his convictions into practice. The second approach is to sift through the internal evidence in his own theological and missiological writings.

Historians have long recognized that committed Christians took an active role in the British administration of the NWP, and that many of them engaged, privately or publicly, in religious and social causes. The connections between them were so close that they formed a network of sympathizers, a school of thought united by common views and goals. The shared ideals that drew these administrators (for the most part Haileybury graduates from the 1820s and 1830s) together were evangelical, expansionist, and reformist (PENNER, 1970: iii). Under the leadership of James Thomason, Lieutenant General of the NWP (1843—1853), these Christian administrators coalesced even more tightly.

Thomason was strongly influenced by the piety and social consciousness of the Clapham sect, the evangelical wing of the Church of England led by

---

[32] As a continental designation for Lutherans, evangelical can be dismissed here. The Oxford Dictionary of the English Language concisely summarizes the vicissitudes to which this word has been subject.

Charles Simeon, a Cambridge clergyman. Simeon's influence on Charles Grant of the EIC's London-based Board of Directors is well documented. For nominating candidates to the Indian chaplaincy, Grant depended upon Simeon's advice, and many of them were his own curates. As a child, Thomason had been entrusted to Simeon's care, imbibing from him the deeply-felt concern for non-Christians that so often characterizes Evangelicalism. Like most nineteenth-century Evangelicals, Thomason was equally committed to India's social and economic development. This was characteristic of the balance between pietism and activism that the Thomasonian school maintained.

Administrators who looked to Thomason for leadership in matters of government and religion linked themselves with missionaries, especially Evangelicals, wherever they served. Pockets of Evangelicals, consequently, existed in most provincial centers where Muir served. The Benares Division was one; Allahabad and its Sadr Board of Revenue headed by R. M. Bird, a prominent Evangelical under whom Muir served, was another (PENNER, 1970: 21—23).

PENNER hesitated, with justifiable caution, to classify Muir as a full-fledged evangelical Thomasonian. To some extent Muir did adhere to the above-cited pattern. His frequent contributions to missionary periodicals underlined his sympathy for, if not allegiance to, Evangelicals. Definitely on their periphery, Muir never publically declared his solidarity with them. Rather, having qualms about their often ill-informed enthusiasm, he professed support for their proselytizing in principle only.

Along with Muir's evangelical sympathies were others that, in modern language, are called ecumenical. British Evangelicals, generally speaking, have been less separatist-minded than their American counterparts. Muir, likewise, valued unity more than doctrinal purity. There is no evidence whatsoever that Muir disdained Dissenters or that he thought their missionary activities infringed upon Anglican prerogatives. More than once he contributed to the Baptists' Friend of India, to mention only one denomination whose relations with the officially recognized clergy were far from cordial. The John Wenger Collection of the BMS Archives contains numerous letters from Muir, in which the two correspondents pondered over Sanskrit equivalents for biblical terminology. To attribute this kind of ecumenical cooperation to Muir does not detract from his standing as an Evangelical, quasi or otherwise.

The depth and durability of Muir's commitment to Evangelicalism can be tested by examining memoranda submitted by him to government while superintending the Benares Sanskrit College (1844—45). These documents are revealing because the situation in which they were written was so anomalous. An appointment such as Muir's was a calculated risk, regardless of the degree to which he was a fully persuaded Evangelical. How would the faculty and student body react to this principal, a qualified Sanskritist but author of the MP (first published five years earlier), which purported to overthrow the very religion the College was meant to preserve and even rejuvenate? If nothing else, Muir's appointment is evidence that Thomasonians tried to bring Christian influence — or pressure — to bear on that religion.

The test must not be phrased in terms of a general plan for infusing into the College Western modes of thought allegedly responsible for European technological achievements. The issue is whether or not Muir tried to steer the pandits and students toward Christianity either as a religion to which they should convert or as a superior statement of truth. One finds that Muir influenced the curriculum according to a perspective that was firm though unaccompanied by the defiant gestures one would expect from a "flaming Evangelical."

When the Benares Sanskrit College (founded by Jonathan Duncan in the late eighteenth century) began to deteriorate in the early 1840s, Muir, whose reputation as a Sanskritist came to the attention of his superiors in government, was selected to diagnose its ills. A harshly worded memorandum was submitted to the education department soon afterward. Muir did not restrict his criticisms to the pandits' tedious traditional teaching methods. At the outset the report condemned, in sweeping generalizations, the religious and philosophic content of the courses themselves. "The metaphysical systems are notoriously characterized by grave errors, the Vedanta being decidedly pantheistic, the Nyaya maintaining the eternity of matter, and the Sankhya in one of its branches being of an atheistic tendency: and even the astronomy which the scientific books of the Hindus teach is the exploded Ptolemaic" (Muir, 1844). The aggressively ethical overtones of this statement made it more an accusation than a description, but this is what the Thomasonians expected to hear from him.

In point of fact, Muir only had a moderate revision of the curriculum in mind, foreseeing just one draconian measure: cancellation of courses in judicial astrology. The dilemma for him was whether or not an institution established by government for public enlightenment could countenance a craft that seemed, from the Western point of view, so obnoxious. "Perhaps the teaching of astrology should be interdicted at once ... and the pandits directed to restrict their prelections to arithmetic, algebra, mathematics and astronomy. The only other mode of proceeding I see would be, without formally prohibiting astrology, to omit all recognition of it and prescribe that so much time should be devoted to the acquisition of other branches as should leave no time for its study" (Muir, 1844). Later, Muir did ban this course from the College, and even though astrology attracted the greatest number of students because of its utility in earning a brahmin's income, its banishment failed to provoke protest (Muir, 1845a). One cannot say that Muir's action was motivated by Evangelicalism, stemming as it did from an almost universal prejudice among his European colleagues.

Muir's manipulation of the philosophy curriculum aimed at depriving the *darśanas* of all vestiges of revelation. This he attempted to do by forcing pandits to abandon their way of teaching, which he thought was tantamount to indoctrination, and to adopt free debate instead. Upon arrival in Benares, he found that each pandit taught his branch of philosophy dogmatically, demanding explicit credence from students. Although Vedānta dominated the other systems, Muir knew that precedents existed for proponents of one *darśana* to call into question the conformity of others to *śrūti* ("Revelation"). This openness to inquiry seemed to him a forum for relativizing Hinduism, subjecting it to a priori reasoning, and for introducing Christianity as an alternative. "This degree of toleration in regard to doctrine would... appear to point out a way in which these metaphysical systems... may from being sources of error, be converted into tolerable instruments for strengthening the reasoning powers. As it is the practice of pandits to argue publically, ... it would seem that they could have the less objection to the students being examined thereon in such a manner as to require them to compare the several systems with each other, and bring them to the test of reason" (emphasis added; Muir, 1844).

The phrase "test of reason" is a clue to Muir's status as a quasi-Evangelical. From the total context of his writing, it is clear that, in his nomenclature, reason was a code-word for the Judeo-Christian tradition and its Western superstructure. The assumption was that right reasoning is consonant with Christian doctrines. Evangelicals, too, were influenced by the Enlightenment, and their dependence on rational argumentation was more conspicuous in Muir's time than today. But Muir equated the mind's assent to doctrine with faith itself, allowing gnosis to eliminate a category of religion deemed essential by full-blooded Evangelicals.

In actuality, Muir did nothing of the sort proposed in his memorandum, even though he was given plenipotentiary powers by government. Students were not required to undergo examinations requiring them to compare the *darśanas*, even if only for the sake of mental exercise, vis-à-vis Western standards of truth (Muir, 1845a). The one change Muir introduced was a series of lectures for the college pandits on European "mental philosophy," which he delivered in Sanskrit (Muir, 1845a).[33] By his own account, "The lectures on mental philosophy interested some of them, as according with their natural turn for abstruse speculation" (1845a). But most noteworthy was his attempt to desacralize Śrūti, to introduce a serpent into this garden of Hindu thought. One can see that this was the intention of his farewell address to the College, delivered in February of 1845. "There is one point in the character of Bhaskara [a twelfth-century mathematician-astronomer] which I would commend to your particular notice and imitation. He was a mathematician in the true sense of the word, and, as his works evince, a real lover of truth. An enlightened young pandit, Bapu Dev,[34] who has studied his writings, informs me that he is in no instance content to receive any truth

[33] These lectures were published as Vyavahārāloka (1845).

[34] Bapu Dev became a celebrity among British educators in the NWP. L. Wilkinson, political agent at Bhopal, was impressed by his analytic skills and taught him Western astronomy, to which be readily assented. Bapu Dev's translation of Sūryasiddhānta is in the Bibliotheca Indica Series.

on the authority of the ancients, but invariably requires demonstration.[35] You should in like manner see that all your opinions rest on sufficient evidence, moral and demonstrative, according to the nature of the subject" (Muir, 1845b).

In this connection it is relevant to note that Muir's successor as principal, James Ballantyne, acted far more belligerently. This Scottish Sanskritist, an outspoken but respected scholar, used colorful language habitually. In a letter to Thomason, he insisted that the Sanskrit courses in the College "should pay tribute instead of scowling defiance" (Ballantyne, 1855b). This was not bombast, as his publications in Church Sanskrit and others amalgamating Hindu and Western science prove.[36] Ballantyne's avowed intention was to make "each educated Hindu a Christian" (1855b). His route to this end was indirect but purposeful: he enforced Muir's suggestion that students answer examinations requiring replies in Western terms, for example the following: "Refute the atheistic assertion that the works of nature are no proofs of the pre-existence of an intelligent creator, because all which we see must necessarily have had some form, and that it might as well be in its present form as any other" (Ballantyne, 1855a: xxxiii). With a note of triumph, Ballantyne reported that his Hindu students responded faithfully according to Paley's natural theology, in which he had instructed them (1855a: xxxiii).

Although at this juncture the evidence is mostly circumstantial, the overall impression Muir left behind is coherent: his commitment to Evangelicalism was consistently indecisive. One can cite as evidence that, even though he shared the Thomasonians' concern for Hindus, he was not dominated by anxiety about their alleged vulnerability to an awful and imminent divine wrath. Concerned but not anxious, Muir saw Hinduism's resistance to Christianity as intellectual, whereas solid Evangelicals would have regarded it as immorally based. A "false religion" must be brought to the "test of reason," but one that stifles truth because of ethical obtuseness must, in their parlance, be made subject to the lordship of Jesus Christ. Muir's fluctuations between these two poles is the reason for calling him a quasi-Evangelical in this study.

The evangelical half of Muir proved to be less than domineering when he superintended the Benares Sanskrit College. There he faced not only Hinduism in the abstract, a phenomenon to be studied, but as a religion to be professed. His constituents were those who, it was thought, needed the faith he embraced. But there is no reason to think that Muir either castigated Hinduism or expressed his bias in more than ambiguous terms. He nudged but never pushed the pandits and students toward Christianity, preferring

---

[35] *Atra gaṇitaskandhe upapattimān evāgamaḥ pramāṇaṃ* ("In the mathematical department, it is only the scripture which is attended by demonstration that is proof"; MUIR, 1910: 63—64).

[36] See, e. g., Candrabhramaṇavicāra: Does the Moon Rotate? The Question Argued in Sanskrit and English by Pandits of the Benares Sanskrit College and James R. Ballantyne (1857).

instead to eulogize dispassionate rationality. Of course, he was confident that, if properly executed, this course would lead them to his own religion. This drift toward a more rationalistic posture, which made his theological fluctuations even more pronounced and episodic, stemmed from a process of thought exemplified by his Theology of Conciliation.

According to Muir's reflections, conciliation is not only a theological and ethical imperative but a self-evident pedagogical principle as well. Rather than being an end in itself, a benevolent humanism, conciliation subserves reconciliation, which is God's redemptive activity. The Bible's clearest testimony to the truth of this position, Muir claimed, was the pattern of conduct established by the Apostle Paul, who acted by the following rule: "Give no offense to Jews, or to Greeks, or to the church of God. For my part I always try to meet everyone half-way, regarding not only my own good but the good of the many, so that they may be saved" (NEB, I Cor. 10.32—11.1). Muir elaborated his interpretation of this passage for missions in numerous articles, summarizing them in an essay entitled "Conciliation in Matters of Religion" (1843). The major thrusts of this publication are mentioned below and elucidated by means of an earlier article that commented controversially on the possibility of salvation without faith in Jesus Christ. This discussion is followed by references to sources that influenced Muir.

The subtitle of the monograph edition (1849) of Muir's essay, The Proper Adaptation of Instruction to the Character of the People Taught, made explicit that he understood conciliation primarily as a pedagogical exercise. His theological presuppositions, however, remained ambiguous. Be that as it may at this point, Muir delved into his subject with avidity, offering pragmatic advice about interreligious dialogue. His essay had a utilitarian aspect, and it became a manual for missionaries.

In the context of pedagogy, conciliation becomes the "study of the most probable means of recommending truth, both human and divine, to the minds of men" (Muir, 1843: 86). Along this line of reasoning, the *raison d'être* of missions is identical with that of academic disciplines: to impart knowledge in the most effective manner. Missions are to Christianity what rhetoric is to a professor. As a teacher experiments with different methods, hoping to find one that is right for an individual or groups of similar people, the missionary does likewise. The analogy breaks down, however, because the missionary approaches others who did not request his help and who already owe allegiance to another religion. To alter their loyalty, Muir argued, requires guidelines that derive from but also surpass ordinary pedagogics.

The first principle the missionary must learn is that opposition to his message may result as much from the exasperating manner in which he presents the Gospel as from serious objections to its content. "Zeal and honesty in a disputant," Muir warned, "are not alone sufficient to justify a reasonable hope of success" (1843: 86). The missionary must subject his words to scrutiny, weeding out whatever is harsh. He must cultivate empathy and stop thinking that he wages a real, if bloodless, battle against some kind of satanic power. Otherwise, the missionary mistakenly assumes that what he "sees clearly and feels strongly... must be seen and felt by others in the same manner" (Muir, 1843: 88). The way to correct this myopia is to remember that people are different. Muir urged missionaries to be regulated by the wisdom of a pedagogue, bearing in mind "not only the importance of the end to be gained, but also the peculiar character of those persons who are to be influenced" (1843: 86).

Muir was aware that most missionaries, bent on dethroning Hinduism, would reject his advice, demurring that "regard to the prejudices... of mankind, is an abdication of the prerogatives of the delegates of God; and that all caution in exploring the least obstructed approaches to the human heart is but a resort to that 'wisdom of the world' which St. Paul denounces" (1843: 89). This notwithstanding, Muir, whom E. SHARPE has called a "bridge between scholarship and Protestant missions" (1965: 36), never faltered in pressing missionaries to devote a few of their number to the study of Sanskrit literature. An earlier article may be quoted here, in which Muir expressed this idea more comprehensively than in his essay on conciliation.

"It is manifest that [the missionary] can carry no weight with learned Natives, if his conversation does not indicate that he does not vituperate at random the doctrines he assaults. If either confessedly or apparently he has never investigated the merits of those systems, he will be exposed to the imputation of impugning that of which he knows nothing, on no better grounds than those of foreign prejudice... The more extensive the missionary's acquaintance with Hindu literature, and the freer his acknowledgment of all its unobjectionable portions, the more credit will he be likely to gain for pure and honest views, and an enlightened wisdom" (Muir, 1838a: 190).

With reference to results, Muir encouraged missionaries in India to be especially patient and grateful for long-term changes, rather than expect abrupt conversions. Convictions with regard to religion alter by slow degrees. The missionary must, therefore, be sensitive, discerning the exact state of mind of his partners-in-dialogue. He must sympathize with their dilemma: "how can [the Hindu] bring himself to believe that a religion originating in a far distant region, whose records are contained in foreign languages, the character of which he is therefore precluded from examining personally can have any just claim on his attention" (1843: 111). If the missionary expects to overcome this barrier and gain the trust of his audience, he must never indulge in "abrupt and irritating assaults" on the doctrines they revere. His approach must be "calm, cautious, and conciliatory," searching for some "little oasis of truth, reason, or good feeling in the hearer's mind," whereby he may lead him "by an affectionate and gradual process of Socratic reasoning" to the point where conversion is the outcome of his own choice (1838c: 65).

Little in this outline of Muir's Theology of Conciliation stems from Evangelicalism. It evinces sincere concern and hope that Hindus will convert to Christianity, but there is no evidence that Muir conceived of the confrontation between the two religions as anything more than a clash of conflicting viewpoints. There is no note of urgency in presenting the Gospel to Hindus in order to save them from a Day of Judgment; no indication that the struggle is with a diabolic power. One would expect to hear these refrains if he had been an Evangelical. His manner was rather that of a patient teacher, trying to make a difficult point to students whose only fault is that they are reluctant to consider new ideas.

Most noteworthy in Muir's Theology of Conciliation is that the issue of real urgency is not how soon or how frequently the Christian message is brought before the Hindu; more crucial is how the missionary addresses him, which is a problem for pedagogics. This position helps to explain why Muir chose to present Christianity by such a roundabout method as Church Sanskrit, which was time-consuming in view of its strict standards of precision. He believed that the evangelization of India could wait without risk until the right methods for formulating the Christian message from the Sanskrit matrix were perfected. That, of course, was an immense task, but he noted that, "It is consoling to reflect that the responsibility of those persons, to whom the true religion is proposed, ... must always be proportioned to the clearness with which its evidences can be exhibited to their mind" (1843: 112). Again, pedagogy is at stake. Divine judgment depends not so much upon the Hindu's response as on the missionary's capacity to make his subject clear.

It has already been stated that the theological presuppositions underlying Muir's Theology of Conciliation were more implicit than explicit. His essay was rather the practical application of those principles than their explication. Why did pedagogy take precedence over an urgent, more evangelical form of proclamation? Muir supplied the answer in the following quotation, in which he commented on a passage from one of St. Paul's epistles (Romans 2.12—15): "It would appear to be a doctrine of scripture that those may be saved who are a law unto themselves, though they never heard the name of him before whom every knee should bow. If this be so, how can it be justifiable to say that the mere rejection of the Gospel entails the ruin of him who does not embrace it? ... It should seem therefore that the only proposition we are warranted in making, is, that those incur condemnation who, with some sense of the value of the Christian revelation, reject it from hatred or a culpable indifference" (1838c: 66—67). Verbal professions of faith, according to Muir's interpretation, are not a prerequisite for salvation, except in the case of those who comprehend that Christ is the "truth." Others who, through no fault of their own, fail to grasp this belief are nonetheless saved if they adhere to the moral law "inscribed" on their "hearts." It was possible for Muir to talk about the "mere rejection of the Gospel" because he claimed that missionaries themselves may be responsible for the resistance of their partners-in-dialogue. As Muir saw it, opposition originates as much from noetic as moral conflicts. This latitudinarianism, uncommon among his colleagues, was at variance with the pietist-inspired exegesis of the same epistle, which stressed the moral wretchedness of mankind (e.g., Rom. 3.23) and its "stifling" of truth (Rom. 1.18). Muir did allow that some forms of resistance to Christianity are "culpable," stemming either from meanness or repeated failure to respond to what has been clearly explained. Into these broad categories many would fall, facing "condemnation."

In spite of this proviso, Evangelicals accused Muir of espousing an incipient universalism. Alexander Duff, editor of the journal in which Muir expressed these thoughts, inserted a harshly worded disclaimer into the article. To Duff he appeared to undermine missionary élan: why propogate Christianity if Hindus, who are safe beforehand in their ignorance, are thereby made culpable for resisting it? Clearly, Muir did not allow this position to jeopardize his participation in missions, for this publication came before, not after, his career in Church Sanskrit. SHARPE was therefore justified in basing on Muir his claim that "the pietist-inspired negative attitude to Hinduism" was not the only one open to missionary-minded Protestants in the nineteenth century (1965: 36).

Muir borrowed his concept of conciliation as a pragmatic issue from Richard Whately, Anglican Archbishop of Dublin, who had attempted a definition of the via media between tolerance and indifferentism. "Conciliation in Matters of Religion" originally appeared as a review of Whately's 1822 Bampton lectures, The Use and Abuse of Party Feeling in Matters of Religion. A strong but circumstantial case can be made for attributing influence to a second, but unnamed, source: Rammohun Roy. Muir's sensibilities regarding interreligious dialogue harmonized with Roy's. They both wanted reasoned, charitable discourse instead of undignified polemics. But despite his restraint, Roy was castigated by the Serampore missionaries, especially Joshua Marshman. Roy replied that, "to introduce a religion by means of abuse and insult, ... is inconsistent with reason and justice. If by the force of argument they can prove the truth of their own religion and the falsity of that of Hindus, many would of course embrace their doctrines, and in case they fail to prove this, they should not undergo such useless trouble, nor tease Hindus any longer by their attempts at conversion" (GHOSE, 1978: 146). It may be that Muir self-consciously tried to demonstrate that he could be irenic toward Hinduism even while endorsing Christianity. Moreover, Muir eschewed the irritating terminology that Roy complained about finding in the Friend of India, such as "Father of Lies to whom [Hinduism] evidently owes its origin," "pretended gods of the Hindoos," and so forth, *ad nauseam* (GHOSE, 1978: 146). Nor did Muir vent moral indignation over Hindu social practices which preoccupied Evangelicals (e. g., *satī*).

Roy's approach to Christianity was, if anything, conciliatory. It is not improbable that Muir's thoughts on interreligious dialogue reified as a result of reading Roy as well as Whately. The latter, of course, is sufficient to account for the character of Muir's Theology of Conciliation. Roy would not be mentioned here were it not that Muir evinced an admiration for the Brahmo Samaj, founded in 1828, the year that he arrived in Calcutta. Muir wrote an article (1847) on the Samaj that complimented its monotheistic stand. Presumably, the reason Roy was not acknowledged in the essay on conciliation was that Muir, who valued his reputation in the missionary community, could not applaud Roy with impunity. The evidence for this connection is indirect and the argument strictly conjectural.[37]

Turning to Muir's hermeneutics, which can be used as a test of his Theology of Conciliation, one finds that he was not an innovator but an imitator. Apart from several neologisms, he added nothing to Church Sanskrit terminology and paid too little attention to the problem of adapting Christianity to the Hindu mind. Whereas Mill moved freely through the religious universe of the Purāṇās, utilizing many of their motifs and stylistic conventions, Muir confined himself to a dense hermeneutics based on word-for-word equivalents for Hindu and Christian ideas. Even his flawless, often elegant, *kāvya* style could not compensate for this cumbrous approach. Western readers are likely to find his verses transparently Christian, even their phraseology; but such ease of comprehension throws into doubt whether his partners-in-dialogue found them so pellucid. He may have been writing in Sanskrit but he was thinking in wholly Western terms.

Although Muir did little by way of contextualization to enhance the intelligibility of what he was saying in Church Sanskrit, he did make an effort to justify his methods before his colleagues. His view of the new hermeneutics was summarized in this succinct *dictum*: "Renovate the spirit without rejecting the existing forms of Indian philosophy" (1838d: 125). He wanted neither to absorb nor eradicate the structures of Hindu thought; rather he hoped to create conditions for their assumption into something higher, believing that Hinduism undergoes spiritual transformation through Christocentric reorientation. Something of that religion is thereby lost but much of the preexisting matrix remains. This was Muir's ideal and Mill's terminology was his *modus operandi*.

But Muir was inconsistent with his own *dictum*, more often rejecting Hindu presuppositions cursorily than adapting them selectively. His dismissal of Vaiśeṣika and Sāṅkhya doctrines about the root constituents of the physical universe is just one random example: "In the beginning there was neither a single atom nor a material nature. Besides God there was nothing beginningless."[38] Clearly, this flat denial was debatable within the context of interreligious encounter, yet Muir refused to recognize any commonality between his world view and that of Vaiśeṣika and Sāṅkhya. One would expect at least a gesture of that kind from the author of "Conciliation in Matters of Religion."

An exception to this pattern of stern rebuttal occurs in Nistāramārgadīpikā, where Muir claimed that Christianity unites Hinduism's allegedly disparate *mārgas* ("paths"). The implication was that, whereas Hindus engage in only one or another of *jñāna* ("knowledge"), *bhakti*

---

[37] Muir's essay on conciliation had a definite impact on M. Monier-Williams, who also went through an evangelical phase. Under Muir's influence, his views on Hinduism moderated (SHARPE, 1965: 37; MONIER-WILLIAMS, 1962: 3).

[38] *Adau na ko 'pi paramāṇur nāpi prakṛtir āsīt / parameśvarād ṛte kim apy anādivastu nāstīti //* (Muir, 1846: 53).

("devotion"), and *karman* ("deeds"), Christians practice all three simultaneously. "This, the true *mārga*, of non-human origin, uses all means of perfection. Truly it is the way of knowledge; the way of devotion; and the way of deeds as well. Men who walk in it do indeed obtain true knowledge of God. In the end, having also attained correct knowledge of themselves, they reach the highest perfection. Men who walk in it and belong to God, being grateful for having seen mercy's supreme manifestation, reverence their saviour and their beloved salvation with steadfast devotion. Men who walk in it know they are powerless to fulfill what is good. They are capable of doing good, however, when they pray to God for spiritual strength."[39] It is not an issue here whether Hindus would have agreed with Muir's contention that people can know, love, and serve God only insofar as he enables them to do so. Nor is it germane to ask whether they would have condoned this assimilation of their three-fold scheme of religious life. What is noteworthy is that readers would recognize landmarks familiar in their own tradition. But one does not find amplifications of Christian ideas to the same extent as this in the MP.

Muir generally left technical terms undefined and without the benefit of contextualization. He chose words carefully, but expected too much from them. One can see why readers were hard pressed to understand him. His vocabulary was borrowed from Hindu sources, but its meaning was galvanized within a Christian context, viz., the ŚKhS. Each tersely worded *śloka* carried the burden of a particular theological doctrine on one or more words appropriated from Hindu philosophy or religion. Consequently, Muir's terms had two functions: pointing toward and beyond something in the minds of his partners-in-dialogue.

Prāyaścitta is one of the clearest examples of this dual function. After reading the Gaṃgāvākyāvalī, in which the Ganges and its purificatory powers are extolled, Muir wrote a treatise entitled Pāpamocanayathārthopāyapradarśana, subtitled "The Inefficiency of the Ganges to Wash away Sin, with a Statement of the True Atonement." The belief that sins are removed by ablutions seemed to Muir a cheap and easy form of grace. To counteract it, he wrote the following: "Atonement (*prāyaścitta*) for the sins of all men was accomplished by the sacrificial death of him who was sinless."[40] Although the meaning and phraseology in Sanskrit are hardly problematic to one who is conversant with Christianity, would this verse

---

[39] *Yathārthamārgo 'yam apauruṣeyaḥ siddher upāyān nikhilān prayuṇkte /*
sa jñānamārgaḥ sa ca bhaktimārgaḥ sa karmamārgo 'pi yathātathāsti //
asmiṃś calanto manujā yathārthaṃ jñānaṃ labhante paramātmano hi /
sveṣām api jñānam avāpya samyak te siddhim ante paramāṃ prayānti //
asmiṃś calanto manujāḥ prakāśam aiśyā dayāyāḥ paramaṃ vilokya /
nistārakaṃ svīyaṃ udāraṃ iṣṭaṃ bhaktyādriyante dṛḍhayā kṛtajñāḥ //
asmiṃś calanto manujāḥ svakīyāṃ jānanty aśaktiṃ sukṛtasya siddhyai /
kiṃtv īśvarād ātmikaśaktidānaṃ prārthya kriyaṃte sukṛtau samarthāḥ //
(Muir, n. d.: 10—11).

[40] *Niṣpāpasya tathā tasya yajñarūpeṇa mṛtyuṇā / aśeṣamārtyapāpāṇām prāyaścittam asādhyata //* (Muir, 1840e: 5).

have made sense to one who was not? Aside from other terms in it, *prāyaścitta* puts several major obstacles in the way of proper interpretation.

Chief of these impediments is that *prāyaścitta* is better understood as penance than as atonement or propitiation. It is more a demonstration of regret or an attempt to terminate undesirable karmic repercussions than an act designed to appease divine justice. Another problem is that the Hindu tradition has scant precedent for substitutionary *prāyaścittas*, although in Dharmaśāstra texts one finds that close relatives may undergo penance for children below the age of responsibility who have committed certain minor sins (KANE, 1953: 78—80). Some writers refer to the Mārkaṇḍeyapurāṇa's account of King Vipaścit's descent into hell as an instance of vicarious suffering or substitutionary atonement (WINTERNITZ, 1972, 1: 562—64; NAKAMURA, 1975: 382—84). But this story's correspondence with the Christian doctrine of Christ's atonement is more apparent than real. The inmates of that hell were released not because justice was satisfied on their behalf by Vipaścit, but rather because the king would not ascend to heaven, a journey made necessary by his merit, unless they would accompany him. In the present state of scholarship, one cannot say that other instances of this sort will not be found.[41] The South Indian *bhakti* tradition, in particular, may be a fertile source for comparisons. Nevertheless, it is reasonable to say that, at least in the classical Hindu tradition, the precedents for vicarious *prāyaścittas* were too few for Muir to have made much sense in the above-quoted verse. There may not be a better word than *prāyaścitta* for referring to Christ's suffering and death in place of others, but surely Muir should have foreseen the benefits of broader contextualizations.

It would be false to portray Muir as if he had no regard for precedent. Although he was too confident that his terminology pointed both to Hinduism and beyond to Christianity, he did not hesitate to coin neologisms when he thought readers would be misled by traditional terms. One such instance was a compound juxtaposing two theretofore antithetical terms: *svārgya* (or *svārgīya*) and *mukti*. It first appeared in the same text cited above, in which Muir tried to avoid two extreme interpretations of the Christian concept of heaven as the realm of the blessed dead. *Svarga* alone, he reasoned, would suggest a localized paradise where pleasure is of limited duration, rather like the heaven from which King Yayāti fell (van BUITENEN, 1973: 195—204). Prevalent notions about *svarga* as a reward for merit also worried him. Without an adjective, *mukti* might connote not immortality but

---

[41] Sometimes cited is the story of Cakra, the merchant's disobedient son, who, when faced with his punishment, volunteered to suffer in place of other sinners. This expression of charity was immediately rewarded with release. Selflessness rather than justice is this story's motif, which may, therefore, derive from the Buddhist *boddhisattva* idea (PENZER, 1925: 229—31; JAGADĪŚALĀLĀŚĀSTRĪ, 1970: 56.140—68; MUIR, 1878: 232). Another story of this type concerns Rantideva, the brahmin whose compassion was so great that he starved himself in order to give food to others. But the reason for this was that Rantideva saw Viṣṇu everywhere (*hariṃ sarvatra sampaśyan*), an explicitly monistic idea which has nothing in common with the Christian concept of substitutionary atonement (PĀṆḌEYA, 1962: 9.21.1—18).

a state wholly beyond time, in which conditions necessary for interpersonal exchanges are extinguished. Muir was not, therefore, content to acquiesce to Mill's claim that "the right idea of it [*mukti*] will follow to the converted Hindu" (p. 41, *supra*).

Because *svārgīyamukti* is a neologism, Muir realized that a paraphrase was in order. In the immediately following verses, one finds this explanation: "But the *mukti* I am talking about is not absorption into Brahman. It is rather an eternal state of being in a sinless heaven affording happiness that is pure. Heaven is not earned by men whose deeds are meritorious. It is gained, on the contrary, by Christ's boundless merit."[42] Muir rarely bothered to facilitate readers' comprehension even with succinct glosses such as this, which, in the case of *svārgīyamukti*, proved to be insufficient when incorporated into the MP.

There will be further occasions to comment on Muir's terminology when the pandits' critiques of the MP are introduced. The preceding paragraphs provide sufficient evidence for one to see that Muir's contribution to Church Sanskrit was not in hermeneutics. His reputation — or notoriety — was built on the content of what he alleged against Hinduism in terms borrowed from Mill.

In the course of three editions, the MP underwent many permutations, stylistic and conceptual, so many that the last had little in common with the first two. The third, which postdated the MP Controversy, will be excluded from this discussion. Both the first and second editions are germane because it is impossible to specify which ones the pandits had read, except Soma., who had access only to the first.

The need for a book like the MP was first publically broached by Muir in April of 1837. Even at that stage he was clearly biased toward so-called Evidential Theology, a popular form of religious a priori reasoning in the late eighteenth and early nineteenth centuries. "A Sanskrit Treatise on the Evidences of Christianity, with a refutation of Hinduism, is a desideratum. The reasoning portion of the learned Hindus should not be left without an explicit statement of the grounds, historical and rational, on which a revelation coming from God must be based, followed by an application of these principles to Paganism and Christianity" (Muir, 1837b: 185). Writing under the pen name Philo-Sungskrit in the following June, Muir submitted to the Friend of India an article critical of fellow British Sanskritists' "ornamental erudition." Would not one of them, he asked, apply himself to a book of the type mentioned above? If not, "The Germans, profound, laborious, and poor, might perhaps be induced by premiums to prepare the requisite treatises" (1837c: 188). Muir reinforced his plea, which did not draw a response, by proposing an outline encompassing the whole project: "Rough Notes of an Essay on Christianity, Mohammedanism, and Hindooism" (1837a: 387—88). Not only was the scope enlarged to include Islam, but the

[42] *Muktis tu yā mayā proktālayo bhramaṇi naiva sā / svarge tv avasthitir nityā nimale puṇyaśarmade // martyair na so 'rjitaḥ svargaḥ svakīyaiḥ puṇyakarmabhiḥ / śrīkhṛṣṭasya tv anantena puṇyenoparjito 'sti saḥ //* (Muir, 1840e: 9).

essay was to be in Urdu instead of Sanskrit. Again, the response was negligible despite the offer of a large reward. But Muir was insistent, raising the issue again in an article urging missionaries to learn Sanskrit in order to "combat... Hydra-headed Paganism" (1838e: 376). In a similar article, he suggested that the so-called pseudo-Veda be revised, stripped of its dross and pretense to prepare it for incorporation into an argument against Hindu "errors" (1838b: 506—07). Others' disinterest convinced Muir at that point to appropriate the project himself.

The MP, of course, was the outcome. A brief treatise consisting of only 379 terse *anuṣṭubh* verses, it was first published by Bishop's College in 1839. Its format was a dialogue between a guru, Muir's alterego, and a perplexed student (*śiṣya*). The major change in the 1840 edition was that many Sanskrit sources were quoted in an attempt to confirm the allegations against Hinduism, whereas the first rarely cited Hindu authorities. The amplified edition totaled 1032 *ślokas*.

Both editions were conspicuously unlike previous missionary productions, which generally attacked Hinduism on moral grounds alone. Muir altered the debate between the two religions by bringing the latest Indological scholarship to bear on the history of Hinduism. Most Western Orientalists seem not to have brought sectarian bias into their profession, but Muir recognized a certain latent threat in their findings, which could be usefully applied to orthodox Hindu presuppositions about *śruti* and *smṛti* ("traditional teaching"). Muir relied on Mill, John Wilson, and an early missionary polemicist in Bengal, George Mundy, for moral judgments against Hinduism. But for textual criticism, which might demonstrate that Hinduism had gone through stages of historical development, he depended upon such Orientalists as H. T. COLEBROOKE, H. H. WILSON, F. BOPP, A. SCHLEGEL, and O. BURNOUF. This procedure was so unusual that its ramifications deserve comment.

By citing such authorities, Muir was reversing an apologetic strategy that worked well against his religion. In the nineteenth century, Christianity's advocates in India were sometimes required to answer arguments drawn from nonorthodox Western scholars. Rammohun Roy, for instance, studied the literature of Unitarians and freethinkers who documented the rise of Trinitarian theology in order to prove its allegedly unbiblical origin. Their findings buttressed Roy's critique of "Christian polytheism." Evangelical missionaries (e. g., Joshua Marshman) were greatly discomfited, being out of contact with developments in contemporary European biblical criticism. Muslims, too, benefited from this strategy. When G. Pfander argued over the Trinity with the *ulamā* at mid-century, he admitted that he was "astonished to find that Dr. Wazir Khan had the books of T. H. Horne, D. F. Strauss, and other German theologians in front of him" (POWELL, 1976: 53). Pfander even attributed his poor performance to this disadvantage. In like manner, Muir's battery of criticisms, derived from Orientalists, forced Hindus to answer unfamiliar arguments utilizing their own religion's historical development in their disfavor.

Mata and *parīkṣā*, the members of the compound Muir selected for his title, combine to form a unique statement to readers about his intentions. His avowed purpose, according to the English subtitles, was to "examine" or "test" (*parīkṣā*) "religions" or "doctrines" (*mata*). There is no mystery about the meaning of *parīkṣā*, but it will be discussed below because it has implications for understanding Muir's method of reasoning about religion. However, the meanings attached to *mata* and to another term used frequently in the MP, *dharma*, are problematic.

One can see ambiguity in Muir's use of *mata* in the title, where it stood both for religion and doctrine. It is one thing to refer to Hinduism but quite another to speak of a Hindu creed or doctrine. Similarly, one readily recognizes that Christianity and the Christian creed are not necessarily equivalents. Muir compounded this ambiguity by preferring *dharma* as a word for religion, even though *mata* appeared in the title. These words were used as synonyms for that idea, but never interchanged as words for doctrine, for which *mata* was used exclusively. The dominant use of *dharma* was evident at the very beginning of the MP: "There are, O guru, a great many different religions (*dharma*) in the world, the doctrines (*mata*) of which are contradictory, and [the same is true] with respect to customs."[43] Although *mata* and *dharma* alternated without much consistency, one can see a pattern dimly. It is hardly conceivable, moreover, that Muir used this pair of words arbitrarily. *Mata* and *dharma* must have acquired "religion" as a meaning before he used them that way. The task, then, is to locate where and when this sense was acquired before Church Sanskrit came into existence. What may be the case is that Christians and other religious minorities in India, anxious lest they be overwhelmed by Hindus who outnumbered them so greatly, found in *dharma* a term to express their sense of self-conscious identity. In this connection, it will be worthwhile first to note how Christians used *mata* and *dharma* in the period antedating Muir.

As the past participle of a root (*man*) meaning to cogitate, *mata* is generally translated "thought" or "idea." It also stands for a set of interrelated ideas, "doctrine" or "creed." The philosophical systems (*darśanas*) are also called *matas*, as are the teachings of Śaivas and Vaiṣṇavas. The word is well suited to that in religion which derives from or relates to intellect. *Dharma* concerns what one does, but *mata* what one thinks. Hindu authorities may have used *mata* to distinguish between schools of thought, but they could not make it allude to anything more than the noetic dimension of religion.

Mata was used rather more in South than North India by Christian authors. In the early seventeenth century, de Nobili used *mata* (Tamilized as *madam*) in a way that betrays his anxiety to impress upon Hindus the *sui generis* character of Christianity. To *madam* he added *mey*, an adjective, in order to specify his religion as the "true" one. By this same word he denoted

[43] *Saṃsāre 'tīvabāhulyaṃ dharmāṇāṃ vidyate guro / viruddhamatayuktānāṃ bhinnānāṃ cāpi rītiṣu //* (Muir, 1839: 1.1; all references are to the first edition unless otherwise specified).

other religions, adding less than tactful adjectives: *poy madam* meant "false religion"; *piṛa madaṅgal* were "foreign religions" (TILIANDER, 1974: 58—60). *Mata* has certain properties which render it useful for expressing the idea of Christianity as a creed, but as an all-purpose word in Sanskrit it conveys a one-sided impression of religion. In addition to being a means for expressing exclusiveness, de Nobili may have thought that, compared with Hinduism, Christianity consists more of *mata* than *dharma*.

Turning north, one finds that Carey used *śikṣā* instead of *mata* for doctrine (διδαχή; e. g., Mt. 7.28). But he, too, recognized that the meaning of *mata* converges with religion at least on one side. In 1805, three years before the Dharmapustaka was published, his press at Serampore published a tract entitled Khrīṣṭīyanerder Mat Ki. In his Sanskrit New Testament, proselytes were *matāvalambins* (Mt. 23.15; Acts 2.10, 6.5). W. Yates and J. Wenger were even more explicit: *yihudīyamatagrāhin* (Acts 13.43). In spite of *mata*'s limitations, no lesser Sanskritists than de Nobili, Carey, Yates, and Wenger were attracted to it, and their examples may have been sufficient for Muir to incorporate it into his nomenclature.

Probably each of these Sanskritists thought *mata* was a more neutral term than *dharma*, but they were strongly attracted to the latter anyway, for reasons which need elucidation. Although *dharma* regulates a Hindu's relation to the divine, it seldom stands for what he conceptualizes it to be, whereas *mata* does. There are some notable instances, however, where *dharma* includes not only its usual meanings but refers also to an ideology of the divine. These may have served as precedents for its adaptation in Church Sanskrit. First are noted the variety of ways in which Christians have applied the word.

Dharma was little used by de Nobili, probably because its connotations are different in Tamil and because a Tamil word, *aṛam*, is often used instead. *Darmam*, the Tamilized pronunciation, appears only once in de Nobili's catechism, Kuṛippiḍam, in a compound with *vaḷḷi*, which meant "the road of *dharma*," an expression for the Christian way of life (TILIANDER, 1974: 51). One finds *dharma* more frequently in Church Sanskrit in North India. Carey's title for the Bible, Dharmapustaka, does not mean a book about religion, for the Bible is hardly that, but rather "book of righteousness." What is most noteworthy is that this name designated the entire Bible, not just the law books of the Old Testament. *Dharma* was put to other uses; most significantly it stood for θρησκεία ("religion"; Acts 26.5; Yates and Wenger, *dharmamata*) and *dharmika* for θρῆσκος ("religious"; James 1.26). Besides what was previously noted, proselyte was rendered by *dharmāvalambin* (Acts 13.43). *Sarvadharmapūraṇa* meant "fulfilling all righteousness" (δικαιοσύνη).

But in most of these instances *dharma* was out of alignment with its general development in Hinduism. *Dharma* as δικαιοσύνη spiritualized or internalized the meaning of that word rather more than it had theretofore been. Whereas *matāvalambin* is a meaningful compound, *dharmāvalambin* is somewhat disconcerting in the Christian context of conversion, because a Hindu can always change his *mata* but never his *dharma*. As W. HALBFASS has noted, *dharma* was nonetheless capable of assimilating even Christian connotations: "Es ist symptomatisch, daß der Ausdruck *dharma*, der doch hinduistischer Selbstbehauptungsbegriff par excellence ist, dergestalt auch auf die fremde Botschaft und ihre Träger angewendet wird" (1981 : 393). But none of these applications of *dharma* stretches its meaning so much as θρησκεία. If *dharma* can mean *mata*, but not vice versa, then *dharma* became a word both for religion and religious creed in addition to its traditional meanings. Where, then, had this word acquired such connotations before Church Sanskrit came into existence?

The place to start this search for precedents is Bengal, where Church Sanskrit first flourished. J. O'CONNELL found that Gauḍīya Vaiṣṇavas sometimes used *dharma* as a word to express their self-awareness over against other groups, especially Muslims (*yavanas* or *mlecchas*). Instances of *dharma* compounded with *hindu* or *hindura* occur in the Caitanyacaritāmṛta and the Bhaktamālā, Bengali texts belonging to the early seventeenth and late eighteenth centuries respectively (O'CONNELL, 1973: 343—44). Each case involved "confrontation and strained relationships between Hindus and another group or type of people" (1973: 341), but nowhere did *dharma* imply anything ideological. Rather, within its purview were only customary rights belonging to Hindus, which Muslim officials (*qāẓī*) had violated (O'CONNELL, 1973: 342). One can say, therefore, that Gauḍīya Vaiṣṇavas found in *dharma* a useful word for distinguishing themselves from non-Hindus at the social, if not ideological, level (cf. DIMOCK, 1976: 5—6).

Tantrists in Bengal took *dharma* a step closer to the border line with θρησκεία, since by it they designated both their praxis and conception of the divine. The Mahānirvāṇatantra (speculation about the date of which varies widely, even so far as to posit its origin at a date not much before Carey; DERRETT, 1968a: 168) was one of the basic texts of the *kauladharma*, the *dharma* of goddess Kālī's family (WINTERNITZ, 1972, 1: 595). Its philosophy has much in common with Sāṅkhya and Advaita Vedānta, but it also prescribes a ritualistic ideology necessary for liberation, consisting of *mantras* (prayerlike formulas), *yantras* (mystical diagrams), etc. All of these combined, its philosophical understructure and ritualistic ideology, are encapsulated in the term *dharma*. As Tantrists use the word, its implication seems to be that only they possess *dharma*. Because this is the Kali Age, and the Vedas, Smṛtis, and numerous Purāṇas are no longer authoritative, the goddess has assigned the new dispensation to the Kaulas (WOODROFFE, 1971: 5—10). One finds, therefore, that the Mahānirvāṇa extolls itself as the *dharma* of *dharmas*: "As the footmarks of all animals disappear in the footmarks of the elephant, so do all Dharmas disappear in the Kula-Dharma" (WOODROFFE, 1971: 382).[44] An expression such as this is on the border line with θρησκεία.

Jains were another religious minority anxious to preserve and assert their distinctiveness. Missionaries and Jain apologists had one trait in

[44] *Karipāde vilīyante sarvaprāṇipadā yathā / kuladharme nimajjanti sarve dharmās tathā priye //* (AVALON, 1929: 14.180).

common: both were inclined to dogmatically declare the supremacy of their own religion. One example in this vein from the Kṣatracūḍāmaṇi, an eleventh-century text written by Vādībhasiṃha, suffices. In this passage (11.105), *dharma* and *mata* are juxtaposed in such a way that the former clearly signifies the noetic dimension of religion. Vādībhasiṃha there urges the man who wants supreme beatitude to take refuge in the Jain religion (*dharma*), which is likened to a lion that destroys elephants, a figurative expression for wrong doctrines (*durmata*).[45]

The Prabodhacandrodaya, an eleventh-century Hindu allegorical drama in which personified philosophies and religions compete with each other, took note of Jain preoccupation with *dharma* in this sense. The Diagambara, depicted in the play as a lowbred debauchee, always asks others about their *dharma*. He queries the Buddhist, who denounces the idea of an eternal *ātman*, about the person who taught him that *dharma* (*kena te īdṛśo dharma upadiṣṭaḥ*; Nambiar, 1971: 72). When the Kāpālika enters the Jain asks what his conception of *dharma* and *mokṣa* is (*kīdṛśas tava dharmaḥ kīdṛśas tava mokṣaḥ*; Nambiar, 1971: 76). These exchanges are not unlike Christians asking one another whether they are Roman Catholic or Protestant; in both cases *dharma* defines the group designation and vice versa.

Although most of the instances cited above are on the border line, there was some precedent for writers in Church Sanskrit to make *dharma* into an equivalent for θρησκεία. Like other minorities, Christians seized upon it as a way to distinguish themselves from others and to say that one religion — theirs — is true and others false. This does not mean that Carey, Mill, or Muir read the texts mentioned above and deliberately adapted from them. The point is rather that *dharma* did approximate the meaning of the word religion often enough, and when these Sanskritists wanted a word to convey this idea, pandits were able to bring it to their attention with some justification.

The present writer thinks that in Muir's case an argument can be made in favor of a closer connection with Jain literature. Of course, Muir may have named the MP without giving a thought to Jain authors; but it must be noted that there are books in their religion known as Dharmaparīkṣas. One text by that name was composed in Sanskrit by Amitagati in the late tenth century and another in Apabhraṃśa by Hariṣeṇa in the early eleventh. Both authors appear to have relied on a predecessor by the name of Jayarāma, whose Prakrit Dharmaparīkṣā is presumed lost (Muni, 1944: 41). These two texts were mechanically translated into many other dialects used by Jains. K. K. Handiqui noted that, "Jaina writers often indulged in what is called *dharmaparīkṣā* or the examination of the relative merits of different religions with a view to demonstrating the superiority of Jainism to the others" (1949: 329). A. N. Upadhye added that Amitagati contrived his text in such a way

[45] *Evaṃ nirmaladharmanirmitam idaṃ śarma svakarmakṣayaprāptaṃ praptum atuccham icchatītarāṃ yo vā mahecchо janaḥ / so 'yaṃ durmatakuñjarapraharaṇe pañcānanaṃ pāvanaṃ jainaṃ dharmam upāśrayeta matimān niḥśreyasaḥ prāptaye //* (Handiqui, 1949: 330).

that a Hindu named Vaiśramaśreṣṭhin became a "pious believer (*suśraddhā*) with firm faith in Jina." The author achieved this result because he scrutinized "the credentials of other religions by criticizing their deities and mythology" (Muni, 1944: 47). Muir's approach had much in common with this literature. If one substitutes Christianity for Jainism, they would be virtually the same, except for the satirical style that one finds in the Jain texts.[46]

It is not improbable that the author of Original Sanskrit Texts knew the Dharmaparīkṣā literature and named his text accordingly. These books resemble each other not only because they debunk Hinduism but also because they apply *dharma* as a word to distinguish their religions from Hinduism. Muir substituted *mata* for *dharma* in his title probably because the former is more neutral. Be that as it may, they were synonymous in the MP. The chief connection between that text and the Dharmaparīkṣas is that Muir, Amitagati, and Hariṣeṇa subjected Hinduism to a brutal rationalistic analysis, a subject which now brings this discussion to *parīkṣā*. (Hereafter, "Dharma" is not italicized when its broader meaning, "religion," is connoted.)

If sophisticated readers, for whom Muir was writing, did not associate *parīkṣā* with the literature just described, they would at least have associated it with Dharmaśāstra nomenclature, in which it refers (alternating with *vicāra*), to investigative procedures in a legal hearing. Additionally, as a term for the tertiary stage of discourse upon a subject in philosophy, *parīkṣā* refers to the process of testing and examining an idea already adumbrated and elaborated at the primary (*uddeśa*) and secondary (*lakṣaṇa*) levels (Jhaḷakīkara, 1893: 449). By using *parīkṣā* in his title, Muir alluded to himself as an impartial judge whose approach to religion was logical and philosophical. The MP was actually a kind of treatise in the philosophy of religion, and its method of reasoning on that subject requires some comment.

One must not overlook the fact that the MP was a *parīkṣā* of religions (*mata* in plural) instead of, for instance, "the religion" (*tanmata-*) or the "false religion" (*asatyamata-*). Muir hoped to make explicit, by not adding a modifier to *mata*, that his *parīkṣā* was applicable to all religions, not excluding his own. A synopsis shows that not only the title but the book as a whole was designed to convey an impression of strict neutrality. The implication, dubious in the judgment of his critics, was that Christianity would be rejected with all the others if it failed to pass the test of objective scrutiny. Muir claimed to have searched for the one religion endowed with

---

[46] The first verse of an episode in Uddyotana Sūri's eighth-century Prakrit romance, Kuvalayamālā, entitled Dharmaparīkṣā in Ratnaprabha's Sanskrit digest, reads as follows: *tadākarṇya rājā dharmaparīkṣārthaṃ devatāgṛhe kuladevatāṃ śrīyam ārādhayām āsa.* Śrī brought a mysterious manuscript inscribed in Brāhmī to Dṛḍhavarman, a Hindu king. Unbeknownst to him, it listed the basic tenets of Jainism. Learned Hindus and Jains were assembled and the king ordered them to expound their doctrines to determine which corresponded with the ms. Naturally, the Jains won and the king converted (Handiqui, 1949: 329—30; Upadhye, 1970: 69—71).

authority (*pramāṇatva*) among the many that claim allegiance from mankind. Of course, Christianity was that religion. This was a conclusion to which he said he had come by testing each one to determine whether or not it possessed the characteristics (*lakṣaṇas*) of divine origin (*īśvarotpatti*). Despite a chapter on the "Necessity of Divine Guidance" (*aiśanītyāvaśyakatā*) and a statement that "men's minds are blind in matters of religion" (*dharmasya viṣaye tarhi mānavā andhamānasāḥ*, 1.9), Muir's method of reasoning about religion was rationalistic, distrustful even of his own scripture's appeal to divine inspiration. If Christianity is authoritative, he argued, then it is so because it has met certain qualifications imposed upon it by reasoning human minds.

Whence came this mode of reasoning about religion, especially to one who has been characterized here as owing a debt to Evangelicalism? The *lakṣaṇas* that Muir alleged are characteristic of the true religion must be viewed in their historical context. From a contemporary perspective, one will probably find them tailored to suit his purpose, which was to enhance Christianity. Tailored they undoubtedly were, but to a particular set of mind prevalent among Europeans who defended Christianity in terms of objections David Hume had raised against it. In order to elucidate Muir's way of thinking about religion, it is useful to briefly discuss nineteenth-century Evidential Theology and analyze one segment of his *parīkṣā* dealing with credibility of miracles as an illustration of it.

Historically, Christian thinkers have posited certain spheres in which either God alone has the prerogative of knowing truth, or man as well. Roman Catholics have traditionally bifurcated reality into Nature and Grace, whereas Protestants usually differentiate between General and Special Revelation. Nature, then, is a sphere in which God reveals to man certain general truths, his deity and omnipotence, for instance. If man reasons properly, he will know at least that much about God. An Anglican cleric, William Paley (1743—1805), systematized this kind of thinking, although he was not the first to do so. Like others, Paley presupposed that reason and revelation are not antithetical; they reciprocate, confirming each other (LeMahieu, 1976: 163). One sees, according to his pre-Darwinian view of nature, the benevolent hand of God everywhere, adapting means to ends. Nature is a great mechanism and everything, even the gullet of a seagull or the pouch of an opossum, are designed for specific purposes. "God, man, the Bible, nature, reason, ... were all linked in Paley's coherent vision of the universe. His was a theology of purposeful relationships, a theology in which a rational observer could reveal the ways of God to man" (LeMahieu, 1976: 172). This was the sum and substance of Evidential Theology.

One finds echoes of Paley throughout the MP, the details of which can be noted in the synopsis. Early in the first chapter (17—22), Muir claimed that nothing is so "suggestive of a maker" (*kartṛdarśaka*) than the human body, the components of which are connected by arteries and veins (*nāḍi*) and bones (*asthi*). Muir borrowed this argument from chapter eight of Paley's Natural Theology, "Of Mechanical Arrangement of the Human Frame."

From the same section Muir derived an argument against the theory that the phenomenal world is a dream-like illusion, from which one's senses must be withdrawn. God designed the senses, Muir argued, so that man can perceive the created world. If true, *māyā* would imply that God had frivolously equipped man with sense perception (5.133—50). *Pratyakṣa* ("direct perception") is the *pramāṇa* ("means of knowledge") that verifies the world's existence. Oddly, at this point in the second edition (6.464), Muir cited for support a passage in the Prabodhacandrodaya that criticized Vedānta because its *māyā* doctrine contradicts *pratyakṣa.* This was a serious lapse of judgment on Muir's part, for he was apparently oblivious to the fact that this judgment was attributed to Egoism (*ahaṃkāra*), an allegorical character allied to Delusion (*moha*).[47] This faux pas may partly explain why the pandits called him an "infidel" (*nāstika*). Be that as it may, Muir can be better understood when one sees him in the context of an intellectual milieu no longer in vogue.

This study has already referred to the ascendancy of Empiricism in Europe and to the fact that missionaries often addressed Hindus as if David Hume himself was their partner-in-dialogue, testing the credibility of their claims about biblical miracles against rationalistic criteria. But the Hindus who debated with John Wilson in Bombay never called into question the possibility that Jesus Christ abrogated "laws of nature," which was, in any event, a concept alien to Indian thought at that time. Rather, their ire was aroused when missionaries disparaged Kṛṣṇa's miracles (*vide* p. 27, *supra*). Muir, too, had Hume in mind as much as Hindus when he wrote about miracles in the MP, and Paley was much in evidence again. So pervasive was this theologian's influence in the early nineteenth century that even a quasi-Evangelical in the Indian mofussil, writing for Hindus, was not exempt from it. The reason for his dependence on Paley was that the latter's View of the Evidences of Christianity was considered the outstanding reply to Hume by an orthodox churchman in that age. Muir's Paleyan approach to reasoning about miracles becomes apparent by examining the criteria he proposed in the MP for verification.

Besides being contrary to laws of nature, Hume asserted that miracles cannot be substantiated by the testimony of witnesses for four reasons, of which only the first and fourth are quoted here. "For first, there is not to be found, in all history, any miracles attested by a sufficient number of men, of such unquestioned good sense, education and learning, as to secure us against all delusion in themselves; of such undoubted integrity, as to place them beyond all suspicion of any design to deceive others..." (Hume, 1975: 116). "Every miracle, therefore, pretended to have been wrought in any of these religions (and all of them abound in miracles), as its direct scope is to establish the particular system to which it is attributed; so it has the same force, though more indirectly, to overthrow every other system" (1975: 121).

---

[47] *Pratyakṣādipramāsiddhaviruddhārthāvabodhinaḥ / vedāntā yadi śāstrāṇi bauddhaiḥ kim aparādhyate //* (NAMBIAR, 1971: 29).

Hume's logic was that miracles are beyond reasonable belief because the witnesses were probably charlatans, if not simply dull-witted. All religions claim miracles on their behalf, but all cannot be true. All must, therefore, be false (LeMahieu, 1976: 108).

Paley disagreed, amassing citations from Roman writers to confirm a probability argument in favor of the witnesses' credibility. Many "professing to be original witnesses of the Christian miracles, passed their lives in labours, dangers, and sufferings, voluntarily undergone in attestation of the accounts which they delivered, and... also submitted, from the same motives, to new rules of conduct" (Paley, 1838: 203). Contradicting Hume's aspersions, Paley alleged that, "There is not satisfactory evidence that persons pretending to be original witnesses of any similar miracles, have acted in the same manner" (Paley, 1838: 203). Suffering demonstrates sincerity (but not veracity according to Hume); men do not resist oppression for an untruth. Paley's "seminal assumption," according to LeMahieu, "was that consistency disproved fraud and harmony established truth" (1976: 101). But underneath this noble assertion lay the more dubious proposition that "the early disciples demanded and got reasonable evidence — visible signs perceived by the senses — that solidified their faith" (1976: 105).

These are the same lines of thought along which Muir reasoned in the MP. For the sake of "supernatural proof" (*adbhutasiddhi*), God entrusts to the "founder" (*pravartaka*) of the true religion a power for doing "wonderful deeds" (*camatkārakriyā*). These must be recorded immediately by witnesses (*sākṣin*) and must withstand the scrutiny of opponents. To Muir, Christianity's credibility stands or falls with this issue. One can see his concern growing in each edition. Whereas the first stated the position theoretically, over eleven hundred *ślokas* were devoted in the third to citations culled from Roman writers.

This procedure may seem irrelevant, since most Hindu readers would not have doubted that Christ performed miracles. But Muir had another purpose. He wanted to make clear that, rather than being accessible to historical analysis, Hindu miracles are lost in the oblivion of an unrecorded past. The MP, therefore, became his attempt to do in the case of Hinduism what Paley had already tried to do with Islam, viz., demonstrate that miracles are merely ornamental in that religion instead of at its very center, as in Christianity.

In one sense, then, Soma., Hara., and Nīla. were arguing against Paley and a theological school of long standing in Europe. Anachronistic though it may seem from a contemporary perspective, they took it seriously as a threatening form of irreligious reasoning. Nīla., especially, directed some very biting criticism against Muir's Paleyan apologetics. One can also say that Muir was arguing in the MP for a very truncated, abstract Christianity. Whatever he derived from Paley was designed more to change minds than convert persons. Descriptions of Christ's moral character are found in the MP, but they are secondary to the discussion of miracles. In so doing, Muir displeased Mill, who wrote the following to Bishop's College, disapproving of its intention to publish another edition of the MP: "The instructor gives no hint to his heathen pupil of anything more being required of him than the isolated mental reception of the philosophy of Christianity: ... no hint of the primary necessity of being joined by baptism to the Church as the body of Christ" (Mill, 1842).

A synopsis of the 1839 edition of the MP follows (numbers refer to chapter and verse). Significant variations in the subsequent editions are discussed in the notes only. English equivalents of Sanskrit words are given as Muir meant them, not as they might be understood by Hindu readers.[48]

Chapter One: Description of God's Attributes (*Īśvaraguṇavarṇana*)

1—2 Student: There are many religions, each contradicting the others. One doubts whether they can all be true.

3—13 Teacher: Truth is hard to find, but error is everywhere. People are blind about religion, even those who reflect on it carefully. Intelligent people ought to test religions, accept the true one (*saddharma*), and reject the false (*anṛta-*) ones.

14 Student: What are the characteristics (*lakṣaṇas*) of the true religion?

15—21 Teacher: Before stating these, God (*īśvara*) must first be described. All people except atheists (*nāstika*) say that God exists. The earth, created (*asarji*) by God, displays his majesty, skill and mercy. He is a river of mercy (*dayāsindhu*), who gives food to creatures according to their species (*svadharma*).

22—31 God (*parameśvara*), a spirit (*ātman*) who is holy (*puṇya*), is hostile to sin (*pāpa*). He has given people the power (*śakti*) to distinguish between good and evil (*puṇyapāpavivekin*). Even wicked kings know they must conform to law (*dharma*). God, who made man's conscience (*narāntaḥsthitavāṇī*), will reward good deeds and punish sins in the next world.

32—34 God is omnipresent (*sarvavyāpa*) but distinct from all that he created. There is no absorption (*laya*) of souls (*ātman*) in him.

Chapter Two: The Necessity of Divine Guidance (*Aiśanītyāvaśyakatā*)[49]

1—2 Student: Do all devout people worship God, who conceive of him as omniscient, the creator of everything (*viśvakartṛ*), etc.?

[48] Muir's MP was only the first of many *parīkṣās*, which missionary presses printed in vast quantities, such as J. Newton's Rāmaparīkṣā (1867), W. F. Johnson's Śivaparīkṣā (1876), and Lal Bihari De's Vedāntaparīkṣā (1896) and Vālmīkīyarāmāyaṇaparīkṣā (1904).

[49] In the 1840 edition this was entitled "The Propriety of Examining Religions" (Mataparīkṣaṇaucitya).

3—7 Teacher: Because religions in different countries are dissimilar, the human intellect (*nṛbuddhi*) is proven to be feeble and incapable of deciding what truth is. People of different races (*vaṃśa*) follow religions that blaspheme God (*vibhu*), worshipping other spirits (*bhūta*). Even learned men cannot attain God by intellect.

8—15 Salvation (*mukti*) is eternal happiness (*nityaśreyas*). It cannot be obtained by good merit (*puṇyadharma*). Whether they are charlatans (*vañcaka*) or confused (*bhrānta*), people claim their scripture is divine (*aiśa*). But one should not think all are therefore false.

Chapter Three: Description of the Characteristics of the True Religion (*Satyadharmalakṣaṇavarṇana*)

1 Student: What are the characteristics of the true scripture? And the false?

2—10 Teacher: God gives the true scripture certain signs (*cihna*) in order to remove doubts about it. The first is that the founder (*pravartaka*) must have had power to work miracles. The true scripture was given to prophets (*bhaviṣyavādin*), who gave life (*jīva*) to the dead. Those who claimed authority, but were devoid of such power, were charlatans or simply confused.

11—14 If accounts of those miracles had not been recorded for the sake of people's confidence (*pratyaya*) at a later time, would they not doubt whether they were contrived (*kalpita*) for prestige?

15—25 People should question the authority (*pramāṇatva*) of miraculous accounts. Even those transmitted by tradition (*paramparā*) may be false, because poets lauded their heroes (*vīra*), mixing truth with error. Stories about *daitya*s and *sura*s ought to be doubted, yet people trust them uncritically. No god does these deeds today, so pandits must ask whether or not they are true.

26—32 The second means of proof (*pramāṇa*) God gave to the true scripture is excellence (*śreṣṭhatā*, *sattā*). God is holy; his scriptures must be holy, too. Other scriptures containing shameful stories are not divine; they originate from human ignorance.

33—38 The third characteristic is universality (*sāmānyatā*). There is one God, one human species (*nṛjāti*), and one religion (Dharma). A scripture good for only one race (*vaṃśa*) derives from man, not God.

Chapter Four: Presentation of Christianity (*Khṛṣṭīyamatapradarśana*)

1—3 Student: If all scriptures but one originate in delusion (*mohaja*), which one has these three characteristics?

4—6 Teacher: Only Christianity (*khṛṣṭīyadharma*) possesses all three.

7—16 In Judea (*yahūdya*) there were prophets who foretold the future, including Christ's incarnation (*avatāra*). Christ, Son of God (*vibhoḥ sutaḥ*), born of a virgin (*vimalakanyā*), healed diseases. Killed by wicked people, he nonetheless lives again (*punar jīvan*). He ascended to heaven (*svarga*) before the eyes of his disciples (*śiṣya*).

17—19 Student: By what means of proof (*pramāṇa*) can I know that Christ did miracles?

20—24 Teacher: They were done before many witnesses, including even Christ's enemies (*vairin*). Shortly after his ascension, his life was recorded, the veracity of which was admitted even by adversaries.

25—28 During Christ's time, Greeks and Romans were known worldwide for erudition. They, too, found that account accurate.[50]

29—37 The first Christians adhered to their religion (*mata*) despite being beaten (*pīḍita*), because they believed Christ did miracles. Who would follow that religion (Dharma), risking suffering, unless it had been tested?

38 Student: How do we know at what time and under what conditions those records were written?

39—47 Teacher: Christ became incarnate in the beginning of the Vikrama Era. Our means of proof is a literary tradition founded soon afterward, the books of which have been dated. Christianity's origin is not hidden and the facts about it have never been doubted.

48—49 Student: But is this religion actually the best (*śreṣṭha*)?

50—52 Teacher: No religion besides Christianity has commandments (*ājñā*) so holy and contents so pure (*amala*).

53—58 Unlike us, Christ was sinless, leading people to the way of salvation (*muktimārga*). He taught them to love and fear God. Besides this chief duty (*mukhyadharma*), Christians must be honest, etc.

59—60 Student: The prophets taught these duties; why, then, was Christ's incarnation necessary?

61—62 Teacher: Christ became incarnate to save people from the punishment their sins deserved.

63—69 Only Christianity is universal (*sāmānya*). No one is excluded from its benefits by reason of caste. The whole human species has sinned. Christ came for its justification (*viśuddhi*) and deliverance (*uddhṛti*). Westerners (Yavanas) and Indians, the cultured (*saṃskṛta*) and barbaric, have all become coheirs (*sahabhāgins*) because of his grace (*prasāda*).

70 Student: What in Christianity should we think about most carefully?

---

[50] The 1840 edition quoted Mahābhārata 8.30.85a: *sarvajñā yavanā rājañ śūrāś caiva viśeṣataḥ* ("The Yavanas [Ionians, Greeks or Westerners in general] are omniscient, O king, and preeminently brave").

71—77 Teacher: People's wickedness (*bhraṣṭatā*) especially, which resulted from an original (*ādya*) transgression of God's command (*īśājñollaṃgha*). People are born with a multitude of sins (*aghasaṃcaya*) deserving punishment here and in the next world. Because of Christ's atonement (*prāyaścitta*), God forgives the sins of those who repent.

78—84 One who is righteous (*dharmika*) is not released from suffering caused by sin. Faith (*śraddhā*) is thereby tested and attachment to the world (*saṃsārāsakti*) broken. The traits of a Christian are meekness, etc.

85 Student: Who is the Holy Spirit? The Son of God?

86—92 Teacher: This recondite subject is beyond human intellect. There is one tri-natured (*trirūpaka*) God (*īśvara*). The Father is God; so is the Son and Holy Spirit. The father conceived of Salvation; the Son made atonement; and the Holy Spirit sanctifies (*puṇyīkaroti*).

93 Student: Explain this salvation (*mukti*) located in heaven (*svarga*).

94—100 Teacher: The Christian scripture does not make this clear. But those who go there will always be holy. There is joy there but not grief, because they meditate on God's splendor (*tejas*). Their happiness is superior to bodily pleasure (*śārīrikasukha*). One should ask God for that salvation in heaven (*svargīyamukti*).

101—03 They will be dreadfully punished who refuse this salvation.

Chapter Five: Deliberation on the Indian Scriptures (*Bhāratīyaśāstravicāra*)

1—2 Student: What do you think about the sages' teachings, to which I adhere?

3—7 Teacher: Impartial (*apakṣapāta*) and accustomed to grasping truth (*satyagrahaṇaśīlaka*), I will tell you whether the three characteristics are found in the Indian scriptures.

8—16 One does not find in them the first *pramāṇa*, viz., miraculous power in their founders. They are, therefore, not divine. Children and fools may believe the stories about *daitya*s and *sura*s, but not intelligent people. They are contrived, born of delusion (*mohaja*). People should trust only those accounts of miracles that were done before witnesses and recorded.

17—26 The Vedas were not written down but orally transmitted, and one cannot determine when they were composed. The true account of their origin is concealed in darkness. The same is true of the Smṛtis and Purāṇas. They do not merit the pleasure that intelligent people find in them.[51]

[51] In the 1840 edition at this point, the pupil asks whether or not Brahmā revealed the Vedas. The teacher's reply is based on Western textual criticism. The Vedas were not formed at once but over time, because the lists of contents

27—28 Student: Why, then, have they been accepted for so long?

29—40 Teacher: People always think about God and fear the afterlife because of their sins. They do not test stories about *devas* and *devīs*. Their teachers were in awe of stars, the sky, the oceans, and mountains, seeing divinity everywhere. To events with natural causes, they attributed divine powers. The followings of those deities gradually increased as their devotees contrived stories glorifying them. As it happened in the West, so it happened in India to Durgā, Śrī, Śiva, and Viṣṇu. The attributes (*guṇa*) of the one God were assigned to many gods.

41—43 Vālmīki and other poets lauded their heroes, attributing false incarnations to them. Rāma and Kṛṣṇa were not gods but men of valor and ability.[52]

44—50 The Purāṇas are mixed with much that is unbecoming. Their accounts, supposedly true, are simply embellishments of poets. Their authors did not see miraculous events with their own eyes, and people now believe those stories merely on the authority of their authors.

51—52 Student: Is not the second characteristic of the true religion found in the Indian scriptures?

53—64 Teacher: Only that scripture is divine in which God is worshipped as holy, unchanging (*avikāra*), etc. Man-made scriptures attribute blasphemous qualities to God, the reading of which encourages people to sin. Brahmā, Viṣṇu and Śiva acted reprehensibly.[53]

(*anukramaṇikā*) appended to the Vedas are inconsistent; various kings are euologized who lived after creation; and the Vedas are written in different types of language, ancient and recent. One can see in their language different stages, Muir asserted, quoting Ṛg Veda 1.2.1a and Sāyaṇa's paraphrase. How, then, could they have been revealed at once?

[52] In the 1840 edition, Muir followed H. T. Colebrooke's euhemeristic explanation of the deification of Rāma and Kṛṣṇa: "I suppose both heroes to have been known characters in ancient fabulous history; but conjecture that... new fables have been constructed, elevating those personages to the rank of Gods" (Colebrooke, 1858: 284). To illustrate this development, Muir contrasted an ancient text, Chāndogya-Upaniṣad 3.17.6, which mentions Kṛṣṇa only as the son of Devakī, with the later Kṛṣṇa cult. As evidence of change in Rāma's cult, Muir contrasted the early literature on him with the mystical interpretations of his name in Rāmapūrvatāpanīya-Upaniṣad 1.1—6 (Deussen, 1963: 805). Muir claimed, as an instance of contradiction, that the fabulous longevity attributed to Rāma in the Rāmāyaṇa was at variance with the life span Manusaṃhitā 1.83 allowed for persons in that *yuga*.

[53] In an appendix to this section in the 1839 edition, Muir quoted Bhagavad-Gītā 3.21 and 4.7—8, the latter being the verse which says that God descends when *dharma* wanes and *adharma* waxes. But neither Brahmā, Indra, or Śiva were fit for such a task because of their licentious behavior, Muir asserted. To this discussion the 1840 edition added the conversation between Śuka and a certain king in Bhāgavata-purāṇa 10.33.27—39, in which Śuka vindicated Kṛṣṇa's dalliance with the cowherdesses (*gopis*) in mystical terms — a subterfuge to Muir's mind (Muir, 1873: 49—53). He then quoted Bhagavad-Gītā 3.21ff., alleging that Kṛṣṇa failed to keep the high moral standards he himself set in that passage.

65—66 Brahmā is no longer worshipped and Śaivas and Vaiṣṇavas castigate each other's *iṣṭadevatā*: "Those who profess the worship of Bhava (Śiva), and those who follow their doctrines, are heretics and enemies of the sacred *śāstras*" (WILSON, 1976: 3)[54]; "From even looking at Vishṇu, the wrath of Śiva is kindled, and from his wrath, we fall assuredly into a horrible hell; let not, therefore, the name of Vishṇu be pronounced" (WILSON, 1976: 3).[55]

67—69 Sūrya, Agni, and others were worshipped in the original Veda, but not Viṣṇu. Brahmins recite the Vedas because of the meter, but they do not understand their meaning. Pārvati, Lakṣmī, Rudra, Kṛṣṇa and others became popular later.

70 Some scriptures prohibit and others endorse image worship (*mūrtipūjā*). "Those who (in their ignorance) believe that Isvara is (only) in images made of clay or stone, or metal, or wood, merely trouble themselves by their devotion. They can never attain Liberation without knowledge" (WOODROFFE, 1971: 373).[56] "But he goes to the highest place, who has made a beautiful golden image of various jewels and worships it according to precept. He would go to hell who thinks of an image as stone."[57]

71—72 The Purāṇas are mutually contradictory, full of shameful stories.

73—77 Bhāskara's Siddhāntaśiromaṇi described the world as round and situated in space (*ākāśaśūnyastha*). But the Purāṇas contradict this, saying it is lotus-shaped or resting on a turtle's back.[58] Sailors exploring the earth have never seen the seven seas of ghee and so forth described in the Purāṇas. A scripture with errors like these could not be divine.

---

[54] *Bhavavratadharā ye ca ye ca tān samanuvratāḥ / pāṣaṇḍinas te bhavantu sacchāstraparipanthinaḥ //* Bhāgavatapurāṇa 4.2.28, MUIR, 1873: 381. As other examples of hostility to Śiva, Muir quoted Bhāgavatapurāṇa 1.2.26 (GUPTA, 1964) and Padmapurāṇa 6.163.2, 9, 11 (MAṆḌALĪKA, 1893—94).

[55] *Viṣṇudarśanamātreṇa śivadrohaḥ prajāyate // śivadrohān na sandeho narakaṃ yāti dāruṇaṃ / tasmān na viṣṇunāmāpi na vaktavyaṃ kadācana* (Padmapurāṇa). From the same Purāṇa, Muir quoted 6.163.10 (MAṆḌALĪKA, 1893—94; WILSON, 1976: 3), which gave the opposite opinion of Viṣṇu.

[56] *Mṛcchilādhātudārvādimūrtau īśvarabuddhayaḥ / kliśyanti tapasā mūḍhāḥ parāṃ śāntiṃ na yāṃti te //* (AVALON, 1929: 14.119). As another instance of prohibition, Muir quoted Śātātapasmṛti: *apsu devā manuṣyāṇāṃ divi devā manīṣiṇāṃ / kāṣṭhaloṣṭheṣu mūrkhāṇāṃ yuktasyātmani devatā //* (ĀPṬE, 1905).

[57] *Kāṃcanīṃ pratimāṃ kṛtvā nānāratnamayīṃ śubhāṃ / pūjayed yas tu vidhinā sa yāti paramaṃ padaṃ // pratimāyāṃ śilābuddhiṃ kurvāṇo narakaṃ vrajed /* (text unidentified).

[58] Golādhyāya 21: *bhūmeḥ piṇḍaḥ śaśāṃkajñakaviravikujejyārkinakṣatrakakṣā // vṛttair vṛtto vṛtaḥ san mṛdanilasalilavyomatejomayo 'yam // nānyādhāraḥ svaśaktyaiva viyati niyataṃ tiṣṭhatītyādinā //* ("This round terrestrial ball, composed of earth, air, water, ether, and fire, surrounded by the circles of the orbits of the moon, Mercury, Venus, the sun, Mars, Jupiter, Saturn, and the stars, has no other support; but by its own power stands fast continually in the sky, etc." MUIR, 1910: 63; *idem* 1868a: 489).

78 Student: What other defects (*doṣa*) do you find in the Indian scriptures?

79—83 Teacher: What good is repentence (*anutāpa*) if one can be cleansed of sin by merely bathing in the Ganges? Those who bathe in it are deluded (*vimohita*), not knowing what holiness (*pavitratā*) is.

84—95 Suffering (*duḥkha*) results from sin. It is God's punishment. If the Ganges releases people from sin, why not also from suffering? There is no power in the Ganges to remove sin or attachment to it. If it cannot heal diseases of the body, how can it remove sin?

96—97 Student: Do not Christians do the same, who trust in Christ for their salvation?

98—103 Teacher: True, Christians are saved by faith (*viśvāsa*), but only if they repent.

104—05 Student: I am averse to the Tantras, but what about the Vedas and six systems of philosophy?

106—08 Teacher: If one follows the Vedas, one ought to reject the Purāṇas. Sometimes the Vedas describe God accurately; but Indra and Agni are also worshipped there, and they ought to be rejected by those who worship God as spirit (*ātman*).

109—18 God is both omnipresent and distinct from all that was created, but the Vedas deny this. Vedānta conforms to Śrūti, but one who knows God's majesty (*māhātmya*) would not say "I am Brahman." What a great difference there is between God, infinite and holy, and man, weak and sinful!

119—21 Student: Pandits say the *ātman* is infinite but in bondage to this world of *māyā*. What do you say?

122—26 Teacher: The world (*saṃsāra*) is not *māyā* but real (*vāstava*). The pandits' assertion is unprovable. Our perception (*pratyakṣa*) of the world as real is undeniable.[59] What we perceive by the senses could not be other than real.[60]

127—32 The *ātman* is not holy and infinite but sinful and perishable (*antavat*), nor is it one, but many.[61] Its afflictions are not illusory but real, given by God as punishment for sin. If people are parts (*aṃśa*) of God, they would possess all the attributes of divinity.

---

[59] Here Muir quoted Prabodhacandrodaya, see n. 47, *supra*.

[60] The 1840 edition followed Colebrooke, who argued that *māyā* was a late accretion to Advaita Vedānta: "I take it to be no tenet of the original Vedāntin philosophy, but of another branch, from which later writers have borrowed it, and have intermixed and confounded the two systems" (Colebrooke, 1858: 242). For support Muir quoted the Sāṃkhyapravacanabhāṣya 1.22 (GARBE, 1895: 16), according to which *māyā* is a modern doctrine derived from Buddhist Vijñānavādins.

[61] To show a lack of unanimity in the *darśanas* on the question whether the *ātman* is one or many, Muir quoted against Advaita Vedānta Brahmabindūpaniṣad 1.12 (DEUSSEN, 1963: 648), Sāṃkhyakārikā 18, Kapilasūtra 1.149, and Yogasūtra 1.24.

133—39 The relation between sense and sense object shows how marvelous God's mind is. Our eyes, for example, were designed to perceive external objects (*bahiḥsthaviṣaya*).

140 Student: What about Yoga as a means to detach oneself from sense objects?

141—50 Teacher: Instincts (*rāga*) are necessary; God put them in us for good. People's lives (*jīvas*) are protected by instincts such as hunger and thirst, and they would be slothful without them. Wordly activities would cease. Only by effort do men achieve the things they want.

151—61 People were not created for their own ends but for community (*saṃgati*). They do well who devote their activities to God and love their neighbors. When they suffer misfortune, they do not disparage the world, but say instead that God gave them misfortune for their improvement. *Saṃnyāsa* (renunciation) is not holy; it blasphemes God.

162 Student: Then what do you think of the philosophical systems?

163—64 Teacher: The Mīmāṃsā, Nyāya and Sāṅkhya are mutually contradictory. They are refuted by the three means of proof I proposed.

165 Student: But does one not find the third characteristic in the Indian scriptures?

166—67 Teacher: The kind of conduct prescribed by the Dharmaśāstras is found only in India. Those outside the four castes are unable to follow the Indian scriptures.

168—78 Brahmins are called the gods of the earth, but an honest brahmin should accept *kṣatriyas* and *vaiśyas* and *śūdras* as equals. Brahmins have no qualities that others do not also have. Thus, the scriptures of India deny equality between men (*nṛsamatva*).

179—80 Student: Will not what you say displease those who are learned in the Indian Dharmaśāstras?

181—89 Teacher: The true religion, by which people are saved, must be proclaimed to everyone. I derive no satisfaction from refuting other religions. I know how subtle Hindu minds are and how beautiful their poetry is. Their grammatical science is sophisticated and they have many other good qualities. But they err in religion (Dharma), not knowing the way to salvation. All examiners (*parīkṣakas*) who think carefully about my argument (*tarka*), will attain truth by the Holy Spirit's grace (*prasāda*).

Somanātha (Subājī Bāpu): The First Apologist

There is reason to believe that the name Soma. was a pseudonym adopted by a Maharashtrian, Subājī Bāpu, a progressive *jyotiṣa* ("astrologer") and religious liberal who enjoyed the patronage of Lancelot Wilkinson, a little-known British civil servant and Orientalist. Although the author of the MPŚ identified himself as Soma., the existence of a real person by that name is questionable due to a cryptic note written in English on the final folio by an anonymous hand (the ms.'s donor?). According to this unknown informant, the actual writer was none other than the aforementioned pandit.

The veracity of this information was contested, unfortunately for unspecified reasons, by no less an authority than J. R. Ballantyne, who wrote the entry for the MPŚ in the IOLR's cataglogue of Sanskrit mss. (KEITH, 1887: 625—26). Considering Ballantyne's arrival in Benares shortly after the MP Controversy subsided and his acquaintance with two disputants (Muir and Nīla.), one must take his judgment seriously.

However, the present writer thinks that the anonymous notewriter must have been better informed than Ballantyne. Comparison of Soma.'s MPŚ with Subājī's writings supports this position, for such analysis reveals more than merely casual correspondence. Subājī's Westernized scientific perspective and broadminded tolerance clearly resonate in Soma.'s stanzas. It appears that Ballantyne was not inclined to pursue the problem of authorship so far as to inquire into Subājī's other contributions to Sanskrit and vernacular literature.

The following sections review two phases of Subājī's career predating the MPŚ. The main features repeated in Soma.'s critique of Christianity are noted, keeping two purposes in sight: identification of the two authors as one and the same; and elucidation of factors responsible for shaping the outlook of this neglected Hindu apologist. Before commencing with this discussion, it must be admitted that, although the resemblance between Subājī and Soma. may be so compelling as to leave little room for doubting their joint identity, one can only surmise as to the author's reasons for disguising himself. As ingenious as any explanation of his secrecy might be, this is not the place to indulge in psychoanalytic speculation.

This precaution notwithstanding, it can be said that Subājī — or Soma. — exhibited traits symptomatic of one who experienced uncomfortable tensions. Probably these were consequences of his involvement with Wilkinson, a relationship which made him the brunt of ridicule by fellow pandits. What emerges is the image of a critical mind in transition, faced with challenging dilemmas. Without far more information than actually exists, these tensions can only be pointed out, not treated as the basis for a psychohistory.

Insofar as Subājī's career has been documented, it was inextricably linked with that of his patron.[62] One finds no trace of the pandit either before or after Wilkinson's tenure as the EIC's political agent in such Central Indian cities as Bhopal and Sehore. After his benefactor's premature death sometime in the mid-1840s, Subājī ceased to be mentioned in the Orientalist periodicals that featured him prominently on several occasions during the previous decade. Although his renown was of brief duration, the acclamation of Western colleagues was enthusiastic. His route to celebrity was deter-

[62] Biographical information about Wilkinson is scant. A privately circulated encomium, apparently written by Muir, was published in 1853: Brief Notice of the Late Lancelot Wilkinson of the Bombay Civil Service (London).

mined by his patron, an ardent amalgamator of Hindu and European astronomy. At first a reluctant collaborator in Wilkinson's projects, he eventually became a "zealous defender of the system of Copernicus" ("Proceedings of the Asiatic Society," 1837: 401). It is possible to observe this transition, which was tantamount to a kind of conversion, beginning with its early stages.

Keenly interested in the social application to India of advancements in Western science, especially astronomy, Wilkinson published an article in 1834, entitled "On the Use of the Siddhāntas in the Work of Native Education," in which he outlined plans for modernizing Indian ideas about the physical universe. Unlike other publications of missionary-educators in that period, this one did not assume that Hindus trained in European theories would convert to Christianity. Rather, Wilkinson aimed primarily at spreading more accurate understanding of physical science throughout the Central Provinces, regardless of the effect this might have upon changing patterns of religious affiliation. But this is not to say that a secondary benefit — one that would be advantageous for missions — was neither envisioned nor hinted at: the weakening of popular Hinduism by demonstrating that Purāṇic cosmography, with which it is inextricably mixed, is defective on the grounds of irrefutable scientific reasoning. Progress in this direction, it was thought, would be accompanied by a commensurate decline in the prestige of the brahmins, who were the guardians of antiquated astronomical notions. In his view, modernization of physical science would be minimal as long as popular beliefs derived from the Purāṇas were regarded as trustworthy explanations of natural phenomena. The way to bring about the reversal he anticipated was to discredit myths with facts.[63] In the Siddhāntas, technical treatises on astronomy and mathematics often at variance with the Purāṇas, Wilkinson thought he had found a natural ally: "Till conviction of the truth of the Siddhāntic system, as to the size and shape of the earth, is felt, the popular absurdities of the Purānic cosmogony will never be abandoned" (1834: 511).

Curiosity about the methods by which Hindu astrologers, "generally so ignorant, succeeded in predicting eclipses" drew Wilkinson's attention to the Siddhāntas (1834: 510). Finding inadequate the Tithīcintāmaṇi and Grahalāghava, handbooks popular at that time for solving astronomical equations, he turned to the nearly forgotten treatises of Bhāskarācārya and Āryabhaṭa, discovering that, for example, both authors believed in the daily revolution of the earth upon its own axis. Moreover, he found that they "spared no pains to expose and ridicule the monstrous absurdities of the Jain Sutrās and the Purāns" (1834: 505—06).

Wilkinson recognized that the Siddhāntas were in the past, and could be in the future, bridges between two, generally aloof, communities of scholars.

[63] Retrospectively, one may think this a dubious tactic. There is evidence, however, that it was sometimes effectively used by missionaries as a tool for conversion. See, for example, the caustic article by one of Duff's converts at the Scottish Church College, "Physical Errors of Hinduism" (CR 11.397ff.).

Bhāskara and Āryabhaṭa "always professed in their writings the greatest admiration for the learned men of the West, the Ionians, or 'Yavans'; whilst the Purāns have denounced those who hold any communication with men of these nations, termed the lowest of the low" (1834: 506). However, the intricate theories of those two astronomers had nearly fallen into oblivion during the nineteenth century; pandits generally only vaguely recollected the contents of their treatises. Wilkinson advocated bringing them again to the forefront of dialogue. His dictum was like Muir's: guide the pandits to that which they do not know yet by means of that which they know already. Grateful to their European instructors, he prophesied, astrologers would become genuine astronomers, adding to their classical tradition theories current in the West.

Subājī's role in Wilkinson's scheme for revitalizing the Siddhāntas was crucial. Yet not only in his case had his patron's technique been effective. A nucleus of *jyotiṣas* gathered around this Western proponent of the new science: "My own pandit and the brāhmans of Sehore, who have become converts to the Siddhānta and our system, all express the utmost anxiety to get globes if possible in Hindī, convinced that they will prove to others as they have done in their own case, the readiest means of demonstrating to them the truth" (Wilkinson, 1834: 512—13). Among these students Subājī was the most enthusiastic. In 1836 he published a Marathi tract, entitled Siddhāntaśiromaṇiprakāśa (hereafter cited as ŚSP; subsequently translated into Hindi as Bhūgolasāra by Oṃkara Bhaṭṭa),[64] "explaining the correct system of astronomy." He thereby proved that he had indeed become a zealous Copernican ("Proceedings of the Asiatic Society," 1837: 401). Subājī's treatise was not unchallenged, having been attacked by Poona pandits in a not yet located brochure. Subājī defended his newfound perspective on astronomy in still another tract, Avirodhaprakāśa ("Proceedings," 1837: 616).

Subājī was not easily converted to Copernicus. Beginning as early as 1824, he and his patron began to discuss the physical sciences. Wilkinson's account of the final breakthrough is worth quoting at length:

"I had... entertained in my private service a *siddhāntī* who possessed a higher degree of knowledge of his profession, and having had an opportunity of making myself whilst at Kota in some degree acquainted with the Hindu astronomical books, I had communicated a knowledge of them to my own Shāstrī, by name Subhājī Bāpu, a man of wonderful acuteness, and intelligence, and sound judgment... The arguments by which I had for the previous eight years of our connection in vain endeavored to impress on Subhājī Bāpu a conviction of the truth of the real size and shape of the earth and other important physical facts, now carried to his mind the clearest conviction when shewn to be precisely the same as those of their own

[64] The Asiatic Society of Calcutta has a copy of a Sanskrit version of this same text, published in 1837 (Madras: Church Mission Press) with Telegu characters, to which an appendix written by Wilkinson was added. A Bengali translation also exists.

astronomical authors. His was the master mind; and it exercised its influence over the minds of all the other pandits. He was lost in admiration when he came fully to comprehend all the facts resulting from the spherical form of the earth... He lamented that his life had been spent in maintaining foolish fancies, and spoke with a bitter indignation against all those of his predecessors who had contributed to the willful concealment of the truths that had once been acknowledged in the land" ("Proceedings," 1837: 401; emphasis added).

Orientalists and EIC officials alike applauded Subājī vigorously. The globe he had requested in 1834 was presented in 1837 — in silver. Minutes of an Asiatic Society meeting record that, as a token of appreciation, he was given "two handsome silver emblematical inkstands, representing a jotishi pandit seated between two globes, expounding their use from the Siddhāntas — and around the stand, richly embossed, the twelve signs of the zodiac — a Sanskrit couplet on each expressing that it was presented by the Governor General in Council" ("Proceedings," 1837: 401).

Could Subājī, so highly acclaimed by European colleagues and so resentful — if we are to believe his patron — of fellow pandits, have been attracted to Christianity in addition to Western science? Such may have been the case, if Wilkinson's translation has not thoroughly distorted his pandit's declamations. In the only material bearing on this matter from the first phase of his career, one finds terminology usually associated with Christian faith. Yet it is impossible to say whether this is the real Subājī speaking or whether Wilkinson's hopes were projected into his words: "[The ŚSP] will bear the test of even a severe criticism. It is full of philosophical reflections. From the different productions of different countries mutually necessary he argues the intention of Providence to unite all mankind by commerce in the bonds of an interested affection. He hence infers the restrictions laid on Hindus against travelling abroad to be violent and unnatural. He assails the folly of astrological predictions, and upholds the wisdom and mercies of Providence in veiling the future from our curiosity, and in keeping us all instant in our duties by an unfailing hope" ("Proceedings," 1837: 402; emphasis added). Aside from the curious remarks about the role of economics in the divine plan for international relations, this statement may indicate that Subājī was indeed oscillating between religions. Especially curious are the remarks about Providence, since there is no exact corollary to this Christian concept in Hinduism. Conversion to another religion is, of course, preceded by discontent with one's own. Yet the most one can say is that Subājī found much to scorn in Hinduism, especially brahminic teachings about the nature of the universe. If they meant more than this, a tentative step toward embracing Christianity, it was revoked not long afterward in the MPŚ.

Antagonized by the ŚSP, the pandits of Poona may have thought that Subājī's adherence to the new science was betrayal, a form of collusion with an alien, non-Vedic system; that the *jyotiṣa* was less than a stalwart Hindu for doing so. Railing against rules prohibiting voyages by sea may certainly have been ground for suspecting his orthodoxy, but cross-cultural dialogues on science were by no means proscribed. Wilkinson rightly noted that regulations restricting contact with non-Āryans do not appear to have inhibited earlier astrologers and astronomers in their relations with the outside world. Testifying to this is the interrelatedness of Babylonian, Greek, and Hindu science, especially evident in the Siddhāntas. One even finds passages encouraging ecumenicity. WINTERNITZ, for example, cited a verse from the Vṛddhagargasaṃhitā: "The Greeks are barbarians, but science is firmly established among them; they are on this account honoured equally as sages; what to speak of a Brāhmaṇa, who is a scholar of Astrology."[65] Subājī cannot be faulted, therefore, for collaborating with Wilkinson; nor can his support imply that he was a crypto-Christian.

In this connection it is useful to take note of a general but not always sharp distinction maintained by Hindu thought: the difference between secular (*laukika*) and divine (*alaukika*) knowledge (*vidyā*). Whereas the domain of the former is comprised of astronomy, astrology, and other sciences or pseudoscience, the domain of the latter is knowledge that is inaccessible to the unaided human mind, such as metaphysics, soteriology, and ethics (MAHADEVAN, 1969: 27). Usually this dichotomy is more apparent than real; *alaukika* and *laukika* elements are frequently juxtaposed, resulting in a curious combination of science with theology in Purāṇic literature and theology with science in Siddhāntic texts. A further consequence of this connection between secular and divine knowledge is that traditional Hinduism has been somewhat reluctant to reappraise apparent verities in the *laukika* domain. This observation helps to explain why it took Subājī more than ten years to become a Copernican. Nonetheless, the precedent was there for those who wanted to draw a provisional line across the two fields of knowledge.

The corollary to this distinction between *laukika* and *alaukikavidyā* is the idea that certain types of *śāstras* have mainly, if not exclusively, one or the other within their purview. For instance, the Siddhāntas are authoritative only in the former; the Purāṇas in the latter. A faulty scientific notion espoused by a Purāṇa is not a stumbling block to devout Hindus, since accuracy in that dimension of knowledge is not its *raison d'être*.

Oddly, it was Muir himself who confirmed that Subājī resolved contradictions between the Siddhāntas and Purāṇas in exactly this manner. Although it appears that Muir was not acquainted with Subājī, he at least knew him second hand through the medium of the Hindi translation of the SŚP. Muir informed readers of the Friend of India that the tract's author was not alarmed at inconsistencies in the above-mentioned texts, some affirming and others denying the sphericity of the earth and its suspension in space. "In a little Hindoo tract on Astronomy, by a Joshee, of Malwa, which I have seen, this discrepancy is admitted; but the writer does not seem to regard it as fatal to the sacredness of the Poorans or other books he refers to, but gets

[65] *Mlecchā hi yavanās teṣu samyak śāstram idaṃ sthitaṃ / ṛṣivat te 'pi pūjyante kiṃpunar daivaviddvijaḥ //* (WINTERNITZ, 1967: 654).

over the difficulty by saying that the error arose from the Pouranist or other Poet, whoever he may be, stepping out of his province, and handling a subject he was ignorant of'' (1837d: 228).

Soma.'s treatise, unlike the SŚP, was not scientific in scope. The MPŚ, after all, was a critique of Christianity, especially its evangelistic excesses; it was an apology for Hinduism, not the new science. He neither amalgamated Hindu and Western astronomy, nor alleged that brahmins had conspired to supress "truths that had once been acknowledged in the land." *Alaukikavidyā* was Soma.'s special concern. This distinction notwithstanding, the author was also fascinated with *laukikavidyā*, British technology in particular. "Steamships" (*uṣmapota*) and "flying machines" (*ākāśayānayaṃtra*; 2.8—10; citations by chapter and verse) were singled out admiringly as evidence of European cleverness (*cāturya*). Further evidence of this *laukika* orientation is that Soma. scolded Muir for denying in Bhāratīyavarṇana that the EIC demanded payment of tolls (*śulka*) by travellers (*yātrika*; 2.14—16). But even these scant *laukika* elements do not relate to physical science. One reads with surprise, therefore, that Soma. described himself as "learned in scientific truths" (*jñātavijñānatattva*; 3.45). This claim would be quite enigmatic if Subājī's early career was not in the background.

Soma.'s reiteration of Subājī's distinction between Siddhāntic and Purāṇic spheres of authority is additional evidence of the authors' joint identity. As cited above, Muir knew beforehand that Subājī's respect for the Purāṇas had not been undermined by apparent contradictions with the Siddhāntas. Nevertheless, the MP (5.73—77; see p. 78, *supra*) drew attention to discrepancies between popular notions about the earth's shape and Bhāskarācārya's description of it in the Golādhyāya. Subājī's explanation of this alleged contradiction was repeated in the MPŚ, where he again claimed that religious texts aim at magnifying God's glory, sometimes at the expense of scientific accuracy. "If there is falsehood somewhere, because a particular motive is applied, it would not make a scripture defective; it would subserve some purpose or other. Therefore, the description of the earth, etc., mentioned in Purāṇas and other scriptures, would not be false, since it describes *īśvara*'s omnipotence" (3.13—14).[66]

Subājī may have been, in comparison with other pandits, extraordinarily receptive to the new science, but there was ample historical precedent for collaborating with Wilkinson in *jyotiṣavidyā*. What is more, he became a Copernican, albeit only after eight years of dialogue, without undergoing a religious crisis and loss of confidence in the Purāṇas. His estimate of the integrity of past generations of brahmins may have depreciated, but faith in the sources of his tradition was unshaken. To use current terminology, his outlook was modernized but not Westernized. Thanks — paradoxically — to his patron, who led him to Copernicus via Bhāskarācārya and Āryabhaṭa, Subājī's transition was organic, not disjunctive.

---

[66] *Prayojanaviśeṣeṇa prasaṃgāc ced asat kvacit / duṣṭaṃ na tena śāstraṃ syāt tattadarthopakārakaṃ // bhūmyādivarṇanam ataḥ purāṇādāv udīritaṃ / asat tan na bhaved yasmād īśvaraiśvaryavarṇanaṃ //.*

Yet the MPŚ shows signs of tension supressed in the SŚP. Certainly not a dilettante, Subājī tested every exotic theory imported by Wilkinson into Sehore against the criteria of the Siddhāntas, finding them inadequate in one particular respect: the age of the universe, or the date of creation. With regard to this question, the old science with its scheme of *kalpas* ("aeons") was in one sense superior to the new, which in Wilkinson's time was pre-Darwinian and still encumbered with theology (e. g., Bishop Ussher's chronology of creation based upon biblical geneologies). Subājī's contempt may have been masked in the SŚP, but it was vented in the following rebuke, the most stinging in the MPŚ, to which, ostensibly, not even Wilkinson was exempt: "For this very reason, that they say creation occurred six thousand years ago, they were previously like animals" (2.21).[67] In other words, only people in a low state of mental development, who recently in the cycle of rebirth were not much better than animals, could conceive of such an unsophisticated idea as one that posits a creation that occurred a mere six millennia in the past. Tension may account for the disdain, since it is grossly inconsistent: whereas European scientific naivety is a debility due to *karman*, similar fallacies are committed by Hindus only when they make pronouncements outside their sphere of competence.

Wilkinson still dominated the second phase of Subājī's career; only the project changed, from science to social criticism. His patron's opinion about backwardness in physical science moderated. Unjust class divisions, mutually exclusive *varṇas* (castes) were a greater malaise: "There is no evil in Indian society, which has been so much deplored by those anxious to promote the enlightenment of the people, as the institution of caste" (Wilkinson, 1839: 2). Instead of following his benefactor's lead as before, Subājī became stubborn, repudiating this indictment of Hindu society. The reason for this reification was that Wilkinson's critique impinged upon *alaukika* verities. Although he himself chaffed under certain restrictions imposed upon his *varṇa*, such as proscription of sea-voyages,[68] Subājī's criticisms were not wholesale but selective. Relations with Wilkinson remained cordial, yet this phase was a turning point: Subājī recognized the danger of disjunction, a loss of continuity with his past, in following his patron farther. One finds backtracking but not backlash in the pandit's writing during this period. Indeed, his conservatism was matched by generosity to those outside the pale of B h ā r a t a, India.

The second phase of Subājī's career was marked off from the first by publication of Wilkinson's little-known contribution to Indology, an edition of the Vajrasūcī attributed to Aśvaghoṣa, to which the pandit's commentary, the Laghuṭaṃka (LṬ), was appended.[69] Early nineteenth-century Orienta-

---

[67] *Ata eva hi te sṛṣṭeḥ ṣaṭsahasragatābdakaṃ / vadaṃti prāg yatas tasmāt paśuprāyā hi te 'bhavan //.*

[68] Subājī also criticized restrictions on the remarriage of widows in an untraced Marathi tract, Paraśurāmakṣetrasthā (WILKINSON, 1841: 3).

[69] The Wujra Soochi: or Refulation [sic] of the Arguments upon which the Brahmanical Institution of Caste is Founded. By the Learned Boodhist Ashva Ghosu. Also the Tunku by Soobajee Bapoo. This edition, bound in a red cover suggestive of

lists and missionaries alike were intrigued by this Buddhist author's witty and caustic assault upon distinctions based on caste.[70] Aśvaghoṣa subjected brāhminical prerogatives to intense ridicule, deftly citing inconsistencies in their own canonical texts. To those who thought, as Wilkinson did, that the *varṇas* are inimical to social improvement, publicizing the Vajrasūcī promised to be an effective means to undermine vested interests. Subājī, however, was unable to assess the Buddhist's treatise so positively; it was, after all, his own society whose warp and woof Wilkinson wanted to unravel. "When I announced our intention of printing the work to my learned and enlightened Shastree Soobajee Bapoo, his prejudices in favour of the institution took the alarm and induced him to request me to print along with the Boodhist attack on the institution, such arguments as suggested themselves to him in support of it. . . . His reply to Ushwa Goshu, entitled the Tunk — or Lughoo Tunk, from its being an abbreviation of a longer work, is accordingly offered to the public along with our Author. In this Bapoo manifests the same talent and learning, and all things considered liberality of sentiment and regard in truth which have ever distinguished him amongst his countrymen" (Wilkinson, 1839: 4).

Having reviewed the SŚP, one can easily recognize what "enlightened" implied in Wilkinson's unstinting praise of the pandit: it meant, of course, that Subājī had become a Copernican. Yet, no space in the MPŚ was devoted to defending the new science. The question, then, is whether other forms of Subājī's "learning" and "liberality of sentiment" are resonant in Soma.'s remarks. In answering this, it should not be overlooked that the phraseology and not only the contents of the two treatises harmonized. Ballantyne should not have underestimated the significance of nearly identical verses concluding the LṬ and MPŚ. The author's highly detailed geographical locations (Ajaṃtā, or Ajaṃtāgraṇī, part of Sehore, a city near Bhopal in Malwa) and deference to Wilkinson testify to their joint identity.[71] Unlikely as it might be, two distinct scholars, neighbors in the same borough, initiated into Wilkinson's nucleus of *jyotiṣas* popularizing the new science, may each have written one of the two treatises now before us. Several resonances in particular, however, indicative of Subājī's erudition and broadmindedness, make this an unlikely possibility.

Buddhism, was published in Bombay in 1839. Also included was a translation prepared by BRIAN HODGSON, British resident in Nepal. Whether or not Aśvaghoṣa wrote the Vajrasūcī is uncertain. For a discussion of the problem, see WINTERNITZ, 1972, 2: 265—66.

[70] A summary of Western interest in this text will be found in A. WEBER, 1859: 1ff. WEBER mistakenly attributed a translation of the Vajrasūcī to a missionary named PERCIVAL in Ceylon. This translation was actually by WILLIAM MORTON, a missionary in Calcutta, which appeared in a Jaffna periodical, the MS (1846, 152, 161, 169—70, 177).

[71] The final verse of the LṬ, with variations in the MPŚ noted in parentheses, reads as follows: *deśe mālavanāmake ('sti) 'tra nagarī bhūpālanāmnī (varā) śubhā tasyāṃti śihūranāmakapurī yasyām ajamṭāgraṇīḥ / vilkinsann iti sāhibo vijayate tasyāśritānāṃ sabhāmadhye ('bhūn mahitā mahītalajanaiḥ śikṣeyam anvīkṣitā) 'bhul laghuṭaṃka eṣa viduṣāṃ toṣāya doṣāpahāraḥ* // (LṬ: 60; MPŚ: 3.47).

Neither text, both simply dated 1839, mentioned the month in which it was written. Which preceded the other is impossible to ascertain; nor can it be precluded that they were produced simultaneously or nearly so. What is clear is that subjects occupying the writer's mind in one treatise were transferred to the other as well. The first correspondence indicating that the Buddhist critic triggered a chain of thoughts in Subājī's mind that carried over into both the LṬ and the MPŚ revolves around quite an arcane issue: was Rāvaṇa, the *rākṣasa* ("demon") of Laṃkā, a brahmin? To this recondite subject, originating in Aśvaghoṣa's assertion that one does not become a brahmin by studying the Vedas, Subājī attached great importance. The Buddhist argued this question along the following lines, rendered according to HODGSON's translation: "Do you declare that by reading the *Vedas* a man becomes a Brahman? This is palpably false: for it is notorious that the *Rakshasa* Ravan was deeply versed in all the four *Vedas*: and that, indeed, all the *Rakshasas* studied the *Vedas* in Ravan's time: yet you do not say that one of them thereby became a Brahman. It is therefore proved that no one becomes a Brahman by reading the *Vedas*" (Wilkinson, 1839: 8—9).[72] Subājī straightforwardly contradicted Aśvaghoṣa in the LṬ, citing the axiom *vedamūlam idaṃ brāhmyaṃ* ("brahminhood is rooted in the Vedas"; v. 43 of Bhartṛhari's Nītiśataka) which he applied to Rāvaṇa. "One becomes a brahmin by the Vedas alone, because the Vedic mantras are necessary in all of a brahmin's ritualistic activities. Rāvaṇa was not only a brahmin but an *āhitāgni* as well. 'Only because of delusion' does one say 'he was not a brahmin'" (Wilkinson, 1839: 37).[73] To prove his point, the widely read pandit cited two verses from the Adhyātmarāmāyaṇa, an appendix to the Brahmāṇḍapurāṇa. Śuka, a spy, uttered the first in a reprimand addressed to Rāvaṇa as a brahmin: "Therefore being a Brāhmaṇa and the son of Paulastya, why art thou like an ignorant person always running in vain after sensual delights?" (Nath, 1913: 143).[74] Subājī also noted that, during Rāvaṇa's funeral, the *rākṣasa* was referred to as one who had maintained the sacrificial fire (*agnihotra*).[75]

Soma.'s reference to Rāvaṇa in the MPŚ is more than obstruse: it is enigmatic, a flash of insight without amplification. Interpretation of the sole occurrence, 2.22—24, is puzzling in relation to the MP, but connecting it with 5.65—66 is the most likely solution. Muir had argued there (see p. 78,

---

[72] *Vedenāpi brāhmaṇo na bhavati kasmāt rāvaṇo nāma rākṣaso 'bhūt tenādhītāś catvāro vedāḥ ṛgvedo yājurvedaḥ sāmavedo 'thārvavedaś ceti / rākṣasānām api gṛhe gṛhe vedavyavahāraḥ pravartata eva na ca te brāhmaṇāḥ syuḥ / ato manyāmahe vedenāpi brāhmaṇo na bhavatīti /* (WILKINSON, 1839: 5).

[73] *Brāhmaṇasya samastakarmasu vedamantrāvaśyakatvāt vedenaiva brāhmaṇo bhavati / rāvaṇo brāhmaṇa eva pratyutāhitagnir api / brāhmaṇo nety uktir mohād eveti //* (WILKINSON, 1839: 37).

[74] *Atas tvaṃ brāhmaṇo bhūtvā paulastyatanayo 'pi san // ajñānīva sadā bhogān anudhāvasi kiṃ mudheti //* (Adhyātmarāmāyaṇa, 6.4.53—54).

[75] *Cityāṃ niveśya vidhivat pitṛmedhavidhānataḥ // āhitāgner yathākāryaṃ rāvaṇasya vibhīṣaṇaḥ // tathaiva sarvam akarod bandhubhiḥ sahamantribhir iti //* (Adhyātmarāmāyaṇa, 6.12.36—37; cf. WEBER, 1859: 237—38).

supra) that Hinduism is out of equilibrium, each sect vaunting its own *iṣṭadevatā* at the expense of others. Soma. responded by saying that religious preferences are universal, not faults peculiar to his coreligionists. Muir failed to perceive, he seemed to allege, that an excess of devotion, manifesting itself through intolerance, can be a mask behind which genuine piety thrives. To illustrate this principle, Soma. cited the hostility of Rāvaṇa, Rāma's archfoe, toward Viṣṇu, the supreme deity. Here the author may have followed the Adhyātmarāmāyaṇa, according to which this *rākṣasa* attained *mokṣa*, despite contempt for Viṣṇu, because his mind was constantly focused on him as the Supreme Spirit. What cannot be accounted for is the *vedabhāṣya* ("commentary on the Vedas") attributed to Rāvaṇa.[76] "Something is indeed praised in Jain and Buddhist books, though it is the superiority of their own respective *īśvara*. But it is like that everywhere. Śāktas, Vaiṣṇavas, Śaivas, and others are mutually opposed. Nevertheless, in their respective books they inquire into gods other than their own. There was a *rakṣasa*, Rāvaṇa, despiser of Viṣṇu and brahmins, who made a commentary on the Vedas. In it there is praise for *avatāras* and so forth" (2.22—24).[77] In each case the context was different. Rāvaṇa did not appear as a brahmin in the MPŚ, nor as a pious but prejudiced *rākṣasa* in the LṬ. Yet it is hard to discount as improbable the liklihood that Aśvaghoṣa raised an issue with ramifications spilling over into both of Subājī's 1839 treatises. The obscure origins of the Rāvaṇa reference speak in favor of this hypothesis.

Aśvaghoṣa's Vajrasūcī may have activated Subājī's "prejudices" in favor of the *varṇas*, but he was nonetheless charitable toward non-Aryans, *mlecchas*, and in this the LṬ and MPŚ were fully agreed. Hindu opinion about the status of barbarians diverges, some authorities maintaining that the *varṇāśrama* system is nonexistent outside Āryāvarta, while others claim that all *mlecchas* are *śūdras* (KANE, 1941 : 383—87). This *jyotiṣa* conformed to the latter viewpoint,[78] except that he went beyond it in assessing salvific possibilities in non-Hindu religions. Whether or not *mlecchas* are the object of divine solicitude seems not to have been a question weighing heavily upon

[76] There was a Rāvaṇa — some would say the *rākṣasa* of Laṃkā! — who wrote an early commentary, now lost, on the Vaiśeṣika-Sūtras: the so-called Rāvaṇabhāṣya or Vaiśeṣikakaṭandī. For details, see JAMBUVIJAYA, 1961: 12—14; SHASTRI, 1964: 103—07; KUPPUSWAMI SASTRI, 1929: 1—5. Soma., however, specified a *vedabhāṣya*, not a commentary on a *darśana*. Tradition is silent on this possibility, though the following comment by KUPPUSWAMI SASTRI, unelaborated and relegated to a footnote, is worth further attention: "When I was in Lahore in November, 1928, ... I happened to see in the Lalchand Library there a manuscript of the Rg-Veda-padapāṭha [but not a *saṃhitāpāṭha*] attributed to Rāvaṇa" (1929: 5).

[77] The final word, *kīrtitaḥ*, unintelligible in the original, is emended as *kīrtanaḥ*. *Jainabauddhaprabandheṣu kiṃcid asty eva kīrtitaṃ / kiṃtu svasveśvarādhikyaṃ tat tu sarvatra tādṛṣaṃ // śāktavaiṣṇavaśaivādyāḥ parasparaviroddhinaḥ / paraṃtu tattadgrantheṣu tadanyeṣāṃ nirūpaṇaṃ // viṣṇudvijadveṣakartā rāvaṇo yas tu rākṣasaḥ / vedabhāṣyaṃ cakārāsminn avatārādikīrtanaṃ //*.

[78] For example: *itaravarṣeṣu ca / śeṣeṣu cāṃtyajajanā nivasaṃti sarve iti ekaiva jātir vihitā /* (WILKINSON, 1839: 54).

the minds of ancient pandits,[79] but it was significant to Subājī and even more so to Soma. For them the issue was not whether but how *bhagavān* has made provision for *mlecchas*. Parallelisms in their treatment of this issue will be noted here, whereas fuller discussion is reserved for the sections on tolerance and Christianity's place in the general scheme of Dharma.

Ritualism preponderates throughout much of Hinduism, and, likewise, in Subājī's LṬ. Spiritual felicity was predicated of *mlecchas*, despite severe handicaps, chief of which is the absence of brahmins to perform ceremonies on their behalf. According to Subājī, there are natural rather than moral factors to account for this disability. *Mlecchas* are not the offspring of *pratiloma* ("contrary to caste") marriages; they are *śūdras* simply because circumstances, such as geographical location, militate against brahminical oversight. Taking a rather strained example, Subājī referred to arctic regions where days and nights are sometimes monthlong. Ablutions (*snāna*) in such conditions are impractical; nor are sunrise and twilight ceremonies (*saṃdhyā*) feasible. If brahmins, as instructed by scripture, are to eat twice-daily only, how will they survive four-week intervals between meals? But surely *bhagavān* is concerned with preserving life. *Mleccha* cultures are monocaste by virtue of necessity (Wilkinson, 1839: 54; Weber, 1859: 253).

Where others stopped thinking, Subājī started asking whether there is a way for *mlecchas* to circumvent brahminical rituals. His answer was that *bhagavān*, supremely compassionate (*atiparamakāruṇika*), prepared a means for them to attain *svarga* or even *mokṣa*. Thus, in the following passage one finds a clear expression of the universal *avatāra* doctrine (Wilkinson, 1839: 54—55; Weber, 1859: 252—53): "Since it is impossible for people who live [in *mleccha* countries] to perform ritual activities, *bhagavān*, having undertaken to become an *avatāra*, bestowed on them a theistic [Weber, "monotheistische"] scripture, in their very language, so that they might attain contentment — but only by good behavior other than this" [e. g., *snāna* and *saṃdhyā*].[80] Paralleling this liberality are many, often redundant, verses in Soma.'s MPŚ, two of which are cited here. If the liklihood that *mlecchas* will attain *mokṣa* was implicit in the LṬ, it became explicit in this text. Salvific possibilities in non-Hindu religions are unlimited, according to the broadminded Soma. Yet, this universalism was based not on essential identity but on insurmountable disparities in human nature. "Since God

[79] No less a scholar than D. C. SIRCAR would dispute this point. Referring to Bhagavad-Gītā 4.7—8, he claimed that "This was said not with reference to the people we now call Hindu, but with reference to all peoples. And thus, not only the Buddha, but Christ, Muhammad, Nānak and other great religious teachers may all be taken as Avatāras,..." (1971: 91—92). Whether the Bhagavad-Gītā had *mleccha* populations in mind is, of course, moot. The liklihood is great that SIRCAR's interpretation is due to modern Hindu universalism. Dogmatic exclusivism, a fault which cannot be attributed to the Gītā is one thing; concerned, informed awareness of other religions is quite another.

[80] *Tatratyānāṃ karmakaraṇāśakyatve 'pi taditarasadācaraṇenaiva kṛtārthatāsiddhyarthaṃ bhagavatā teṣv evāvatāraṃ dhṛtvā tadbhāṣayaiva seśvaraṃ śāstraṃ vihitaṃ* //.

made men with particular natures, those belonging to a specific race must follow a particular scripture uttered by God. If only one scripture is agreeable to God, why did he, lord of the world, not make mankind single-natured? For this very reason, that he made spatial, temporal, and other differences, it would be perfectly certain that differences between scriptures would also be quite pleasing to Him."[81] The obvious corollary was divine unity despite human diversity. Soma., therefore, enjoined his audience to worship this multifaceted God: "Worship him, the universal *ātman*, true lord, who is honored as 'Buddha' in the Buddhist *darśana*, 'Jina' in the Jain scripture, known by the name 'Christ' in the Christian religion, as 'Allah' in the Mohammadan religion, and by the names 'Arka,' 'Pramatheśa,' 'Śakti,' 'Giriśa,' 'Śrīśa' and so forth in the threefold [science], various Tantras, and Purāṇas."[82]

From this study a tentative pattern emerges: a mind obsessed and struggling with newly acquired knowledge, yet cognizant of a theological framework into which *laukika* and *alaukikavidyā* must fit. His points of reference were shifting, but if he was tempted by Christianity, there is no corroborating evidence that he was attracted to the figure of Christ. If that religion had, in his view, any advantage over his own, it was that it had fostered a somewhat superior rational and technological civilization in Europe. Nonetheless, on rational grounds, Christianity, too, was defective in physical science. The irony is that, if Wilkinson attempted to convert his pandit, he failed, for in revitalizing the Siddhāntas he inadvertently refurbished Subājī's confidence in his own tradition.

It is not implausible that Soma.'s broadminded tolerance was inspired, in part, by prolonged and fruitful collaboration with Western colleagues. He risked his prestige in the Hindu community once before by publishing the SŚP. Perhaps he feared the MPŚ was a too mild critique of Christianity for fellow pandits; perhaps he thought it would appear overly inclusive to his exclusivistic benefactors. One cannot say whether his motive was this or otherwise in seeking anonymity as Soma.

The IOLR ms. of the MPŚ, the only one known to exist, contains many scribal errors. Consisting of 107 verses spanning seven folios, it is subdivided as follows: chapter one, "A Brief Exposition of the Unity of Religions" (Mataikyasaṃkṣepa); chapter two, "The Teaching Establishing the Compatibility of All Religions" (Sarvamatāvirodhavyavasthāpanopadeśa); and a third untitled chapter. Like Muir's MP, the MPŚ was a dialogue between two interlocutors: a *śiṣya* puzzled by Christianity and a *guru*, Soma.'s alterego.

---

[81] *Viśeṣavaṃśajair grāhyaṃ pṛthakśāstraṃ vibhūditaṃ / pṛthaksvabhāvā vibhunā yatas tena kṛtā narāḥ // yady ekam eva śāstraṃ ced iṣṭam īśasya tarhi saḥ / ekasvabhāvāḥ kṛtavān prajāḥ kiṃ na jagatpatiḥ // ato hi deśakālādibhedasya karaṇād bhavet / bhedo 'py abhīṣṭaḥ śāstrāṇāṃ īśasyeti suniścayaḥ //* (Soma., 1839: 2.29—30, 32).

[82] *Buddhaḥ saugatadarśane jina iti syādvādaśāstre mataḥ khṛṣṭaḥ khārṣṭamate mahaṃmadamate allāha ākhyāmitaḥ / yaś cārkapramatheśaśaktigiriśaśrīśādināmnoditas trayyāṃ taṃtrapurāṇabhitsu bhaja taṃ sarvātmakaṃ satpatiṃ //* (Soma., 1839: 2.51).

HARACANDRA TARKAPAÑCĀNANA: THE SECOND APOLOGIST

Attention now shifts from Central India to the ambiance of Calcutta where the Christian community's reaction to Hara.'s MPO was swift and censorial. The Calcutta Christian Observer, deeming it a "silly book full of falsehood and bitter invectives," smugly predicted that, "If the enemies we shall by and by have to contend with in India are not more formidable than this brahman, our task will be an easy one" ("Hinduism and Christianity," 1841: 311—313, *passim*). Likewise outraged was the prominent Bengali clergyman, Krishna Mohan Banerjea, who charged that Hara.'s title (An Answer to the [author] of the Mataparīkṣā) was a "flagrant misnomer," his assertions "glaringly incorrect, absurd, utterly subversive of all religion," and that he was guilty of "effrontery" in writing "without any regard to the rules of common courtesy" (Banerjea, 1841: i—iv, *passim*). Whereas Christians scoffed, conservative Hindus, if not more moderate elements such as the Brahmo Samāj, heartily endorsed Hara. as a "defender of the faith."[83]

No doubt Hara. was tactless and pugilistic. If Subājī epitomized finesse in interreligious dialogue, Hara. was his antithesis. What little persuasive power he had could not compensate for the insults heaped on his partner-in-dialogue. Muir was impugned as "Hinduism's great foe" (*hindudharmātivairin*, 1.3; p. 1; citations by chapter, verse and page), an "infidel" (*nāstika*, 1.20; p. 3), so "blind" (*andha*), "confused" (*bhrama*), and "prejudiced" (*pakṣapāta*) that he delighted in the "fall [of others] from caste" (*jātibhraṃśa*, 1.40; p. 5). Also rankling upon Hara. were the missionaries and evangelists (*pravarttakas*) from whom there was no escape either in the marketplace or on the main roads, with their constant refrain, "Convert to our religion (*asmākaṃ dharmam ālambya*) and be happy forever!" (1.2; p. 1). Reserved for special contempt were so-called Hindu-Christians. "Only that man falling into the net of bewitchment of dissembling priests, because of the beauty of the daughters of priests and others and because of covetousness for liquor and meat and whatnot, who is deluded, desirous of acquiring profits, who has neither deliberated upon his own religion nor looked at the defects in Christianity, would become a Christian."[84] As if oblivious to the sting in these insinuations, Hara. pledged himself to further dialogues — but only if Muir guaranteed to bear the cost of printing and remunerated him for his efforts (3.3—4; p. 16).

Compared to Soma's MPŚ or Nīla.'s ŚTV, Hara.'s MPO may be the nadir of Hindu apologetics, but its vulgarity may also be its strength. It has no grandiose claim to sophistication in analyzing religious topics; yet it is

---

[83] Several contemporary sources ("Hinduism and Christianity," 1841: 311; Banerjea, 1841: iii) mention that the MPO was translated into Bengali and serialized in the Prabhākara, a Calcutta newspaper, accompanied by recommendations from leading Hindu citizens.

[84] *Kevalaṃ dhūrttapṛṣṭānāṃ māyājāle patan janaḥ / madhyamāṃsādilobhena pṛṣṭakanyādirūpataḥ // mohito bhogalābhecchur avicārya svakaṃ mataṃ khṛṣṭadharmasya doṣaṃ vā nāvekṣya khṛṣṭako bhavet //* (1.6—7; p. 1).

studied here because it is an early, and in some respects original, contribution to the defense of Hinduism. And though it is calumnious, the MPO is not a puerile, anti-Christian chapbook throughout. Its caricature of converts might easily be falsified, but it condemns the Khrṣṭadharma (Christianity) for substantive reasons, unfortunately muted by Hara.'s penchant for polemics.

Secondary sources give no information whatsoever about the circumstances in which Hara. lived or died. The MPO, on which this biographical profile depends exclusively, only partly bridges this lacuna. One would presume that, as an intelligent Bengali brahmin residing in Calcutta, Hara. would have been aware of the exotic currents of thought blending in that metropolis. The MPO conveys the image of a dilettante, certainly not a scholar, sampling a little of the Bible, a bit of church history, a morsel of Western free thought, and a tidbit of the new science. All these left impressions on Hara., which were utilized against Christianity in the MPO. By examining them one learns something about the milieu in which this apologist moved.

Hara.'s denunciation of Christianity was dogmatic, which is not only to say that its tone was imperious: traditional, systematized beliefs about the nature of Vedic revelation were applied to the field of apologetics. The nub of his critique of the MP was that, whereas the Bible is a recent book, the Vedas are eternally preexistent (*sanātana* or *nitya*) and are coeval with creation. Therefore, "Only that religion is true which has prevailed on earth since the time of creation, and not one that arose subsequently" (1.16; p. 2).[85] One can see that, in this context, Muir's insistence on the Bible's historically verifiable origin and authorship must have worked in his disfavor (MP 4.20—47; p. 75, *supra*). In taking Muir to task in this way, Hara. faithfully voiced long-standing, orthodox Hindu presuppositions, for which one need not search far. Commentators generally found their precedent for this concept of revelation in Manu 1.23. According to the scholiast Kullūka Bhaṭṭa, "The same Vedas which [existed] in the previous mundane era were preserved in the memory of the omniscient Brahmā, who was one with the supreme spirit. It was those same Vedas that, in the beginning of the [present] *kalpa*, he drew forth from Agni, Vāyu, and Sūrya: and this dogma, which is founded upon the Veda, is not to be questioned..." (MUIR, 1873: 6). To Hara., then, the Bible was but a book of yesterday, compared with the unfathomable antiquity of the Vedas.

What is especially puzzling about the MPO is that orthodox reasoning of this kind made an ally of European free thought and Unitarianism. Throughout the text, traditional dogmas were juxtaposed with an odd assortment of references to strains of Western thought, inimical not only to Christianity but to Hinduism as well. It was pointed out above (p. 64) that, in the Roy-

[85] *Tasmāt sṛṣṭiṃ samārabhya yo dharmaś calito bhuvi / sa eva satyo nānyo 'sti dharmaḥ kālāntarotthitaḥ //*. Creation (*sṛṣṭi*) here means the initial unfolding of each new *kalpa*.

Marshman and Khan-Pfander debates, Unitarians and continental biblical critics were widely quoted, with considerable success, against Evangelicals. Hara. also utilized these strands of criticism as apologetical tools without, so it would seem, actually endorsing their substance. Yet, this observation applies only to the Sanskrit text of the MPO, not to its short English introduction, in which Hara. descanted more like a Western Pyrrhonist than an orthodox Hindu.

"I am aware of the inutility of discussions on this subject, and that it is impossible to prove the truth or falsity of any scheme of faith.

Revelation itself implies a miracle. The first votaries must believe in humble reverence, the person really or falsely designating himself, as the chosen of God. Each succeeding race of believers yield a blind and a more pious acquiescence.

A Moslim asserts that Mohumud was the Prophet of God, because he has asserted his divine mission and his assertion is recorded in the Koran. If I must break the silence which is most prudent on such occasions, I reply, that I admit that Mohamad made these pretensions, but that I consider him to be an imposter or insane, — at least on this subject. I have no pious prejudice in favor of the Koran, and reply without hesitation. The Moslim makes equally short work of the Christian or Hindu faith.

The truth of a revelation cannot be proved by an appeal to the beauty of its perceptive [sic] morality, nor can its falsity be established by impugning deformity to its institutions. The standard of beauty and deformity is arbitrary and man with his limited reason is not able to scan the objects of the precepts, which he believes to have been divinely revealed" (Tarkapañcānana, 1840: i—ii).

What, then, actually was Hara.'s attitude toward reasoning about religion? It is significant that the first, one might think agnostic, sentence above was contradicted by the final *śloka* in the MPO: "If only Christianity could be made clear, I vow that, along with my colleagues, I will convert to it" (3.5; p. 16).[86] Either of two alternatives may account for this apparent alliance between dogmatism and skepticism. According to the one view, Hara. attempted, albeit ineptly, to repudiate Muir's allegedly objective methods for verifying subjectively apprehended religious truths in order to show that skepticism is the only alternative to dogmatism. According to the second, Hara. believed that skepticism is the guardian of dogmatism, at least when aimed at beliefs other than one's own. The former views skepticism as a danger to be eliminated by dogmatism; the latter sees doubting other dogmas as a means to enhance one's own. Again, it may be either that, unless one consents to the dogma of eternally preexistent Vedas, one will plunge into agnosticism, or that the only way to preserve one's belief in that dogma is to skeptically question the claims of other religions. Whichever formulation is correct, there is ample evidence that, in the cosmopolitan

---

[86] *Yadi bodhitam eva syāt tadāhaṃ bandhubhiḥ saha / khṛṣṭadharmaṃ grahīṣyāmi pratijñeyaṃ kṛtā mayā //.*

milieu of Calcutta, Hara. encountered Unitarianism and Western free thought, which influenced the Pyrrhonistic preface. Whether he sympathized with or actually disdained those trends, Hara. utilized them effectively against Christianity.

Unitarianism was introduced to Calcutta early in the nineteenth century, and it became especially popular in some wings of the Brahmo Samaj. To the chagrin of Evangelicals, the presence of heterodoxy disproved their claims to equilibrium in Christian doctrines. Unitarian literature began about the time of Hara. to circulate in Bengali translations.[87] Western free-thought, too, made inroads, particularly Tom Paine's manifesto for rationalism, The Age of Reason, to which Hara. had access in English and Bengali (S. DAS, 1974: 46).

From writings such as these, Hara. learned that Christianity in its own territory was not the united front it seemed to be in India. Moreover, the church hierarchy, in Hara.'s view, seemed vindictive and bent on suppressing its opponents: "Since many fearless, intelligent men, such as Hume, Tom Paine, the great Voltaire, Palmer, Paine, and Gibbon confuted these priests, the priestly classes, answerless, called them infidels" (2.55; p. 15).[88] These same sources may account for Hara.'s interest in apparently contradictory biblical accounts. Problems in Jesus' geneology were pointed out in 2.26—28 (pp. 11—12); discrepancies about who first discovered the empty tomb in 2.29—34 (p. 12); inconsistencies in calculating the appearances of the resurrected Christ in 2.35—38 (pp. 12—13). Also fuel for his rationalistic critique was an apparently unfulfilled prophecy regarding a kingdom (*rājya*) to be established in Bethlehem, but which was destroyed immediately after Christ's birth (2.23—24; p. 11). Epiphany, too, was problematic, the maji having been led to the birthplace by a rising star: "The English are of the opinion that a star is motionless and, indeed, unconscious. How did it point out the way, knowing about Christ's birth?"[89]

Muir may have alleged that Hinduism is sect-ridden, but Hara. found Christianity equally plagued with denominationalism. This observation need not be attributed to Western critics of that religion, for any resident of

---

[87] For details on Unitarian penetration of Calcutta, see chapter one, "Unitarian Social Gospel and the Foundations of Hindu Modernism," in D. KOPF's The Brahmo Samaj and the Shaping of the Modern Indian Mind (1979). See S. LAVAN's Unitarians and India (1977) for information about Unitarian literature circulating in India in the nineteenth century.

[88] *Hiyumaś caiva ṭām peno valṭāyas tathā paraḥ / pāmar peno gibānādyo bahavo vijñamānavāḥ // tarkayām āsur etebhyaḥ pṛṣṭebhyo nirbhayā yataḥ / tasmāt tān nāstikān āhuḥ pṛṣṭavargā niruttarāḥ //*. Whether the name Paine is mentioned twice because of the author's oversight or because different personages were meant is not known. "Pāmar" seems to equal "Palmer." This may have been Thomas Fyshe Palmer (1747—1802), an English Unitarian whose unusual and ill-fated life may have become known in India. Unjustly accused of sedition and exiled to Australia, he died while escaping to Macao (Dictionary of National Biography, 1917, vol. 15.162—64).

[89] *Acetanaṃ hi nakṣatram iṃlaṇḍīyamate sthiraṃ / kathaṃ jñātvā khṛṣṭajanma darśayām āsa paddhatiṃ //* (2.45; p. 13).

Calcutta could see for himself that it was a divided faith. Most major branches of Christendom were represented in the environs of the metropolis at that time: among Protestant churches, there was St. John's Cathedral (Anglican), St. Andrew's (Scottish Presbyterian), and Lal Bazaar Chapel (Baptist), along with Roman Catholic and Eastern Orthodox congregations. Hara. was stunned by such diversity: "How could that religion, the religious customs of which would constantly change, deserve respect from intelligent men endowed with reasoning? These 'Catholics,' 'Protestants,' 'Presbyterians' and other 'Dissenters' are changing successively" (2.46—47; pp. 13—14). This criticism was sarcastically aligned with the general one that, as a religion, Christianity was a late arrival. "As the world-creator was powerless at the time of creation to establish religious customs, he, [taking] the form of Christ, established them afterwards; when Christ died, the world-creator, [assuming] the form of the pope and others, established them" (2.48—49a; p. 14).[90] This proliferation of sects did not deter Hara. from noting that many Westerners in Calcutta never attended church at all (2.50; p. 14).

Hara. was also familiar with the distinction made by church historians, and effectively used by nineteenth-century anticlericalists, between pre- and post-Constantinian Christianity. This so-called Great Divide, before which it was an oppressed religion and afterwards an oppressor, may have come to Hara.'s attention while reading the same Unitarians and free thinkers mentioned above. Though this is illative one would think this the case in view of his extreme disdain for the way that Christianity spread after Constantine endorsed it early in the fourth century, a subject on which Western critics of the church have discoursed ever since. "West of Persia lies Turkey where there is a city called Constantinople. The ancient Turkish capitol is also there. Formerly, there was a certain king there, named Constantine. This deluded king stupidly converted to Christianity and strove to propagate this worthless religion by fraud, distributing wealth, craft, and force. He made citizens everywhere in his realm convert to that religion. From then until now its propagation comes by nothing other than royal decree. Men don't convert to it of their own will."[91]

For whom did Hara. write the MPO? Ostensibly, it was Muir, indicted by name throughout, and his colleagues in missions, who would have been flustered and somewhat hard-pressed to obviate the arguments Hara. had

---

[90] *Sarvadā parivarttaḥ syād yasya dharmasya rītiṣu / kathaṃ tat tarkayuktānāṃ mānanīyaṃ manīṣiṇāṃ // kethālikaḥ prateṣṭāṇṭas tathā ḍiseṣṭaraḥ paraḥ / presbeṭerīyān ity ete parivarttā yathākramaṃ // sṛṣṭikāle jagatkartā dharmarītivinirmitau / na śaktaḥ khṛṣṭarūpeṇa paścāt sā tena nirmitā // khṛṣṭe mṛte 'pi popādirūpeṇaite vinirmitāḥ /* (2.46—49a; pp. 13—14).

[91] *Āste turuṣkadeśas tu pārasīdeśapaścime / kānaṣṭāṇṭīnopalākhyaṃ nagaraṃ tatra varttate / turuṣkarājadhānī ca tatraivāste cirantanī / kānaṣṭān iti vikhyātas tatraiko 'bhūn nṛpaḥ purā / asau mūrkhatayā khṛṣṭadharmaṃ jagrāha mohitaḥ / pracārayitum aicchac ca dharmaṃ etad akiñcanaṃ / chalena dhanadānena kauśalena balena ca / grāhayām āsa taddharmaṃ svarājyasthān samastataḥ / rājaśāsanamātreṇa tataḥ prabhṛti kevalaṃ / pracāro jāyate 'dyāpi nṛṇāṃ svecchā na tadgrahe //* (2.53: pp. 14—15).

gleaned from Unitarian and free thought literature. Hara.'s comments on the post-Constantinian expansion of Christianity, exaggerated though they were, effectively countered Muir's claim that his religion's universality (*sāmānyatā*) was spiritually rather than socially oriented (MP 3.33—38, 4.63—69; pp. 74, 80, *supra*). The historico-critical approach to reasoning about religions, reflected in the MPO, gained currency in Muir's time, and its threat to Evangelicalism was widely recognized. As long as Hara. dealt with Christianity on these grounds, he was sure of gaining an attentive, if not appreciative, audience.

Whatever impact Hara.'s rudimentary historico-critical arguments may have had, they suffered in the eyes of Western critics because of juxtaposition with a crude canard scandalizing the Virgin Mary, which is why the Calcutta Christian Observer charged the author with libel. By incorporation of the following story, the MPO appears also to have been intended as a chapbook for native readers unfamiliar with the new religion, whose credulity could be stretched.

"Christ's mother, named Mary, stayed in a certain temple until the age of sixteen, and was loved by many priests. Having become pregnant, she gave rise to doubt in her husband, who, therefore, always worried whether it was so or not. Agitated with worry, he saw in a vision an angel, which had approached and said from above, 'Don't worry! By God alone is this one, whose soul is righteous, conceived in your wife. Therefore, O husband, you should not suspect adultery.' Thus, when news of the vision was publicized everywhere those very priests conspired to conceal their offense. Those who are intelligent must consider whether co-habitation with men could be the cause of pregnancy or whether the vision could be credible.[92] ... What would the truth be? Either she made it known to conceal her offense, or he actually saw what he did in the dream... Thus, though a bastard, even the priests extolled him, and thinking 'I am a righteous-souled one,' he began to preach religion. Trusting his words, having scarcely considered anything, dull-witted people became his ardent servants. As the priests attributed miraculous activity [to him] in order to conceal their offense, so did they, too, become bereft of sense, deluded by their own magic. In the book, they made the fantastic proclamation that, 'This is God.' Thus was this religion propagated over the earth."[93]

[92] Having noted that, whereas Matthew 1.18—25 attributes the vision to Joseph, according to Luke 1.26—38 it came to Mary, Hara. then proceeded to use both masculine and feminine pronouns.

[93] *Merināmnī khṛṣṭamātā bahubhir yājakair vṛtā / ekadevālaye 'tiṣṭhat ṣoḍaśābdavayo 'vadhi // tatra garbhānvitā bhūtvā janayām āsa saṃśayam / svāmino niścayaṃ vāpi tataḥ so 'cintayat sadā // svapne cintākulatvena tena dṛṣṭaḥsamāgataḥ / devadūto jagādoccair mā cintā kriyatām iti // īśvareṇaiva dharmātmā janito 'sti striyāṃ tava / na śaṃkā vyabhicārasya tasmāt kāryā tvayā naya // evaṃ svapnasya vṛttānte sarvatra prakaṭīkṛte / svīyadoṣāpahārāya yājakās te 'pi saṃmatāḥ // vicārayaṃtu vidvāṃso yuvatyāḥ puruṣaiḥ saha / vāso garbhasya hetuḥ syāt svapno vā syāt pramātmakaḥ // tayā cet svīyadoṣasya gopanārthaṃ niveditaṃ / svapne dṛṣṭam evam evaṃ tena kiṃ satyatā bhavet // evaṃ sa jārajāto 'pi yājakair api saṃstutaḥ / dharmātmāham iti jñātvā*

The origins of this contrivance are obscure. One is reminded of the Pharisees' insinuation that Jesus was a "bastard," a "wine-bibber" and "glutton" (Luke 7.34), and the canard may have occurred to the author as he read the New Testament — between the lines. At least the purport appears to be the same: illegitimate offspring tend to be blasphemers. Innuendo impugning a teacher's birth is of course useful in exposing new doctrines as heterodox, but the utter naivety with which Hara. introduced this canard suggests that the credulity of native readers might not have been taxed at all, and that, on the contrary, they were familiar with this kind of story. The likelihood that this Jesus-*jātaka* (birth narrative) was folkloric is reinforced by the existence of many so-called Iblīs or Qiyāmat (Satan) stories, popular in nineteenth-century Bengal, some of which describe how the devil started scandals about Mary when she was pregnant (HUSAIN, 1960: 30—33).[94]

Be that as it may, Hara. clearly ranged over many diverse arguments and forms of reasoning about religion in his search for material antagonistic to Christianity. The cosmopolitan milieu of Calcutta aided this venture into apologetics, for it brought him into contact with new patterns of thought derived from the West. Unlike Subājī, Hara. had no overriding theological scheme into which to fit the disparate elements he collected. Yet, despite the unreconciled juxtaposition of foreign and indigenous notions, his haphazard choices happened also to be effective in countering Christianity.

First to respond to Hara. was Muir himself, who, not more than a few months after the MPO appeared, submitted a rebuttal to Calcutta's Christian Intelligencer, "On the Arguments by which the Alleged Eternity of the Vedas May be Refuted" (1840d: 341—47). Muir was not intimidated by Hara.'s apparent alliance with Christianity's Western critics, discerning that the MPO's real substance was orthodox Hinduism. Muffled by vituperation though it was, the claim that the Vedas are coeval with creation was the most effective weapon in Hara.'s arsenal of arguments. He made the Bible tantamount to a sudden bestseller, soon to decline in popularity and disappear. The message to fellow Hindus was plain: "If there is to be faith in a book, let it be in the Veda, since it has prevailed on earth from the time of creation onward!" (Tarkapañcānana, 1840: 1.12; p. 2).[95]

---

dharmaṃ vaktuṃ pracakrame // kṛtvā tadvāci viśvāsam avicārya kathañcana / alpa-buddhijanās tasya jātāḥ sevāparāyaṇāḥ // svīyadoṣācchādanārtham ūcur adbhūtaceṣṭi-taṃ / tathā tanmāyayā te 'pi mohitā hatabuddhayaḥ // īśvaro 'yam iti granthe varṇanāṃ cakrur adbhutāṃ / evaṃ krameṇa dharmasya pracāro janito bhuvi // (2.4—9, 14, 15—19; pp. 9—10).

[94] Suggesting that Hara. may have been influenced by Iblīs folktales, which were composed by Bengali Muslims, does not imply that Islam, according to which Jesus was virgin-born, would condone his aspersions. The illegitimacy argument was also current among Hindus and extended beyond Bengal: Raghunāth Tiwārī's acerbic anti-Christian tract in Hindi, Īsū Caritra, insinuated to its Allahabad audience in 1887 that Jesus was a bastard; Jaffna's Saiva Paripalana Sabhai (*vide* p. 22, n. 5, *supra*) repeated the accusation early in this century (SAVERIMUTTU, 1978: 100).

[95] *Yadi granthe 'sti viśvāso veda evāvalambyatāṃ / yato 'sau sṛṣṭikālādicalito 'sti mahītale //.*

Hara.'s insistence on the Bible's juvenescence was precipitated by Muir's comments on the untraceable origins of the Vedas (MP 5.17—26; p. 76, *supra*). Not having anticipated this reaction, Muir turned to Indologist H. T. COLEBROOKE for arguments to buttress his critique of the orthodox view of revelation:

"Some progress may be possibly made in proving to them that their sacred language has gone through various changes of state and been gradually matured, by adducing the instances of other languages such as the Greek, the Latin and the English. This reasoning might be strengthened by pointing out the coincidences in roots, and other words as well as in inflections between Sanskrit and Latin and Greek. Another part of the argument would be to show by a reference to the mention made of earthly events in the different portions of the Vedas, that they must have been composed or at least according to the Hindu's idea, revealed, at different periods. This would weaken the objection against Christianity, and prove that all the several parts of the Vedas were not simultaneously promulgated at the creation" (Muir, 1840d: 344—45).

Muir then culled from COLEBROOKE's Essays on the Religion and Philosophy of the Hindus the elements of an historico-critical argument against Hara.'s presuppositions about the Vedas. These findings were incorporated into the 1840 edition of the MP, thanks to the MPO.[96] Nonetheless, Muir confessed that he was less than sanguine about the persuasiveness of this approach. "Notwithstanding this difference in style and dialect, the whole of the Vedas including the Upanishads are referred by the Hindus to one period, that of the creation. The difference in dialect does not to the uncritical mind of a Hindu argue any difference in the era of composition. If told that the variation in the inflections of nouns, etc. points to a gradual alteration undergone by Sanskrit in process of time, he seems insensible to the cogency of the conclusion; and replies that the variations which are assumed to belong to different ages, are in fact contemporary forms, the one being scriptural (*baidika*) and the other popular (*laukika*); and that in Sanskrit grammar rules for the formation of the scriptural or vedic as well as the popular forms are to be found" (Muir, 1840: 344).

The MPO caused a sensation in Calcutta itself, provoking an unidentified British "gentleman" to admonish Hara. in three sermons delivered at Christ Church, Cornwallis Square. The minister there, K. M. Banerjea, the first Bengali ordained into the Church of England clergy, was later selected by the Anglican Archdeacon of Calcutta, Rev. Dealtry, to officially respond to the MPO. The outcome was a retort in Bengali, Satyā Sthāpana o Mithyā Nāśana, or according to its English title-page, Truth Defended, Error Exposed (1841).

Unlike Muir, these critics were deflected from the main issue, Vedic versus biblical forms of revelation, by Hara.'s Pyrrhonistic preface and slandering of Christ and Indian converts. The preface to Banerjea's book,

---

[96] *Vide* notes 51 and 52, *supra*.

comprised of the sermons by the anonymous "gentleman," concentrated exclusively on Hara.'s introduction, addressing the Hindu as if he were an agnostic in the Western tradition. Refuting the MPO's caricature of converts was Banerjea's preoccupation, who was himself a prominent convert. "To accuse them of indulging in the hope of obtaining missionaries' daughters is very wrong, because, there are very few if any missionaries here in Calcutta who have marriageable daughters, and to this day no European has been on so intimate terms with a native that the latter might have entertained the hope of marrying the daughter of the former" ("Hinduism and Christianity," 1841: 314). The bulk of Truth Defended, Error Exposed was, like the above extract, a better source of information on intra-Christian than interreligious relations. Clearly, Hara. and his critics were swept into whirlpools of misconception.[97]

The MPO consists of 137 verses covering eighteen pages, including the two-page English preface. The Sanskrit text, divided into three, untitled chapters, was printed in Bengali script, a factor which limited its circulation to northeastern India. Besides the Sanskritized terms of foreign origin mentioned above, Hara. used such non-Sanskritic words as *hindu* and *kabara* (*qabr* in Arabic for "grave," "tomb") in order, by his own admission, to facilitate readers' understanding (*sarvasugamārtha*).

Nīlakaṇṭha Goreh (1825—1885): The Third Apologist

The ŚTV concluded prayerfully: "Glory to you *bhagavān* Viṣṇu, powerful beyond comprehension! I beseech you for faith in the holy Vedic religion."[98] Roughly four years later, on 14 March 1848, the author, a *citpāvana* brahmin, was baptized, stirring up a furor in Benares. Nowadays, Nīla., better known by his baptismal name, Nehemiah, is familiar to students of Indian Christian theology. Though a staunch Anglo-Catholic in later life, Nīla. was a forerunner in the currently popular movement to adopt hermeneutics relevant to Hindu categories of thought. More than a century old, his treatises bearing on that subject still interest theologians. R. Boyd's India and the Latin Captivity of the Church (1974) and K. Baago's Pioneers of Indigenous

---

[97] There is the following — highly slanted — record of an encounter between Hara. and Banerjea: "The Pandit ... was told that Mr. Banerjea was well read in Sanskrit; and so it was a wonder to him a man knowing Sanskrit could have become a Christian. One evening through curiosity he paid him a visit at the manse. Mr. Banerjea received the pandit very cordially and saluted him in right Hindu fashion. The Pandit however showed him no courtesy in return. The reason of this Mr. Banerjea could easily understand; and he by way of retort recited before him in the original Sanskrit the myth of Garuḍa, which put him to the blush. The Pandit then apologized to Mr. Banerjea, and returned home having found a very high opinion of him" (Gosh, 1893: 25—26).

[98] *Namo bhagavate tubhyaṃ viṣṇave 'tarkyaśaktaye / pavitre vaidike dharme śraddhāṃ tvām arthayāmahe //* (Goreh, 1951: 6b.183; p. 85; citations by chapter, verse, and page.)

Christianity (1969), both standard works on new trends in the Indian church, begin with entire chapters bearing on Nīla.'s contributions. Moreover, B. PARADKAR's Theology of Nehemiah Goreh (1969), an anthology of extracts from Nīla.'s postconversion writings, claims — rather extravagantly — that the brahmin became a systematic theologian. Not one of these books, however, took the ŚTV into account, even though it was the counterpoint to all his subsequent writings. His critique of Christianity is studied here not just to bridge a gap in church history, but to fill in a lacuna in the history of Hindu apologetics. Nīla.'s ŚTV, systematic in cerebration, rivalled anything that he later wrote as Nehemiah.

Recounting the events leading to Nīla.'s conversion or its aftermath is not the primary interest here; the epilogue will relate them succinctly. This section has within its purview only the circumstances in which Nīla. encountered Christianity and sought to exorcise Benares of its influence. These are integral to an account of the ŚTV because the evangelistic methods of the day shaped his impressions of the values for which Christianity stood. To reconstruct this situation, Nīla.'s text must be studied not only in relation to Muir's MP but also in the context of dialogues with the missionary who urged that tract upon him, the Reverend William Smith of the Church Missionary Society. Fortunately, there are two biographies of Nīla.: Dwij (1850), written by his partner-in-dialogue, and C. E. GARDNER's hagiological Life of Father Goreh (1900). Especially reliable is Dwij (Twice-Born, a sobriquet for Nīla.), published by SMITH "to show to English readers the nature of the objections raised against Christianity by the brahmans" (1850: 3). As a capable linguist and keen student of Hindu apologetics, SMITH's translations of conversations with Nīla. seem to have minimal prismatic effects. One's understanding of the clash between the MP and ŚTV can, therefore, be more comprehensive than was the case with either the MPŚ or MPO.

Born in Kāśīpurā, a village in the Deccan, Goreh belonged to a family whose forebears held hereditary rights to the office of counselor to the ruler of Bundelkhand. His uncle had been an advisor to the Nawab of Banda, Ali Bahadur. Retiring from public service, the Gorehs, though Maharashtrians, settled in Benares where they endowed and maintained the Annapūrṇachattar, a charitable institution for pilgrims. Unwilling to attend the Benares Sanskrit College because "every Hindu who became acquainted with European learning, lost, in the same proportion, his respect for the shasters" (W. SMITH, 1850: 46), Nīla. was privately tutored in *vyākaraṇa* ("grammar") and the *darśanas*. Most notable in Nīla.'s early life is that, although his background was Śaivite, he turned from Śiva to Viṣṇu as his *iṣṭadevatā*, a change based not so much on preference as reflection upon the sources of his tradition. The reasons for this decision were explained in a letter to M. MONIER-WILLIAMS. "The truth is, that I was a zealous worshipper of Śiva at first. ... But it was an uncomfortable thing for me to find that the great Śankarācārya was an upholder of Vishnu's greatness, and therefore I took some pains to ascertain his views on the subject. I, however, changed Śiva for

Vishnu afterwards, and that for these two reasons. It appeared to me that according to the more venerable and more ancient authorities of the Hindu religion as well as the rites and ceremonies of it, Vishnu occupied the chief place, and not Śiva. Secondly, the great Śankarācārya and his immediate followers were plainly Vishnu worshippers, and Śiva is ignored in their systems. Many parts of the Purāṇa, setting forth Śiva as the supreme being, such as the Sutasanhita of the Skanda Purāṇa and the Śiva Gītā of the Padma Purāṇa, are unquestionably of later date than that of Śankarācārya" (GARDNER, 1900: 35—36).

Although one sees in this incident evidence of a calmly discerning mind, willing to rethink its religious commitments, Nīla. was outraged by bazaar preaching in his sacred city and distressed by its apparent success, sentiments which the ŚTV did not disguise. Missionaries, ostensibly including Smith, were chided for their doctrinaire message: "This is your dogma: there is no other way than faith in God's *avatāra*, known as Christ, acclaimed by your scripture."[99] Hinduism was too profound for such single-minded critics: "One ought not, therefore, to forsake the Vedic scripture, most pure and auspicious, on account of doubts, originating from dullards, about defects."[100] With regard to fellow Hindus who were nonetheless attracted to the Khṛṣṭadharma, Nīla. had this to say: "Oh! I am sorely distressed with those who reject our scripture, giving it only a glance, their hearts agitated by merely apparent defects."[101] Unlike Subājī who remained anonymous, or Hara. who wrote at a distance, Nīla., motivated by these strong feelings, decided it would be, in SMITH's words, "A meritorious act to silence the missionaries; and, driving them from the field, compel them either to leave the country or to confine themselves to the instruction of the Christians" (1850: 37—38).

However, what began in a reactionary fashion quickly became earnest dialogue. Nīla.'s first conversation with Smith occurred in April, 1844. "On his first visit he was reserved, merely asking a few questions on the nature of Christianity; but before he left he expressed his dissatisfaction on discovering that, according to it, man in this life is in a state of probation." (W. SMITH, 1850: 38). On the following day, the missionary received a letter in Hindi from Nīla., detailing his objections to the idea that God brings suffering upon individuals in order to test and toughen their moral fiber. To the problem of evil, and this solution of it, Nīla. attached great importance. But he was unimpressed with Muir's treatment of it in the MP (4.78—84; p. 76, *supra*), which was presented to him on that occasion.

---

[99] *Siddhānta eṣa bhavatāṃ svaśāstraparikīrtite / īśāvatāre khṛṣṭākhye viśvāsān nānyathā gatiḥ //* (1951: 2.9; p. 6).

[100] *Tasmāc chuddhatamaṃ śāstraṃ vaidikaṃ maṅgalāvahaṃ / kṣudrabuddhisamudbhūtair na tyājyaṃ doṣasaṃśayaiḥ //* (1951: 6a.202; p. 66).

[101] *Hantāsmadīyaṃ śāstraṃ ye tyajanti laghudarśanāḥ / doṣābhāsākulahṛdas tebhyaḥ khidyāmy ahaṃ bhṛśaṃ //* (1951: 6b.179; p. 85).

The two did not meet again until April of 1845, an interval of eleven months during which Nīla. composed the ŚTV (dated 1766 in the Śālivāhana era), sending off a copy to Muir, whose reaction is unknown. During this interview, Nīla. submitted to Smith a manuscript in Hindi entitled "Doubts Concerning Christianity," which he had circulated throughout Benares in order to stem the tide of conversions. This document, translated by his partner-in-dialogue, is reproduced here in abridged form because it demonstrates the clarity of Nīla.'s apologetics, always focused on central issues, and because it offers a concise synopsis of arguments elaborated in the ŚTV.

"First Doubt. According to Christianity none can be saved but those who believe in Christ, and yet scarcely any one has heard of Christ! What! has God created many nations and innumerable generations for Hell, and though he had provided the remedy by which they might have been saved, never sent it to them?

Second Doubt. According to the Gospel, Christ is your mediator, and through him... pardon of sin and every other blessing is to be obtained. What! is the sea of God's love and mercy dried up, that the blood and the water of Christ's death and intercession are required to replenish it? But you say, God is just, and therefore Christ died. I ask, is this justice that the innocent should suffer for the guilty, and the guilty escape? Again, where is the use of an atonement, as you state it? Repentence and amendment are what God requires.

Third Doubt. Christ and his Apostles, you say, performed many miracles. This I doubt. Such wonders one hears of everywhere, and learned men have decided that such tales are not worthy of credit. Moreover, wonderful works, which wise men amongst us have related and believed, you won't believe; why, then, should we believe yours?

Fourth Doubt. All religions according with the Ved teach that souls are eternal, and that the nature, or disposition, of God is so essentially just, that from it, as from the *kalpbriksh* [a wishing tree located in Indra's *svarga*], every one receives fruit exactly according to his works. But according to Christianity, God, by a mere act of his will, creates souls; which is both improper and impossible. There are many souls walking disorderly, and are altogether unfortunate: would God knowingly and wilfully have created these? And yet you say, the infinitely wise God has created souls who he knew very well would eventually be miserable in Hell forever! On this supposition I do not ask merely, where is his wisdom gone, but what has become of his justice and his mercy too?

Fifth Doubt. Christianity condemns idolatry: this is wrong. For don't suppose that we look upon the mere image as the creator of the world; but knowing that God's essence is in every thing, we set apart one thing in particular, in order, by meditating upon it, to remember God (as you do with the Bible).

Sixth Doubt. Christianity denies the transmigration of souls. This doctrine involves much injustice. True, for those who after death obtain salvation, it is well enough. But with regard to those who die in their sins, and are never to obtain birth again, the case is very different. Their punishment is not only useless, but it would prove God to be guilty of enmity, cruelty, and injustice.

The doctrine of the Veds and Shasters on this point is far more reasonable. According to them, whatever a soul suffers here is for the sins of a former birth. Thus, by a sensible punishment, they receive correction and instruction; and if they refuse nevertheless to reform, they will clearly be without excuse.

One word, before I conclude, as to what you object in regard to what are esteemed the evil deeds of the gods and incarnations — for instance, those of Krishna. Surely, you would not bind God as you bind yourself! What is sin and what is holiness, but just what God determines to be so? Listening to the story of the divine amusements, whether in Krishna's incarnation, or those of others, is death to evil passions and every sinful desire in man. So that what the Christians say, that the only tendency of Krishna's doings is to increase sin, is all a calumny. If wicked people make these amusements an excuse for themselves committing sin, ... theirs is the sin. God is blameless" (W. Smith, 1850: 59—70, *passim*).

Not the periphery but the core of each religion was adumbrated in this preliminary inquiry, albeit in a rather philosophical mode of expression. It must be noted, however, that the Christianity Nīla. encountered was distinctively Calvinistic in one respect: the doctrine of double predestination. This element was introduced by Smith, not Muir, whose concept of grace tended toward incipient universalism (see pp. 58—59, *supra*), and its ramifications can be seen throughout the ŚTV. By the same token, it must not be overlooked that Nīla.'s remarks bear the imprint of the Vedānta *darśana*, a feature which becomes more evident below.

Nīla. was especially concerned with the epistemology implicit in Muir's MP, for it seemed an irreligious way to reason about religion, reminiscent of Indian materialism. Accordingly, three of six chapters of the ŚTV discussed the relation between faith (*śraddhā*) and reason (*tarka* or *upapatti*). His position was that, without reverential submission to revelation, the whole realm of *parā vidyā* becomes nonsensical, irrelevant to religious life. To Nīla's mind, a challenging apologetic directed against Christianity necessarily presupposed clarification of methods and mental dispositions suitable to reasoning about religion.

The ŚTV was not a sophisticated treatise on epistemology, but it did offer a clear-cut alternative to Muir's proposition that religious truths subjectively apprehended must either be objectively verified or discarded. Nīla.'s first point in rebuttal was that a divine or God-given (*aiśvara*) scripture conveys knowledge which mankind would not otherwise attain by unaided reason. As an autonomous thinker, man is quite obviously handicapped; ordinary means of knowledge (*pramāṇas*) cannot confirm truths embodied by the Sanātana Dharma ("Eternal Religion"), which are beyond perception and inference. This being the case, Nīla.'s second observation was that *śraddhā* is a precondition for intelligent appreciation of the Vedas. The mind bent on objective verification of their contents will, like the *carvāka* ("materialist"), become cynical. *Śraddhā* is a spiritual predisposition of assent to realities outside the realms of sensible perception or logical proof. It is the assurance of things unseen, not because the Vedas' author is omniscient — they are authorless — but because they are self-validating (*svataḥprāmāṇya*). Their substance does not need confirmation, nor can it be confirmed; it is the ground of belief.

There is a notable statistic in this connection: whereas Nīla. used the term *śraddhā* thirty times in the sense described above, Muir used it only once (MP 4.79), preferring *viśvāsa* to connote confidence based on rationality. One will see its dominance in the following extracts, characteristic of Nīla.'s didactic style and selected as representative of his epistemology.

"A divine scripture is profound, its sense beyond the ken of human argumentation. One ought not to look for a defect in it. Human intellects are indeed feeble. The eternal *dharmas* and accounts in Purāṇas and other books are certainly beyond our argumentation, to which one ought not subject them... Stories beyond the ken of human argumentation are seen in your religion, too. It is told that there was, for example, a conversation between a snake and the first woman... Generally characteristic of divinity are stories beyond the ken of human argumentation, augmenting devotion to God alone, which must be reflected upon only through eyes of faith... Ponder in your minds how great is the difference between the human intellect, prone to err, and the divine intention! ... 'Not so! Surely God would promulgate a religion the sense of which is helpful to all, and not one with recondite purport.' If this is what you say, one must demur, since even that which is said to be deeply profound and investigated with a view to its defects is completely comprehended when seen by faith... The intellect's inability to explain subtle meaning easily is famous. Indeed, if it could ascertain truth, what, then, is profound? ... That religion, the meaning of which is grasped by the mind easily, by dullards even, neither partakes of divine truth nor is divine. But our scripture is seen to be deeply profound; proclaimed in the divine speech of the Vedas; possessed of many paths; its truth recondite... Even as you criticize the scripture, faith increases still more through certainty of its profundity... To those who are faithless everything to do with God seems false indeed... An atheistic mind sins worst; it relinquishes even the true sense [of a scripture]. Faith is most beneficial; an honorable man guards it as he would a mother. ... One ought not subject to argumentation those realities which do, indeed, surpass thought. Certainty about the meaning of something profound does not come by way of unsteady argumentation."[102]

---

[102] *Gambhīram aiśvaraṃ śāstraṃ nṛtarkāgocarārthavat | tatra doṣaṃ na saṃpaśyet kṣudrā hi narabuddhayaḥ || purāṇādiṣu yā vārttā ye ca dharmāḥ sanātanāḥ | atarkyāḥ khalu te 'smākaṃ na tāṃs tarkeṇa yojayet ||* (1951: 3.1—2; p. 24) *bhavanmate 'pi dṛśyante nṛtarkāgocarāḥ kathāḥ | yathādyanāryā saṃvāda uragasyeti kathyate*; (3.4; p. 24) *īśabhaktyekavardhinyo nṛtarkāgocarāḥ kathāḥ | śraddhaikacakṣuḥsaṃprekṣyāḥ prāyeṇaiśatvalakṣaṇaṃ* || (3.9; p. 25) *svābhāvikabhramavatī kva buddhiḥ pauruṣī bata | kva caiśam ākūtam iti vicārayata cetasi* || (3.19; p. 26) *nanv evaṃ gūḍhatātparyaṃ*

If speculative or conjectural argumentation (*tarka*), suggestive of intellectual arrogance in the above verses, must be replaced with *śraddhā*, did Nīla. dismiss reasoning about religion altogether? The following extracts show that he saw a positive role in reason (subsequently denoted with a less pejorative word, *upapatti*), in a subservient capacity to *śraddhā*. In this view, reason is subordinate, a device useful either for explicating divine verities on the basis of worldly analogies, or for compelling the mind to acquiesce to eternal realities. And for these purposes, the Mīmāṃsā and philosophical *darśanas* are utilized. Reason can lead astray, but it can also bring the intellect into alignment with faith. Nīla.'s scriptural precedent for this position was Manu 12.106: "He alone, and no other man, knows the sacred law, who explores the [utterances] of the sages and the body of the laws, by [modes of] reasoning, not repugnant to the Veda-lore" (BÜHLER, 1969: 508).

"Those who desire well-being must exercise nothing but faith in the scripture. Indeed, faith is not the culmination of argumentation, which follows intellect. Only in scripture is God taught; in like manner, the ways to worship him; in addition, ritual activities such as sacrifices. So it is and not otherwise... If you deride the scripture from the standpoint of argumentation, then argumentation spoils everything: God has no purpose; there is neither heaven nor hell... Manu said, therefore, that a man is not at fault for using reason consistently with Vedic scriptures in order to understand *dharma*... Believing things in the scriptures to be true, one ought to establish them by means of reason. My opinion is that they are not to be faulted by conforming to reason... Reason conforms only to scripture; not the scripture to reason. Scripture is self-validifying, whereas reason is for understanding it... One must, therefore, use reason conformable — but never contradictory — to things declared in scriptures. Whatever things, therefore, are propounded in Purāṇas and other scriptures are absolutely true. Yet, reason is suitable for explaining them."[103]

---

neśvaraḥ praṇayen matam / taddhi sarvopakārārtham iti cen maivam ucyatām // yad uktam atigambhīraṃ doṣadṛṣṭisamīkṣitam / tad eva śraddhayā dṛṣṭaṃ nitarāṃ sugrahaṃ yataḥ // (3.28—29) *prasiddhaṃ sahasā buddheḥ sūkṣmārthānavabodhanaṃ / tayā jñāyeta cet tattvaṃ gāmbhīryaṃ nāma kiṃ tataḥ //* (3.36; p. 28) *mūḍhair api yadīyārthā gṛhyante sahasā dhiyā / na tad aiśvaratattvena yuktaṃ nāpy aiśvaraṃ matam //* (3.53; p. 29) *asmākaṃ tv atigambhīraṃ vedavācā ca divyayā / proktaṃ bahvadhvabhir yuktaṃ gūḍhatattvaṃ ca dṛśyate //* (3.57; p. 30) *yathā yathā bhavadbhiś ca procyate tatra dūṣaṇaṃ / gāmbhīryaniścayadvārā bhūyaḥ śraddhā vivardhate //* (3.60; p. 30) *bhāti hy aśraddadhānānāṃ seśvaraṃ sakalaṃ mṛṣā /* (3.64a; p. 30) *nāstikyabuddhiḥ pāpiṣṭhā sadartham api muñcati / śraddhā paramakalyāṇī mātevāvati mānavān //* (3.67; p. 31) *acintyāḥ khalu ye bhāvā na tāṃs tarkeṇa yojayet / nāpratiṣṭhitatarkeṇa gambhīrārthasya niścayaḥ //* (3.69; p. 31).

[103] *Śraddhaiva kevalaṃ śāstre prayoktavyā hitecchubhiḥ / na hi tarkasya niṣṭhāsti sa buddhim anuvartate // śāstra eveśvaraḥ proktas tathaiva tadupāsanāḥ / yajñādīny atha karmāṇi tat tathā na tadanyathā //* (4.1—2; p. 32) *tad ākṣipatha tarkāc cet sarvaṃ tarkeṇa lupyati / na prayojanam īśasya na svargo na ca rauravam //* (4.4; p. 32) *athāpi dharmajñānārthaṃ vedaśāstrāvirodhataḥ / naras tarkaṃ prayuñjāno na duṣṭo manur abravīt //* (4.49; p. 37) *satyān matvaiva śāstrārthān upapattyopapādayet / nopapattyanurodhena te dūṣyā iti me matiḥ //* (5.3; p. 39) *śāstrānugaivopapattir nopapattyanugaṃ*

The specifically apologetical application of *tarka* was not explicitly stated in Nīla.'s discussion of epistemology, although its role was clearly implied throughout the ŚTV. However repugnant conjecture might be in itself, its value in deflating the claims of other religions was not disputed. The *khṛṣṭaśāstra* (= Bible) had no claim to *svataḥprāmāṇya*. To Nīla. it had no depth. Rather than finding its doctrines outlandish or inscrutable, he judged them commonplace and pellucid. Thus, one reads such mocking verses as these, interspersed throughout the ŚTV: "If a religion such as yours is being deliberated upon properly in the presence of sensible people, everything seems to have a meaning uttered by fools... Indeed, the meaning of your entire religion is within the ken of infantile minds. It seems, as it were, made by men to suit their own minds."[104]

Nīla.'s treatise consisted of 784 *anuṣṭubh* verses, divided into six chapters: first, "Repudiation of the Opponent's Way of Examining the Authoritativeness of Religion" (Paroktamataprāmāṇyaparīkṣāprakāranirākaraṇaṃ, 28 *ślokas*); second, "Investigation of Faults in the Opponent's Religion" (Paramatadūṣaṇanirūpaṇaṃ, 71 *ślokas*); third, "Beneficial Instruction" (Hitopadeśa, 71 *ślokas*); fourth, "Investigation of the Instability of Argumentation in the Previous Narratives and the Necessity of Faith in the Scriptures" (Śāstraśraddhāvaśyakatākathanapūrvakatarkāpratiṣṭhānanirūpaṇaṃ, 59 *ślokas*); fifth, "Investigation into the Scriptures Self-Validity, which is Independent of Reason" (Śāstrasyopapattinirapekṣasvataḥprāmāṇyanirūpaṇaṃ, 202 *ślokas*); sixth, in two sections, "Repudiation of Suspicions About Defects in Our Religion" (Svamatadoṣaśaṅkānirākaraṇaṃ, 186 *ślokas*).

The ŚTV translation found here is based on the critical edition prepared by S. L. KATRE and published by the Scindia Oriental Institute of Ujjain in 1951. Two fragmentary mss., supplemented by a complete ms. owned by Śrī Bhāu Saheb Katre of Benares, were the basis for this edition.[105]

---

tu tat / svataḥpramāṇakaṃ śāstram upapattis tu tadvide // (5.15; p. 40) *tasmāc chāstreṣu ye proktā arthās tadanukūlagā / upapattiḥ prayoktavyā na viruddhā tu karhicit // ato vedapurāṇādau ye ye 'rthāḥ pratipāditāḥ / satyā evopapattis tu tadbodhāya prakalpyate //* (5.53—54; p. 44).

[104] *Samyagvicāryamāṇaṃ ced bhavatām īdṛśaṃ mataṃ / sudhiyāṃ purato bhāti sarvaṃ mugdhoditārthakaṃ //* (2.176; p. 23) *nūnaṃ bhavanmataṃ sarvaṃ bāladhīgocarārthakaṃ / narair iva kṛtaṃ bhāti prakalpyeva svayā dhiyā //* (3.38; p. 28).

[105] Katre's purpose in publishing an edition of the ŚTV was apologetical as well as academic. He hoped to counteract Nehemiah's most important postconversion book, the Ṣaḍdarśanadarpaṇa, a critique of Hinduism (reissued for the sixth time in 1950), by contrast with his earlier position in the ŚTV (GOREH, 1951: iii—iv).

V. RESISTANCE AND ACCOMMODATION

The MPŚ, MPO, and ŚTV were written to contradict claims made on behalf of the so-called Satya Dharma ("True Religion," = Christianity) and to refute allegations against the Sanātana Dharma (= Hinduism) in the MP. Their contents can first of all be categorized according to whether they refer to the first, second, or third *lakṣaṇa* ("characteristic") posited by Muir. Secondly, they can be arranged with reference either to point-by-point comparisons between Hinduism and Christianity or to an overriding framework for explaining religious pluralism theologically. Both classifications are employed here. Criticisms of the first two propositions advanced in the MP are dealt with below: the necessity of faith-inspiring miracles witnessed by contemporaries and supported by literary traditions, and the excellence (*śreṣṭhatā*) of doctrines embodied in a religion. In the process of confutation, the pandits also rebutted most of Muir's fifth chapter, Bhāratīyaśāstravicāra. Therefore, arguments resisting Christianity are here separated from others defending Hinduism. The third *lakṣaṇa*, universality (*sāmānyatā*), prompted the pandits to theorize about the place of Christianity in the general scheme of Dharma, a subject to be examined individually in the next chapter.

Contra-Christianity

Evidences for the first *lakṣaṇa* (MP 3.2—25, 4.20—47; pp. 14—15, *supra*)

Soma.: "Now, with respect to the truth of Christianity, they say that the proof is that those who proclaimed it did innumerable deeds impossible for men to do. Books are institutionalized in all *mārgas* on earth, teaching about various deeds and so forth in order that people in the future will have confidence in them. They contain miraculous stories about kings and others. Since for men these stories are impossible, they are, therefore, spoken falsely... The date when various [books] were composed is boasted about almost everywhere in [the MP]. There is no delineating between the dates of their composition in [the MP] because the Śaka and other [eras] did not exist at that time.[106] 'For this reason, corroboratory witnesses, the account would not be false,' [says Muir]. According to the maxim beginning

---

[106] Soma.'s purport is that the chronology of the literary tradition (*paramparā*) to which the MP appealed in support of the contemporaneousness of the Bible (MP 4.20—28; p. 75, *supra*) cannot be reconstructed because there were — according to his knowledge — no systems for reckoning time comparable to the Saka or Sālivāhana Era which commenced 78 years after Christ's birth.

'*kumbhīpulāka*,'[107] the other [account] would also be true... But if some believe that Christ alone was the greatest by virtue of his power, then why was he killed by weak men?"[108]

Nīla.: "With regard to this, I ask how contemporary men are supposed to know that this power, expired long ago, existed in the founder of this religion? Why must one think that it was exercised directly before the eyes of witnesses? And why should one think that adversaries tested them? If you say that all this is to be understood according to the book of your own religion, then, look here: why should one not assume [the book has] divine status [simply] because it says so? Besides, would not he who is prepared to falsely say his religion is divine contrive a story in order to substantiate its authoritativeness? He tells another story to substantiate its authoritativeness. But intelligent people do not heed the command: 'Believe it!' ... 'Contemporary writers, too, wrote accurately,' [says Muir]. How could there possibly be certainty about this but for the authoritativeness of the books? 'But surely inaccuracy in contemporary writing is impossible! How could contemporary people believe something that didn't happen?' [says Muir]. One must demur, if this is what you say. You must use here, too, the method you use when perusing the religion of others. For instance, there are stories,

---

[107] *Kumbhī* ("cooking pot") and *pulāka* ("boiled rice"), the first words of a *laukikanyāya* ("popular maxim"), are a variant of the more famous proverb beginning *sthālīpulāka*. According to V. S. APTE's dictionary (1978: Appendix E, 75—76), the latter is used when inferring the character of an entire class on the basis of only one member (e. g., when assuming that all the rice in a cooking pot is thoroughly boiled because one grain is found ready for eating). Curiously, Subājī's *nyāya* seems to have had especial application to astrology and astronomy. Viśvaguṇādarśacampū, written by Veṅkaṭādhvarī in the seventeenth century, contains a typical example (534): *vṛddhihrāsau kumudasuhṛdaḥ puṣpavantoparāgaḥ śukrādīnām udayavilayāv ity amī sarvadṛṣṭāḥ | āviṣkurvanty ākhilavacaneṣv atra kumbhīpulākanyāyāj jyotir nayagatividāṃ niścalaṃ mānabhāvaṃ ||*. *Kumbhīpulāka*, in this connection, justifies the assertion that one can be reasonably confident in all that *jyotiḥśāstra* teaches, because anyone possessed of eyesight can verify that it correctly explains certain astral phenomena (e. g., the moon's waxing and waning, solar eclipses, the appearance and disappearance of planets or constellations, etc.). In the context of the MPŚ, this *nyāya* seems to function as a double entendre: primarily as an indication to Muir that his argument in favor of the reliability of Christian documents applies equally to Hindu literature, and secondarily as a reminder to Wilkinson that the same principle could have been invoked in defense of *jyotiḥśāstra* against Western astronomy.

[108] *Atha yesvasya dharmasya vāstavatve hi kāraṇam | manuṣyāśakyakarmaughakartṛtvaṃ vaktṛṣūcire ||* (MPŚ: 2.4) *Bhāvimartyapratyayārthaṃ tattatkarmādibodhakāḥ | prabaṃdhāḥ sarvamārgeṣu sthāpitāḥ saṃti bhūtale || nṛpādiviṣayās teṣu kathā atyadbhutāḥ sthitāḥ | asaṃbhāvyās tā nṛṣu yat tatas te hi mṛṣoditāḥ ||* (2.6—7) *tattannirmāṇakālaś ca prāyaḥ sarvatra kīrtitaḥ | śakādīnāṃ tadābhāvān na tallekho 'sti tatra ca || tasmād anyonyasākṣitvād udaṃto na mṛṣā bhavet | kumbhīpulākanyāyena satyaḥ syād itaro 'pi yaḥ ||* (2.25—26) *khṛṣṭa evottamaḥ śaktyā kaiścid yadi tu manyate | tadānyair nāśitaḥ kiṃ sa mānavair alpaśaktibhiḥ ||* (2.44). One finds the final thought echoed later in the century in DAYĀNANDA SARASVATĪ's Satyārtha Prakāśa: "Had [Christ] had the power of working miracles, why should he have expired, by crying aloud repeatedly?... But he was not a miracle worker, ... for, had he been so, why should he have undergone that terrible suffering?" (1970: 492—93).

currently coming from various places, about miraculous things, but which are actually also false. Does one not, even now, see intelligent people accepting them? [The story] will be substantiated by additional contrivances other than these. Since you say that hardship, to which others submitted when they converted to this [religion] also is indicative of its divinity, ...it is known that, by faith alone, hardship is endured even though the reward is imperceptible, because one sees people die at Prayāga.[109] ... Moreover, according to your religion, Christ became incarnate on earth at a former time and endowed many men, blind and so forth, with eyesight, etc. This is impossible. If it were so, then why are blind people, who firmly believe in him, not now also possessed of eyesight? Does that compassion no longer exist which God used to have? Or does he treat friend and foe unequally? If at a former time God acted that way for the sake of confidence in the divinity [of that religion], then are not people anxious to have confidence now as well?"[110]

---

[109] Despite the general prohibition of suicide, some Hindu authorities recognize suicide at Prayāga (Allahabad), especially at the confluence of the Ganges and Jumnā, to be efficacious in one way or another for one who is anxious to enter *svarga* or attain *mokṣa*. Besides *tattvajñāna*, ("knowledge of truth"), religious suicide was another means to attain these ends. Voluntary death by drowning or immolation, among other procedures was, therefore, practiced. Opinion differed in accounting for the end attained by suicide. According to the Skandapurāṇa, Śiva whispers *tattvajñāna* to the suicidist. For details, see KANE, 1953: 603—14.

[110] *Idaṃ khalv atra pṛcchāmaḥ sāmarthyaṃ matakartṛgaṃ | cirātītaṃ kathaṃ jñeyaṃ puruṣair adhunātanaiḥ || tasyāpi sākṣibhiḥ sākṣātkṛtatvaṃ jñāyatāṃ kutaḥ | boddhavyaṃ ca kṛtaṃ kasmād vipakṣais tatparīkṣaṇaṃ || svamatagranthato jñeyaṃ sarvaṃ tad iti cet tadā | hanta granthoktitaḥ kasmād aiśvaratvaṃ na manyatāṃ || yaḥ punaḥ svamataiśatvaṃ mṛṣā vaktuṃ samudyataḥ | sa tatprāmāṇyasiddhyarthaṃ kathāṃ no kalpayet kathaṃ || tatprāmāṇyasya siddhyarthaṃ tenaivoktaṃ kathāntaraṃ | mantavyam iti vākyaṃ tu buddhimanto na gṛhṇate ||* (ŚTV 1.14—18; pp. 2—3) *tatkālalikhitāro 'pi yathārtham alikhann iti | niścayaḥ syāt katham iva granthaprāmāṇyam antarā || nanu tatkālalikhite tv ayāthārthyam asambhavi | arthaṃ hy asataṃ manyerañ janās tatkālikāḥ kathaṃ || iti cen naivam ābhāṣyaṃ bhavatā kalpyate yathā | anyeṣāṃ matasaṃcāre yuktiḥ sātrāpi kalpyatāṃ || tathā hi nānāsthānotthā apīdānīntanīḥ kathāḥ | adbhutārthānusaṃbaddhā asatīr api vastutaḥ || idānīm api dṛśyante svīkurvanto budhā na kim | ityādikalpanābhis tadanyābhir api setsyati || aṅgīkṛtyāpi yat kleśaṃ kṛto 'syānyaiḥ parigrahaḥ | tad apy aiśatvagamakam iti yad bhavateryate ||* (1.21—26; p. 3) *apratyakṣe 'pi hi phale dṛṣṭā klesāsahiṣṇutā | śraddhayā kevalaṃ loke prayāgamṛtidarśanāt ||* (ŚTV 1.28; p. 4) *kiṃ ca khṛṣṭo 'vatīryeha narān andhādikān bahūn | netrādyair yojayām āsa prāg ity uktaṃ bhavanmate || tad asambhavi yady evaṃ bhavet tarhy adhunāpi ye | lokās tasmin suviśvastāḥ kiṃ nāndhā netraśālinaḥ || prāg īśvare dayāsīt sā kim idānīṃ na vidyate | kiṃ vā priyāpriyakṛtaṃ vaiṣamyaṃ tatra vartate || yadīśatvapratyayārthaṃ prāk cakāra tatheśvaraḥ | kiṃ pratyayaṃ na kāṅkṣante īdānim api puruṣāḥ ||* (ŚTV 2.15—18; p. 7). In the 1820s Rammohan Roy also belittled the arguments of Evidential Theology. "If all assertions were to be indiscriminately admitted as facts, merely because they are testified by numbers, how can we dispute the truth of those miracles which are said to have been performed by persons esteemed holy amongst natives of this country? ... Have they not accounts and records handed down to them, relating to the wonderful miracles stated to have been performed by their saints, such as Agastya, Vasishta, and Gotama; and their gods incarnate, such as Ram, Krishna, and Narsingh; in the

Noneternal Souls (MP 5.109—18, 127—32; p. 79, *supra*)

Hara.: "Moreover, with respect to his statement that God created *ātmans*, suspicion arises as to whether God is prejudiced. Otherwise, how could one *ātman* come into possession of pleasure and another come into possession of pain? How could God's desire [concerning the pleasure and pain of the *ātmans*] correspond neither to [their] good nor bad deeds?"[111]

Nīla.: "Moreover, since in your religion *jīvas* ["individual souls"] are not thought to be beginningless, but on the contrary, are created by God suddenly, this, too, is clearly not right. This is the ensuing defect: surely God, solitary and melancholic, created people in order to get pleasure! If he created them for the sake of *mukti* ["release"], that would, indeed, be impossible for beings that did not preexist. What does that God want from nonpreexistent beings, whom he has brought into existence, so that he would release them? Grief from seeing others suffer is called compassion. How could there be suffering in nonpreexistent beings? There is not, therefore, compassion in this case either. If God was going to create people intending only to send them to heaven, he would neither have frivolously made them human beings in the meantime nor have given them a place to sin. There is, in newly created *jīvas*, neither a slight possibility of sin nor an inclination, carried over from past lives, toward sin. Why, then, would God create that way? ... Is this God incapable of sending everyone to heaven? Does he desire that they should commit sins after becoming human beings? One does not at all see why those who die right in childhood, or who are retarded since childhood, become human beings ... Moreover, if God makes people intending only to send them to heaven, then why does he require them [to perform] duties, such as worshipping him? If you say that he wants worship in view of the precept for granting *mukti*, then have you not spoiled God's [self-] sufficiency? ... Because he knows past, present, and future, God definitely knows that, 'I will create them, but what is more, they will be sinners.' When God, even though he knows this, goes ahead and creates them, then how could he bring the *jīvas* into being intending to give them *mukti*? Not only is every originated thing thought, as a rule, to be perishable, but if *jīvas* are originated, they would also be subject to destruction. Those who are wise regard being an effect as due to the specific cause of the effect.

---

presence of their contemporary friends and enemies, the wise and ignorant, the select and the multitude? — Could not the Hindoos quote in support of their narrated miracles, authorities from the histories of their most inveterate enemies the Jains, who join the Hindoos entirely in acknowledging the truth and credibility of their miraculous accounts? ... Musalmans, on the other hand, can produce records written and testified by contemporaries of Muhammad, both friends and enemies, who are represented as eye-witnesses of the miracles ascribed to him ... They can assert, too, that several of those witnesses suffered the greatest calamities, and some even death, in defense of that religion ..." (GHOSE, 1978: 614—15). See also DAYĀNANDA SARASVATĪ's objections to miraculous evidences, 1970: 483—84.

[111] *Aparaṃ yac ca tenoktam ātmāno vibhunā kṛtāḥ / tatreyaṃ jāyate śaṅkā kiṃ vibhoḥ pakṣapātitā // anyathātmā sukhī kaścid duḥkhī kaścit kathaṃ bhavet / sukṛte duṣkṛte vāpi sadṛśīcchā na vā kathaṃ //* (MPO 1.65—66; p. 7).

Since God is the specific cause of the *jīvas*, he also, therefore, would be finite. If the specific cause of the effect would remain in existence permanently, the effect would always cohere. That is why one says this cause is finite... When one thinks about it, what difference between these two is demonstrated: the one who brings thieves into existence and the one who would himself be the thief? But in your religion God is construed to actually bring that which is defective into being, since in your religion suffering and defects as well are real. But suffering and defects are simply false from the viewpoint of Brahman and real from the standpoint of those who err, since in our religion they derive from error. The supreme Brahman does not err, indeed. From its viewpoint, therefore, these are false. Our defectiveness is illusory — but this much is peculiar to our religion."[112]

Double Predestination (p. 105, *supra*)

Nīla.: "God, having brought a great many *jīvas* into being, releases only a few of them and throws the others, who have rejected your scripture, into hell. And in hell they experience suffering for an unlimited time; they are never removed from hell again. In any event, among those whom God

---

[112] *Kiṃ ca nānādayo jīvāḥ saṃmatā yad bhavanmate / kiṃ tv akasmād īśasṛṣṭās tad apy addhā na yujyate // īśaḥ kilaikalas tiṣṭhan nirānandaḥ sukhāptaye / lokān sṛṣṭvā sukhaṃ prāpa doṣa eṣa prasajyate // muktyartham asṛjac cen na prāk satāṃ sā hi saṃbhavet / asato 'pi samutpādya kim icchan mocayed asau // pareṣu duḥkham ālakṣya yaḥ śokaḥ sā dayocyate / asatsu hi kuto duḥkhaṃ tasmān neha dayāpy uta // svargaikaditsayā lokā asrakṣyanteśvareṇa cet / vṛthā madhye manuṣyatvaṃ nāghāspadam adāsyata // sadyaḥsṛṣṭeṣu jīveṣu nāṃhaḥsaṃbhāvanāṇvyapi / na cāṃhovāsanā vāpi kuto hīśas tathā sṛjet /* (ŚTV 2.20—25; pp. 7—8) *dātuṃ kim eṣa sarvebhyo aśaknuvan svargam īśvaraḥ / madhye manuṣyatāṃ prāpya kuryur ena itīcchati // bālya eva pramītā ye bālyād bhrāntadhiyaś ca ye / teṣāṃ ca naratāprāpter natarām artha īkṣyate //* (2.27—28; p. 8) *kiṃ ceśaḥ kurute lokān yadi svargaikaditsayā / nṛṇāṃ dharmaṃ svasevādim eṣa kasmād apekṣate // muktidānavidhau sevām icchatīty ucyate yadi / pūrṇakāmatvam īśasya bhavatā kiṃ na dūṣitaṃ //* (2.30—31; p. 8) *mayā sṛṣṭā bhaviṣyanti kiṃ caite pāpinas tv iti / bhūtabhavyabhavajjñatvāj jānāty eva kileśvaraḥ // iti jānann apīśas tān sṛjaty eva yadā tadā / jīvotpādakatā tasya kathaṃ syān muktiditsayā // sarvaṃ cotpattimad vastu niyamenāntavan mataṃ / jīvāś cotpattimantaś ced bhaveyur nāśadharmiṇaḥ // kāryāsāmānyahetor apy āryaiḥ kāryatvam iṣyate / jīvāsāmānyahetau syāt tata īśe 'py anityatā // yadi nityasthiti bhavet kāryāsāmānyakāraṇaṃ / kāryaṃ sadā prasajyeta tato 'nityaṃ tad ucyate //* (2.36—40; p. 9) *utpādako yaś corāṇāṃ svayaṃ coraś ca yo bhavet / kiṃ tāratamyam ubhayor vicāre sati sidhyati // kiṃ tu yuṣmanmate satyaṃ duḥkhaṃ doṣāś ca vai yataḥ / duṣṭotpādakatā satyā vibhau klṛptā bhavanmate // asmākaṃ tu mate duḥkhaṃ doṣāś ca bhrāntijā yataḥ / bhrāntadṛṣṭyaiva te satyā brahmadṛṣṭyā mṛṣaiva hi // abhrāntaṃ hi paraṃ brahma taddṛṣṭyaite mṛṣā tataḥ / asmākaṃ duṣṭatā mithyā viśeṣo 'smanmate tv iyān //* (6b.93—96; pp. 76—77). The idea that an effect exists only as long as its cause (*kāraṇa*) exists is a tenet basic to Sāṅkhya and Advaita Vedānta. In Śaṅkara's commentary on the Vedānta-Sūtras, it constitutes the first proposition in his discussion of *satkāryavāda*, a doctrine of causality in which effects are considered to preexist in their causes (*vide* 2.1.15—18; THIBAUT, 1890: 330—42). This was further developed into the theory of *vivarttavāda*, according to which an effect is not a new entity but the manifestation of the cause in a new aspect. Biblical views on originative causality clearly violate both explanations of cause and effect. For details see LIPNER, 1978: 53ff.

created, the birth of them who went to heaven is better than the senseless creation of them who reside in hell. At the time of creation, did the Supreme Ātman not know that they will experience suffering in hells, having committed sins? And if God, knowing that they must necessarily experience suffering, created them so that they would experience suffering, who, then, is more reprobate than he?[113] ... But in any event, according to our religion, people who have committed many sins experience grievous suffering, the fruit of sin, in places such as hell, and then, in a subsequent life, experience pleasure to an even greater degree by reason of merit. But they do not experience suffering for an unlimited time only. Thus, experiencing pleasure and pain in numerous existences, they also gradually attain *mukti*, on account of knowledge originating from the merit of virtuous conduct... As a father beats his own son, in order to put a stop to bad behavior, and afterwards comforts him, it is likewise proper for God to punish the *jīva* in order to teach it and then give it pleasure and, gradually, *mukti* as well — if it desires what is good for it."[114]

Original sin (MP 4.71—77; p. 76, *supra*)

Nīla.: "If God would make the punishment of one person's sin fall upon another, even though sinless, how could he be just? A father's wicked-

---

[113] Cf. the remarks of the late nineteenth-century Bengali Vaiṣṇava, Bhaktisiddhānta Sarasvatī Ṭhākura (father of the teacher of A. C. Bhaktivedānta Prabhupāda), on Śrī Caitanyacaritāmṛta (Madhyalīlā, 15.163). Vāsudevadatta, Caitanya's disciple, says, "My dear Lord, let me suffer perpetually in a hellish condition, accepting all the sinful reactions of all living entities. Please finish their diseased material life." According to the commentator, "In the Western countries, Christians believe that Lord Jesus Christ, their spiritual master, appeared in order to eradicate all the sins of his disciples. ... Here, however, we find Śrī Vāsudeva Datta Ṭhākura... to be many millions of times more advanced even when compared to Lord Jesus Christ. Jesus Christ relieved only his followers from all sinful reactions, but Vāsudeva Datta is here prepared to accept the sins of everyone in the universe... [He] wanted to completely relieve the conditioned souls from material existence so that they would no longer have an opportunity to commit sinful acts. This is the difference between Śrīla Vāsudeva and Lord Jesus Christ" (PRABHUPĀDA, 1975: 83—84). See also DAYĀNANDA SARASVATĪ's comments on forgiveness in Christianity (1970: 485).

[114] *Utpādya subahūñ jīvāṃs teṣv alpān eva mocayan / anyāṃs tyaktabhavacchāstrān narake kṣipatīśvaraḥ // kālaṃ te 'vadhiśūnyam ca narake duḥkhabhoginaḥ / punar noddharaṇaṃ teṣāṃ nirayād asti karhicit // ye tāvad īśasṛṣṭeṣu svargatās tajjanur varaṃ / ye punar narakāvāsās teṣāṃ sṛṣṭir nirarthikā // teṣāṃ sarjanakāle kiṃ nāsīj jñānaṃ parātmanaḥ / kṛtvā pāpāny amī duḥkhaṃ bhokṣyanti narakeṣv iti // jānann avaśyabhoktavyaṃ tair duḥkhaṃ yadi ceśvaraḥ / asṛjad duḥkhabhogārthaṃ kas tasmād vyasanī paraḥ //* (ŚTV 2.129—33; p. 18) *asmanmate tu ye tāvad bahupāpakṛto narāḥ / bhuktvā pāpaphalaṃ bhūri te duḥkhaṃ narakādiṣu // bhūyo bhavāntare puṇyaiḥ sukhāny api ca bhuñjate / na tu kālaṃ niravadhiṃ kevalaṃ duḥkhabhoginaḥ // evaṃ bhaveṣv anekeṣu bhuñjantas te sukhāsukhe / śukladharmodbhavāj jñānāt kramān muktiṃ prayānty api //* (2.139—41; p. 19) *yuktaṃ tu parameśasya yathā putraṃ nijaṃ pitā / hanti doṣanivṛttyarthaṃ dadāti ca sukhaṃ tataḥ // tathaiva jīvaśikṣārthaṃ daṇḍaṃ datvā tataḥ sukhaṃ / krameṇa mokṣaṇaṃ cāpi yady asau hitam icchati //* (2.145—46; p. 20). See DAYĀNANDA SARASVATĪ on double predestination, 1970: 489.

mindedness never extends to his son. The child's body, indeed, but not his intellect, is derived from his father, because of its relation to semen. Surely one sees in this world a difference between father and son. The son even of a very wicked-minded man is seen to be the crest-jewel of *sādhus* ["virtuous people"]. Intelligence is given by God alone; how could he give it as something that is corrupt? And if this God would give it to them and then punish them, could he be just? Sinning against God by breaking his commands is specifically said to be a defect. But how can this occur in one just born? What, indeed, is this sin of his, that he was born from a corrupt father? Surely birth depends on God, not on man."[115]

Justification (MP 4.71—77; p. 76, *supra*)

Soma.: "If [Christ] destroyed mankind's sin by the sacrifice of his own body, then can that not be done, in order to destroy human sin, by those who, like him, are virtuous?"[116]

Nīla.: "So, nor do I think this remark of yours is well said: 'Christ took the punishment of mankind for the sake of its *viśuddhi*.'[117] To say that one

---

[115] *Yady āgaso 'nyadīyasya daṇḍam anyatra pātayet | puruṣe 'naparādhe 'pi kathaṃ syān nyāyavān prabhuḥ | pitur durbuddhitā putre na prasarpati jātucit | paitro hi śukrasaṃbandhāc chiśor deho na cāsya dhīḥ || tathā hi dṛśyate loke 'py antaraṃ tātaputrayoḥ | sudurmater api suto dṛṣṭaḥ sādhuśiromaṇiḥ || īśadattaiva dhiṣaṇā duṣṭāṃ dadyāc ca tāṃ kathaṃ | datvā ca tāṃ daṇḍayec ced eṣa nyāyī kathaṃ bhavet || īśājñocchedarūpaś ca yo 'parādhaḥ parātmanaḥ | sa eva doṣa ityukto jātamātre tv asau kutaḥ || ko hi tasyāparādho 'sau yad duṣṭād ajaniṣṭa saḥ | janma khalv īśvarādhīnaṃ nādhīnaṃ puruṣasya tat ||* (ŚTV 2.56—61; p. 11). Reflected in this passage are technical assumptions about foetal development. The foetus was widely acknowledged as a product of the union between a father's semen (*śukra*) and a mother's blood (*śoṇita*). But Nīla. was in the mainstream of Sāṅkhya and Vedānta, *darśanas* which hold that these two are insufficient to account for the production of a body. According to these schools, semen and blood operate as causes only in conjunction with the subtle body (*sūkṣmaśarīra*), a psycho-material apparatus guaranteeing continuity of intellect (*dhī, buddhi*) and *karman* between births. As Sāṅkhya elaborates it, this subtle body consists of *mahat, ahaṃkāra*, the eleven senses, and five *tanmātras* which pass from birth to birth upon each death. The *sūkṣmaśarīra*, the support mechanism of *buddhi*, is infected by the latter's ignorance and continues to exist as long as enlightenment is not attained. The corporeal body, then, is a parental product, whereas mental traits are due to *buddhi* and the *karman* it has accrued (for details, see DASGUPTA, 1932: 302—12). With physiological and psychological presuppositions such as these in the background, the Christian concept of original sin could not but appear specious (cf. O'FLAHERTY, 1976: 25—26, 366). Whether one is wicked or not, or blind or not, is due to one's own *buddhi*, conveyed between births by the subtle body, not to vitiated mental and moral capacities transferred biologically from parent to child. It should also be noted that Nīla., by saying birth ultimately depends on God, meant only that the divine function is to create conditions appropriate for the *jīva* to live out its *karman*. Not God but the *buddhi* is the deciding factor in one's mental and moral aptitude.

[116] *Tena svadehayajñena cet pāpaṃ nāśitaṃ nṛṇāṃ | tarhi taddharmibhiḥ kiṃ tan na kāryaṃ nraghanaṣṭaye ||* (MPŚ 2.45).

[117] *Viśuddhi* is untranslated in this quotation because of its susceptibility to two, quite disparate, significations. Muir, following Mill and Wilson, meant by this term forensic justification according to its elaboration in the Pauline epistles (see

person becomes *śuddha* because punishment is taken by another is to depart from the course of justice; certainly, it does not preserve justice. They say justice consists of this: only he who would commit sin deserves punishment; the opposite is called, to the contrary, injustice. Thus, if Christ, contravening justice, makes men *śuddha* out of mercy, then it is pointless for him to take their punishment. Moreover, if sin is destroyed merely by trusting in Christ, then men who delight in sins would commit them at whim.[118] ... Now, if trust along with repentence is required, then repentence is sufficient; what is the purpose of trust?"[119]

Probation (MP 4.78—84, 5.127—32; pp. 76, 79, *supra*)

Nīla.: "Moreover, according to your religion, those who trust in Christ are *śuddha*. Why do people of that sort also experience suffering? If they would experience suffering here even though they trust in Christ, how do we know for sure that they would not be likely to be punished in the next world as well? This statement is by no means proper: God brings people into contact with pleasure and suffering in order to test their nature. Certainly,

---

p. 41, *supra*). Nīla., as the following verses indicate, did not grasp this new connotation. Rather, he apprehended it as "complete purification," in consonance with its traditional meaning. *Viśuddhi* or *śuddhi* was, therefore, understood as ritualistically wiping away sins in order to forestall adverse karmic repercussions. Nīla. considered Christ's substitutionary death inefficacious in this sense, a subject with which he dealt in his comments on probation.

[118] *Vide* Bhaktisiddhānta Sarasvatī Ṭhākur's comment: "Lord Jesus Christ certainly finished the sinful reactions of his followers by his mercy, but that does not mean that he completely delivered them from the pangs of material existence. A person may be relieved from sins once, but it is a practice among Christians to confess sins and yet commit them again" (PRABHUPĀDA, 1975, 84).

[119] *Evaṃ nṛṇāṃ viśuddhyarthaṃ khṛṣṭo daṇḍaṃ gṛhītavān / ity etad api yuṣmākaṃ na manye sādhu bhāṣitaṃ // anyasya daṇḍagrahaṇād anya eva ca śudhyati / iti nyāyapathāpetaṃ na hy etan nyāyarakṣaṇaṃ // aparādhaṃ tu yaḥ kuryāt sa evārhati śāsanaṃ / nyāyarūpam idaṃ prāhur anyas tv anyāya īritaḥ // atha nyāyam atikramya yadi khṛṣṭaḥ kṛpāvaśāt / nṝn śuddhān kurute tarhi tasya daṇḍagraho vṛthā // kiṃ ca viśvāsamātreṇa khṛṣṭe cet syād aghakṣayaḥ / tadāṃhoratayaḥ kāmaṃ kuryuḥ pāpāni mānavaḥ //* (ŚTV 2.167—71; p. 22) *athānutāpasahito viśvāso 'pekṣyate yadi / alaṃ tarhy anutāpena kiṃ viśvāsaprayojanaṃ //* (2.173; p. 22). Roy also reacted strongly to the doctrine of δικαιοσύνη, considering it to be a perversion of justice. "I ask whether it is consistent with the human notion of justice to release millions of men each guilty of sins unto death, after inflicting death upon another person, (whether God or man) who never participated in their sins, even though that person had voluntarily proposed to embrace death? or whether it is not a great violation of justice, according to the human notion of it, to put an innocent person to a painful death for the transgressions of others..." (GHOSE, 1978: 195—96). With respect to the idea that repentence (*anutāpa*) without belief or trust (*viśvāsa*) in a savior is sufficient to remove sin, one finds clear support for Nīla. in Manu 11.228—31. "By confession, by repentence, by austerity, and by reciting [the Veda] a sinner is freed from guilt, and in case no other course is possible, by liberality... He who has committed a sin and has repented, is freed from that sin, but he is purified only by [the resolution of] ceasing [to sin and thinking] 'I will do so no more'" (BÜHLER, 1969: 477). This principle was also clearly enunciated in Mahābhārata 3.198.48ff. (*vide* VAN BUITENEN, 1975: 621).

those who are ignorant of the nature of another test it in order to understand it. What use, indeed, does God, omniscient and an ocean of mercy, have for a test? Testing those who suffered when they reached the age of accountability would surely be proper. Alas! What a pity that those who experience suffering in childhood suffer pointlessly! But the others, who experience suffering in childhood and then die, what is their refuge? If it is heaven, then bringing them into existence is, alas, pointless! If there is not another rebirth for those who have no aptitude, by reason of being mute and so forth, they could only anticipate going to hell. Creating them is purposeless. They have, therefore, become mute and so forth by reason of previously acquired sin. God would surely give them pleasure in yet another existence. There is no equally just punishment for both major and minor sins. For those who have been punished, there is naturally, therefore, another birth."[120]

Heaven (MP 4.93—100, 5.133—50; pp. 76, 80, *supra*)

Hara.: "Pleasure is definitely not experienced in this world without a body. If, in the *mukti*-states, there is a body, there is no impediment to suffering in them, either."[121]

Nīla.: "Moreover, this doctrine is not conducive to the inward peace of good people: a state of being in a place called heaven where there are celestial pleasures is called *mukti*. With time, after men experience pleasure for a long period, anxiety arises even in one who is fond of enjoying those things. In one whose pleasure is this worldly, however, it arises in a very brief time. It is likewise argued that it arises over a long time even towards celestial pleasures... Merit and demerit are produced because of ego-centered activity. Pleasure, pain, and so forth, therefore, revolve like a wheel. While erring thusly and experiencing various sufferings, merit from virtuous deeds arises on account of practicing certain ritualistic activities. From that [merit] comes world-renunciation, deliberation, and tranquility.

---

[120] *Kiṃ ca khṛṣṭe viśvasantaḥ śudhyantīti bhavanmataṃ / tathāvidhā api narāḥ kuto duḥkhāni bhuñjate // yadi khṛṣṭe viśvasanto 'pīha syur duḥkhabhājanaṃ / amutrāpi na daṇḍyāḥ syūr iti niścinumaḥ kathaṃ // nṛsvabhāvaparīkṣārthaṃ sukha-duḥkhādibhiḥ prabhuḥ / tān saṃyojayatīty etad vaco jātu na yujyate // pararūpānabhij-ñair hi tajjñānārthaṃ parīkṣyate / sarvajñasya dayāsindhoḥ kiṃ hi kāryaṃ parīkṣayā //* (ŚTV 2.68—71; p. 12) *jñānāvasthāptaduḥkhānāṃ yujyetāpi parīkṣaṇaṃ / bālyānubh-ūtaduḥkhānāṃ hā kaṣṭaṃ vyarthaduḥkhitā // anye bālyāptaduḥkhāś ca pramīyante tadaiva ye / kā tadgatir yadi svargo hā tadutpādanaṃ vṛthā //* (2.75—76; p. 13) *punarjanmāntaraṃ no cen mūkādyanadhikāriṇāṃ / kāryā syān narayaikāśā sṛṣṭiś caiṣāṃ nirarthikā // tasmān mūkādibhāvaṃ te prāptāḥ prāgarjitāṃhasā / bhūyo bhavāntare tebhyo dadyād eva sukhaṃ vibhuḥ // alpādhikāparādhānāṃ na nyāyyaṃ śāsanaṃ samaṃ / tasmād avāptadaṇḍānāṃ punarjanma svataḥ sthitaṃ //* (2.82—84; p. 13). Roy expressed the same criticism in almost identical rhetorical terms: "If Jesus actually atoned for sin, and delivered men from its consequences, how can those men and women, who believe in his atonement, be still, equally with others, liable to the evil effects of the sins already remitted by the vicarious sacrifice of Jesus?" (GHOSE, 1978: 698).

[121] *Śarīreṇa vinā naiva sukhaṃ loke 'nubhūyate / muktyavasthāsu ced deho duḥkhaṃ tatrāpy abādhakaṃ //* (MPO 1.64; p. 7).

On account of those [qualities], the nature of such things as the body and the *ātman* as well is understood. Because of that [knowledge], nonegocentric deeds therefore, occur. Merit and demerit definitely do not arise from those [deeds]. That very man exists in his own essential nature, whose *ātman* is completely purified in the destruction of remaining *karman* and who is completely released from pleasure and pain. Their intellects purified, they reflect on this *mokṣa* with careful deliberation. But how could there be pleasure for long in the enjoyment of sense-objects? ... This statement is thoughtless: since God put sense-objects in this world and *rāga* into men, world-renunciation is, therefore, improper.[122] In every man and woman, there is desire for sexual gratification. What would come to pass when adulterers think this is given by God? By no means does God wish to destroy us, enticing us with sense-objects like fish with a hook. Who would not, having drunk that wine consisting of sensuality, depart from prudence? And who, having enjoyed sensuality for a long time, would have said, 'I ought to be satisfied.' Like a fire growing ever higher with an oblation, sensuality is not at all extinguished by its gratification. Attachment to sense-objects, therefore, is the root of misfortune. Men ought to assiduously suppress it so that all misfortune will cease. Before those who are wise, therefore, this worthless talk about *mokṣa* as enjoyment of celestial sense-objects is for completely deluding simpletons."[123]

---

[122] By *rāga* Muir meant life-preserving instincts, such as hunger and thirst (MP 5.141—50; p. 80, *supra*). Nīla., however, took this term in its negative aspect as attachment, much akin to greed.

[123] *Kiṃ ca svargābhidhe loke divyabhogayute sthitiḥ / muktir ukteti siddhānto nāntaḥśāntikaraḥ satāṃ // bhuñjatāṃ hi sukhaṃ puṃsāṃ bahukālaṃ tataḥ paraṃ / kālena jāyate trāsa utsukasyāpi tatsukhe // kiṃ tv atratyasukhasyāsau svalpakālena jāyate / kālena bahuna tadvad divyānām api tarkyate //* (ŚTV 2.97—99; p. 15) *sāhaṃkārapravṛtteśca dharmādharmābhisaṃbhavaḥ / tataś ca sukhaduḥkhādi cakravat parivartate // evam hi bhramatāṃ puṃsāṃ nānāduḥkhāni bhuñjatāṃ / keṣāñcit karmaṇāṃ yogāc chuklo dharmaḥ prajāyate // tato bhavati vairāgyaṃ vicāraḥ praśamas tathā / tataś ca jñāyate rūpaṃ dehāder ātmano 'pi ca // tasyārthān nirahaṅkārāḥ pravartante tataḥ kriyāḥ / tataś ca dharmādharmāṇām udayo naiva jāyate // sa vai pumān viśuddhātmā karmaśeṣasya saṃkṣaye / vimuktaḥ sukhaduḥkhābhyāṃ svasvarūpeṇa tiṣṭhati // taṃ mokṣaṃ suvicāreṇa manyante śuddhabuddhayaḥ / viṣayāṇāṃ tūpabhogāt kutaḥ syāt suciraṃ sukhaṃ //* (2.105—10; p. 16) *viṣayāṃs tatra rāgaṃ ca vibhur nṛṣu yato nyadhāt / tasmād yuktaṃ na vairāgyam iti vāg avicārajā // sarvāsu strīṣu nṛṣu ca ratikāmukatā sthitā / matvā tām īśvaraprattāṃ kiṃ bhāvyaṃ pāradārikaiḥ // nāsmān vihantuṃ viṣayaiḥ pralobhya parameśvaraḥ / baḍiśeneva yādāṃsi kvacit kāmayate vibhuḥ // surāṃ kāmamayīṃ pītvā na vivekāc cyaveta kaḥ / kaś ca kāmāṃś ciraṃ bhuktvā tṛptaḥ syām ity avasyati // na jātu kāmaḥ kāmānām upabhogena śāmyati / haviṣā kṛṣṇavartmeva bhūya evābhivardhate // tasmān mūlam anarthasya rāgo viṣayago nṛbhiḥ / sarvānarthanivṛttyarthaṃ niroddhavyaḥ prayatnataḥ // tasmād divyapadārthānāṃ bhogo mokṣa idaṃ vacaḥ / bāliśānāṃ vimohāya tucchaṃ tattvavidāṃ puraḥ //* (2.121—27; pp. 17—18). This passage demonstrates the failure of *svargīyamukti*, Muir's neologism (see pp. 62—63, *supra*), to convey to Nīla. anything positive or attractive. On the contrary, he assessed the afterlife according to Christianity more in terms of *svarga* than *mukti*. Heaven, sphere of the blessed dead, was identified with the often highly anthropomorphic and less than immaterial *lokas* ("worlds" or "heavens") of various deities described in Vedic, Epic, and Purāṇic literature (MUIR, 1870: 305—27; KANE 1953: 165—71). Among the six *darśanas*, only Pūrva-Mīmāṃsā

The Trinity (MP 4.85—92; p. 76, *supra*)

Soma.: "It is a Christian doctrine that the Father, Son, and Holy Spirit are not different, for they are a trinity. What we indeed intend [to say] is fulfilled by this. 'Receptacle of waters' is a name for the ocean. There are other parts [to it] as well, which are by no means distinct [from each other] because it is a great heap of waters. Likewise, along with the supreme God [are recognized] the ranks of [other deities], such as Brahmā, Īśa, and [. . .]. If difference is the conventional meaning [with respect to the divine nature], there is the preeminence of a single [God] in this case also. For this reason, everyone worships the supreme God as one only."[124]

Nīla.: "Though it is said that there is triplicity in God without actually dividing himself, even so his unity is unimpaired. This is, likewise, beyond argumentation. It does not burden the glory of God, which is beyond argumentation, that this cannot be grasped by those whose intellects are deficient and that the mind seems bewildered. On the contrary, it enhances it."[125]

---

regarded *svarga* as mankind's *summum bonum* (see e. g., Pūrvamīmāṃsāsūtra 4.3.15f., and 6.1.1; Basu, 1974: 231, 298). In the other systems, *mukti*, variously defined, superceded *svarga* (see also Bhagavad-Gītā 6.41, 9.20—21). Clearly, no situation, however enticing it might be, could put Nīla.'s mind at ease except the permanency of *mokṣa* (cf. Gonda, 1966: 148). In this respect, his reaction to Muir is reminiscent of the refusal of Mudgala, an ascetic renowned for hospitality, to take *svarga* as his reward. No direct connection with this story in the Mahābhārata (3.247.1ff.) is posited, but citing it will show that Nīla.'s attitude had ample precedent in the sources of his own tradition. Upon being informed that he had access to the highest *lokas*, Mudgala insisted that the envoy of the gods detail their drawbacks. He was informed as follows: "The fruit of acts done, which is enjoyed in heaven, cannot be undone and must be consumed, down to the last of its roots. This I deem a fault, as also the fall at the end of it, the fall of those whose minds had been permeated with bliss, Mudgala. The discontent and resentment after having seen the most brilliant beauties, as are felt by those who dwell in a lower region, are hard to endure. The confusion of consciousness, the harassment by passion, the fear of the one about to fall when his garlands begin to fade are awful faults. . . ." Nīla.'s verdict was not less unequivocal than Mudgala's: "Those who have shared in heaven again fall back down here, therefore I do not covet heaven. I shall search only for that infinite place where they do not grieve, do not suffer, do not chance to fall once they have gone there" (van Buitenen, 1975: 704—05). Nīla. may have misinterpreted the Christian doctrine of heaven, making it a kind of sybaritic paradise, but his abhorrence of *svarga* in any form corresponds well with strains of Hindu thought that assign all celestial *lokas* to the "wishful-fearful thinking of deluded consciousness" (Zimmer, 1951: 453).

[124] *Pitā putraḥ sadātmā ca na bhinnā trinaṭī bhavet / iti khārṣṭīyasiddhāṃtaḥ siddhaṃ iṣṭaṃ hi tena naḥ // vārāṃ nidhiḥ sāgaranāmadheyo bhedās tathānye 'pi mahāṃburāśeḥ / pṛthak kathaṃcin na bhavaṃti tadvad brahmeśa* [. . .] *ādipadaiḥ pareśaḥ // bhedaś ced vyavahārārthas tatrāpy ekasya mukhyatā / ataḥ sarveśvaraḥ sarvair eka eva niṣevyate //* (MPŚ 2.47—49).

[125] *Acchittvaiva yathātmānam īśe traividhyam ucyate / tathāpy ahīnam ekatvaṃ tadvad asyāpy atarkyatā // agrāhyo yat kubuddhīnāṃ muhyatīva ca yan manaḥ / atarkyeśamahimno 'sau na bhāraḥ kiṃ tu bhūṣaṇaṃ //* (ŚTV 6b.145—46; pp. 81—82). The basis for Hara.'s and Nīla.'s positive assessment of Trinitarian Christianity was

Animal Life[126]

Soma.: "Therefore, are not the [adherents] of that religion sinners, committing violence, who injure animals [...]? The worst sin is injuring bulls, helpers in ploughing, and cows, who regularly give of themselves milk, the nectar of juices. This, the zenith of wickedness, will be displayed in the Kali Age by those who pointlessly harm creatures such as cows, who assist us."[127]

Nīla.: "If one does not acknowledge a way to salvation after death for animals and others, then tell us who has seen a way to salvation for human beings either? Animals get hungry and thirsty, copulate, sleep and so forth the same as human beings. They want to get what is good for them and get rid of what is bad for them. Birds and other creatures have such things as houses; rear their families; think about the means and so forth to do these things; distinguish between rain and heat, etc. What is more, without scriptural discernment, animals thoroughly understand fear and the occasion for fear, pleasure and the occasion for pleasure. Now if human beings continue to exist even after death, animals must also — they, too, are creatures of God alone... Does God, compassionate, sufficient, and impartial, expect those whom he created to know him in order to give them pleasure? ... Well, if these animals, created by God according to his desire, who are harnessed to the front of vehicles, their shoulders bruised, suffering from hunger and thirst, afflicted by heat and even tormented by cold in some places, only experience suffering, then God's behavior is obnoxious. But we think that creatures become animals by reason of sins in previous existences. Having experienced the fruit of their deeds, they are released from that [state]. ... Oh, how my heart and those of others as well melt with pity upon seeing them suffer! Does not God's, too, who is compassionate?"[128]

---

not the so-called Hindu Trinity, the *trimūrti* (Brahmā, Viṣṇu, Śiva), but the two-tiered epistemology of Vedānta. According to Advaita, Brahman is apprehended at the lower (*vyāvahārika*) level as *īśvara* manifested variously, by those not yet enlightened; at the upper (*pāramārthika*) level as singular reality by those who have attained *tattvajñāna*. The former knowledge is invalidated by the latter. Smith, the partner-in-dialogue, gave further insight into the Vedāntic terms that Nīla. imposed on the Trinity: "In speaking on the Trinity, he said he could manage that subject very well, because he only looked upon the persons as *upadhī* [*sic*] — manifestations of assumed characters!" (SMITH, 1847).

[126] The MP did not touch upon the subject of nonhuman life, whether it has a soul or not, its purpose and destiny after death. To account for these passages, one must assume that it was widely known and considered repulsive that Christians are not prohibited from consuming beef and other kinds of flesh.

[127] *Atas taddharmiṇo hiṃsāṃ kurvaṃtaḥ kiṃ na pāpinaḥ* / [...] *hiṃsaṃti ye paśūn* // *gāvaḥ sudhārasaṃ kṣīraṃ svebhyaḥ sādhv arpayaṃti yāḥ* / *vṛṣāḥ kṛṣyupakartāras taddhiṃsā pātakaṃ paraṃ* // *svopakārakarān jaṃtūn gavādīn haṃti ye vṛthā khalatāyāḥ parā kāṣṭhā tair eṣā darśitā kalau* // (MPŚ 2.39—41). It should be noted that the slaughter of cows and bulls, a practice identified with Christians by Soma., is a *kalivarjya*, an activity proscribed during the present *yuga*, the Kali (KANE, 1962: 1268—69).

[128] *Paśvāder maraṇād ūrdhvaṃ yadi no gatir iṣyate* / *manuṣyāṇām api tadā kena dṛṣṭā gatir vada* // *kṣuttṛṇmaithunanidrādi paśūnāṃ manujaiḥ samaṃ* / *svahitasya*

Defending Hinduism

Divine Unity (MP 5.29—40; p. 77, *supra*)

Soma.: "According to tradition and sacred texts, the Vedas are preserved by sages. Having the form of various deities, Hari alone is celebrated in them. This, having been experienced previously, has been handed down by those believers. Thus, there is no falsehood whatsoever in differences between deities either. God created man-like deities for the sake of worship and made for them a particular power derived from his own being."[129]

Hara.: "Only the worship of Brahman is shown in scriptures to be foremost. Fools find this way difficult to take, because [Brahman] is difficult to attain. This is why worship of a deity in conjunction with various forms is practiced on earth. Foolish people would gradually attain *mokṣa* by means of that [worship]. As surely as the ocean will be reached by various routes, rivers and so forth, so will Brahman surely be attained by worshipping Śiva, Viṣṇu and others."[130]

---

tathā lipsā jihāsā svāhitasya ca // pakṣyādīnāṃ gṛhādīni svakuṭumbasya poṣaṇaṃ / varṣātapādivijñānaṃ tadupāyādicintanaṃ // bhayaṃ caiva bhayasthānaṃ sukhasthānaṃ sukhaṃ tathā / ṛte śāstrīyavijñānaṃ jānanti paśavo 'khilaṃ // athāsti cen manuṣyāṇāṃ mṛter ūrdhvam api sthitiḥ / paśūnām api tarhy astu te 'pīśasyaiva jantavaḥ // (ŚTV 2.151—55; pp. 20—21) *dayālur āptakāmaś ca tulyadṛṣṭir apīśvaraḥ / svasṛṣṭebhyaḥ sukhaṃ dātuṃ svajñānaṃ kim apekṣate //* (2.158; p. 21) *hanteśenecchayā sṛṣṭā yady ete paśavo nṛbhiḥ / niyojitāḥ svayānādau kṣataskandhāḥ kṣudhāturāḥ // tṛṣārtā ūṣmaṇā taptāḥ kvacic chītārditā api / bhuñjate kevalaṃ duḥkhaṃ kaṣṭaṃ tarhīśaceṣṭitaṃ // vayaṃ tu prāgbhavāṃhobhiḥ paśutāṃ yānti jantavaḥ / bhuktvā karmaphalaṃ tasmān mucyanta iti manmahe //* (2.161—63; p. 21) *aho batāsmadādīnām api tadduḥkhadarśane / kṛpayā dravate cittaṃ dayālor api kiṃ na hi //* (2.165; p. 22). Rammohun Roy expressed similar sympathy for animal life in The Brahmunical Magazine (Ghose, 1978: 184). M. K. Gandhi, too, was known for contrasting the Buddha's mercy for all living creatures with Jesus Christ's "love of man only" (Mehta, 1976: 115). In the beginning of the Vedāntasūtrabhāṣya (*vide* Thibaut, 1890: 7—8), Śaṅkara developed the argument that the "Mīmāṃsā distinction between human beings and animals in terms of intelligence and long-term planning" was, in the final analysis, "reducible to an insignificant difference in degree" (Halbfass, 1977: 234). It would be a mistake, however, to assume that Nīla. considered animals qua animals to be eligible for *mokṣa*. For a thorough discussion of this issue, see Halbfass, 1977: 228ff.

129 *Paramparāmnāyavaśād dhṛtā vedās tapodhanaiḥ / nānādevasvarūpeṇa tatraikaḥ kīrtyate hariḥ // pratipāditaṃ etat prāg anubhūtaṃ tadāstikaiḥ / atha bhede 'pi devānāṃ mithyātvam na kathaṃ ca na // īśena sṛṣṭāḥ sevārthaṃ manujā iva devatāḥ / viśeṣaśaktimattvaṃ ca kṛtaṃ teṣu svabhāvajaṃ //* (MPŚ 3.3—5).

130 *Brahmopāsanam evāste mukhyaṃ śāstreṣu darśitaṃ / tasya duḥsādhyatāhetor mūrkhāṇām durlabhā gatiḥ // ataḥ sākāradevasya bhajanaṃ kriyate bhuvi / tena mūrkhasya lokasya mokṣaprāptiḥ śanair bhavet // yathā samudro gantavyo nānānadyādivartmanā / tathā brahma samāsādyaṃ śivaviṣṇvādisevayā //* (MPO 1.33—35; p. 4). Roy, too, exonerated the worship of deities other than the supreme God in terms of differing mental and spiritual aptitudes. "Lest persons of feeble intellect unable to comprehend God as not subject to the senses and without form, should either pass their life without any religious duties whatsoever or should engage in evil work, — to prevent this they have represented God in the form of a man and other animals and as possessed of all those desires with which we are conversant whereby they may have

Nīla.: "Lord Bhagavān alone is worshipped by every last ritual action prescribed for brahmins in the Veda. ... Indeed, all the deities, Indra and others, consume the oblation thrown on the fire. However, Viṣṇu alone, soul of the sacrifice, is thereby propitiated. When God wants to give the fruit of various deeds to the doers, he gives it only through those [deities], just as a king does by means of servants."[131]

Intrareligious rivalry (MP 5.65—66, 163—64; pp. 78, 80, *supra*)

Hara.: "Whosoever would follow a [particular] path praises it in order to augment his faith, and censures the ways of others. Thus, O student, did praising and censuring deities gradually become approved in this world; but this is not the highest form of activity."[132]

Nīla.: "But we maintain that there is a body by reason of *karman* and *karman* because of the body, a beginningless succession of *karman* and bodies, like seeds and sprouts. Whatsoever God does is so that the *jīvas* will obtain the fruit of *karman*; whomsoever have *karman*, for them there is a just fruit. That conflict between Kṛṣṇa and Śiva, talked about [in the MP], is also for this very reason (the *karman* of the *jīvas*) and, likewise, their victory and defeat. Those two deities, having just one *ātman*, seem distinct on account of differences in [our] viewpoints. How could there be a quarrel between them? And what injury, therefore, could there be to them? However, since those two war against each other prejudicedly, their victory and defeat, therefore, is by reason of varying degrees of *karman*. Actually, God has no prejudice either."[133]

---

some regard to the Divine Being. Afterwards by diligent endeavours they become qualified for the true knowledge of God: but over and over again the Puranas have carefully affirmed, that they have given this account of the forms of God with a view to the benefit of persons of weak minds, and that in truth, God is without name, form, organs, and sensual enjoyment" (GHOSE, 1978: 161).

[131] *Yāvanti khalu karmāṇi dvijānāṃ vihitāni tu / vede tair akhilair īśo bhagavān eva pūjyate //* (ŚTV 6a.87; p. 54) *agnau prattāhutīḥ sarvā indrādyā eva bhuñjate / taddvārā prīyate kiṃ tu yajñātmā viṣṇur eva hi // yadā tattatkarmaphalaṃ karmibhyo dātum icchati / taddvāraiva dadātīśo bhṛtyadvāreva bhūpatiḥ //* (6a.90—91; p. 55).

[132] *Yo yo yat patham ātiṣṭhet tasya śraddhāvivṛddhaye / tatpathasya praśaṃsāsti nindā cāparavartmanaḥ // evaṃ krameṇa he śiṣya devānāṃ stutinindayoḥ / pravṛttiḥ saṃmatā loke na tu sā pāramārthikī //* (MPO 1.36—37; p. 4).

[133] *Vayam tu karmaṇā deho dehāt karmety anādinīm / bījāṅkuravad icchāmaḥ karmadehaparamparāṃ // yad yat karoti ceśas taj jīvakarmaphalāptaye / yasya yasya yathā karma nyāyyaṃ tasya tathā phalaṃ // ata evāsti yaḥ proktaḥ saṃgrāmaḥ kṛṣṇaśūlinoḥ / so 'pi jīvādṛṣṭavaśāt tadvaj jayaparājayau // ekātmānau hi tau devau bhinnau dṛṣṭibhidāvaśāt / tayoḥ kathaṃ syāt kalahaḥ kā ca tasmāt tayoḥ kṣatiḥ // kiṃ tu yat pakṣapātena yudhyatas tau parasparaṃ / tat karmatāratamyena tayor jayaparājayau // nāsty eva parameśasya pakṣapāto 'pi vastutaḥ /* (ŚTV 2.42.47a; pp. 9—10). Nīla.'s precedent for this resolution of intrareligious rivalry may well have been the Harivaṃśa. Śiva there assisted Bāṇa and the Dānavas in a terrible conflict with Kṛṣṇa. Brahmā intervened, telling the two deities that they were actually identical with each other. In a vision, Brahmā had seen the two gods invested with one another's symbols, to which the sage Mārkaṇḍeya gave an explanation beginning with the following: "When thou showest me this auspicious [vision], I perceive

Incompatible *darśanas* (MP 5.163—64; p. 80, *supra*)

Nīla.: "Although there is one accurate knowledge of God's nature, they never say that the attainment of *mukti* has no other mode. With respect to accurate knowledge of the nature of Bhagavān, the teachings in Śrūtis and Smṛtis known as Upaniṣads are the only cause... Nevertheless, those who are dull-witted, their understanding vitiated by argumentation, have no aptitude for truth explained in the Upaniṣads. Thinking that they also must have salvation, God, compassionate and solicitous toward everyone, made ways in other scriptures. Men have an endless number of aptitudes, high and low in nature, on account of the unarguable maturation of their good and bad *karman*. In this world people are observed who, due to their aptitude, are devoid of faith in the Vedānta *darśana*, even though it is pure and substantiated by Śruti. Īśvarakṛṣṇa and others, for instance, knew only the way of Sāṅkhya, and others, such as Udayana, knew the science of logic. Thus, many others, too, whose minds are agitated by argumentation and who give the highest place to disputation, embrace various *mārgas*. Those without aptitude for plumbing the meaning of Vedānta, worshipping Govinda in conformity with their various viewpoints, gradually attain that aptitude by virtue of worshipping God. Knowing Hari accurately, they are released from all bondage. Only by means of knowledge of Vedānta do these numerous *mārgas*, purposeful for those of slow understanding, lead to *mokṣa*. ... As the moon [is pointed out by its proximity to] branches and so forth, God, too, is described in many ways by different *darśanas* in order that those who are slow will understand the truth. The Vedānta *darśana* has stated the pure nature of Bhagavān; the purport of the other systems does not concern its refutation but rather the explanation of it... Moreover, there would be contrariety between *mārgas* by reason of difference in aptitudes, as in this world roads are observed to be opposite on account of differences in location. If someone located in Gayā wants to go to Kāśī, he asks people there and they tell him, 'You must go west,' whereas an inhabitant of Prayāga, wanting to go to Kāśī, asks people there and is told, to the contrary, 'Go east.' Going both east and west, which is by all means contradictory, yields one result on account of being located in different places. By the same token, one way [to salvation] would not be rewarding to [all] men, whose aptitudes are different, on account of the unarguable maturation of their good and bad deeds. Reflecting in these terms, Bhagavān, an ocean of compassion, made various kinds of *mārgas* by which everyone may attain salvation. For instance, among all the scriptures, the Sāṅkhya, Vaiśeṣika and others, likewise the devotional *mārgas* of Vaiṣṇavas, etc., in which their faults are completely done away with by means of much examination and meditation, some people esteem the Vaiśeṣika, some the Sāṅkhya or others, some the

---

thereby no difference between Śiva who exists in the form of Vishṇu, and Vishṇu who exists in the form of Śiva" (MUIR, 1873: 278—81; cf. Viṣṇupurāṇa 5.32ff. with the remarks of GONDA, 1970: 90—91). Isolated passages making the same point are found in many Purāṇas; for further references, see B. N. SHARMA, 1971: 6—15.

Vaiṣṇava *mārga*, and others the Śaiva, etc. This indicates that people have different aptitudes... Yet only one among the *mārgas* yields a direct result; it alone is followed by people whose aptitude is pure."[134]

---

[134] *Yady apīśvararūpasya yathārthajñānam ekakaṃ / mukteḥ sādhanam ity āhur na prakārāntaraṃ kvacit / yathārthabhagavadrūpāvabodhe caikakāraṇaṃ / vedāntā iti siddhāntaḥ śrutiṣu smaraneṣu ca //* (ŚTV 6a.2—3; p. 46) *tathāpi mandabuddīnāṃ tarkadūṣitasaṃvidāṃ / na yeṣām adhikāro 'sti tattve vedāntabodhite // śreyas teṣām api bhavatv iti matvā dayālunā / kṛtāḥ śāstrāntarādhvānaḥ sarveṣām hitam icchatā // atarkyasadasatkarmaparipākavaśān nṛṇāṃ / ānantyam adhikārāṇām uttamādhamarūpiṇāṃ // dṛśyante puruṣā loke yeṣāṃ vedāntadarśane / śuddhe 'pi śrutisiddhe 'pi śraddhābhāvo 'dhikārajaḥ // tathā hīśvarakṛṣṇādyāḥ sāṅkhyam eva gatiṃ viduḥ / tarkavidyām atha pare 'manyantodayanādayaḥ // evam anye 'pi bahavas tarkāndolitacetasaḥ / nānāmārgān prapadyante hetuvādaparāyaṇāḥ // anavāptādhikārās te vedāntārthāvagāhane / upāsamānā govindaṃ svasvadṛṣṭyanusārataḥ // kālenāptādhikārās te īśopāsanagauravāt / yāthārthyena hariṃ jñātvā mucyante sarvabandhanāt // ye caite bahavo mārgā mandabodhaprayojanāḥ / vedāntabodhadvāraiva teṣām mokṣe samanvayaḥ //* (6a.5—13; pp. 46—47) *mandānāṃ tattvabodhāya śākhādibhir ivoḍurāṭ / bahuprakārair īśo 'pi varṇyate darśanāntaraiḥ // śuddhaṃ bhagavato rūpam āha vedāntadarśanaṃ / tadvirodhe na tātparyam anyeṣāṃ kiṃ tu bodhane //* (6a.16—17; p. 47) *kiṃ cādhikārabhedena bhaven mārgavirodhitā / sthānabhedād yato loke virodho dṛśyate 'dhvanāṃ / yathā kāśīṃ jigamiṣur gayāstho yadi pṛcchati / tatratyāṃs te bruvanty enaṃ vraja tvaṃ paścimāṃ diśaṃ // atha prayāgadeśīyaḥ kāśīgamanakāmyayā / pṛcchañ janāṃs tu tatratyaiḥ prācīṃ yāhīti cocyate // prācīpaścimagāmitvaṃ viruddham api sarvathā / bhinnadeśasthiter hetoḥ phalam ekaṃ prayachati // tathaivātarkyasadasatkarmaṇāṃ paripākataḥ / nṛbhyo bhinnādhikārebhyo naiko 'dhvā pradiśet phalaṃ // iti saṃcintya bhagavān karuṇāvaruṇālayaḥ / mārgān nānāvidhāṃś cakre yaiḥ sarve śreya āpnuyuḥ // tathā hi sarvaśāstreṣu sāṅkhyakāṇādakādiṣu / tathaiva vaiṣṇavādyeṣūpāsāmārgeṣu sarvaśaḥ // parākṛtasvadoṣeṣu bahuyuktinirūpaṇaiḥ / kāṇādaṃ manvante kecit kecit saṅkhyādikāny api // kecit taṃ vaiṣṇavaṃ mārgam anye śaivādikāṃs tathā / puṃsāṃ bhinnādhikāritvasyābhivyañjakam asty adaḥ //* (6a.20—28; p. 48) *kiṃ tv eka eva mārgeṣu mārgaḥ sākṣāt phalapradaḥ / sa eva sevyate sarvair janaiḥ śuddhādhikāribhiḥ //* (6a.42; p. 50). There is nothing novel in this attempt by Nīla. to reconcile the six *darśanas*, dismissing their discrepencies as more apparent than real, and to arrange them in hierarchical order with Śaṅkara's Vedānta superior to the others. One finds, for example, the following passage in the Śivamahimnastava (v. 7): *trayī sāṃkhyaṃ yogaḥ paśupatimataṃ vaiṣṇavam iti prabhinne prasthāne param idam adaḥ pathyam iti ca / rucīnāṃ vaicitryād ṛjukuṭilanānāpathajuṣāṃ nṛṇām eko gamyas tvam asi payasām arṇava iva //*. "Though the ways differ which are spoken of in the threefold Veda, Sāngkhya, Yogashāstra, the doctrine of Pashupati and Vaishnava Shāstra; though some take this and others that to be the better, and followers of the various paths both direct and indirect dispute, yet Thou alone art the goal of all, as is the ocean of every river" (AVALON, 1953: 5). In more recent times (as late as the seventeenth century), Madhusūdana Sarasvatī, author of the Prasthānabheda, methodically subjected the principal *darśanas* to an Advaitic critique in order to assess their compatibility with that system. He found them not, at least ultimately, to conflict with each other. The first verse begins as follows: "All scriptures lead, whether directly or indirectly, to Bhagavat alone" (*atha sarveṣāṃ śāstrāṇāṃ bhagavaty eva tātparyaṃ sākṣāt paramparayā veti*; WEBER, 1850: 13). Truth appertains to all; yet only one, Vedānta according to Śaṅkara, is immediately efficacious for *mokṣa*. The illusion of divisions arose in this fashion, according to Madhusūdana: "These different views have only been propounded by [the *munis*], in order to keep off all nihilistic theories, and because they were afraid that human beings, with their inclinations towards the objects of the world, could not be expected at once to know the true goal of man. But all comes right when we understand that

Brahminhood (MP 5.168—78; p. 80, *supra*)

Soma.: "By performing the duties of a brahmin, etc., another person would not acquire that status, because God did not bring him into existence in that caste. That place alone would be best for him, into which, in accordance with his previous *karman*, God would give him birth, on account of [the need to] observe God's commands."[135]

Hara.: "A king is like his subjects; the wise man like a fool. In the aforementioned subject, however, there is a distinction [between castes] in consequence of *karman*. Brahmins, attending closely to *dharma*, are always entrusted with matters concerning the gods; standing in the way of those who do evil deeds, they tell others what their *dharma* is; enduring the pain of austerities, they are calm and have subdued the power of their senses. But, when a contemptible act is committed, there is some sort of expiation [for it]. The superiority of the brahmin over the *śūdra* is, therefore, enjoined by the scriptures, and for this reason people esteem brahmins as the highest. But brahmins devoid of the aforementioned conduct are regarded as *śūdras*, and neither in the scripture nor in this world do they enjoy respect."[136]

Nīla.: "Since brahmins are under orders for the sake of the world's functioning, they must necessarily, therefore, perform religious activities by God's command. God created brahmins because the world is dependent on sacrifices.[137] Brahmins must, for this reason, necessarily perform ritual

---

men, from not understanding their true object, imagined that these Munis would have propounded what is contrary to the Veda, and thus, accepting their opinions, have become followers of various paths" (MÜLLER, 1899b: 82; cf. MUIR, 1868b: 194—96). In much the same spirit of compromise, but with a different scheme of reconciliation, the Sāṅkhyapravacanabhāṣya of Vijñāna Bhīkṣu resolved apparent contradictions between the *darśanas*, distinguishing between practical (*vyāvahārika*) and essential (*pāramārthika*) truths (*vide* MUIR, 1868b: 196—203).

[135] *Viprādeḥ karmakaraṇān nānyas taddharmatām iyāt | na yad utpāditas tasmin varṇe bhagavatā hi saḥ || svaprākkarmānurodhena janma yatreśvaro 'rpayet | tad eva tasya śreṣṭhaṃ syād īśvarājñānupālanāt ||* (MPS 3.31—32). *Vide* Bhagavad-Gītā 18.47—48.

[136] *Yathā prajā tathā rājā yathā mūrkhas tathā budhaḥ | pūrvokte viṣaye kiṃ tu viśeṣaḥ karmayogataḥ || viprāḥ sadā devakārye niyuktā dharmatatparāḥ | pareṣāṃ dharmavaktāraḥ kukarmaparipanthinaḥ || tapaḥkleśasahāḥ śāntā nirjitendriyaśaktikāḥ | yatra kutsitakārye 'sti prāyaścittan tu yādṛśaṃ || śūdrasya brahmaṇas tasmād adhikaṃ śāstracoditaṃ | ato lokais tu manyante brāhmaṇā uttamā iti || pūrvoktācāraśūnyās tu brāhmaṇāḥ śūdravat smṛtāḥ | śāstre loke 'pi dṛśyante mānabhājo na te tathā ||* (MPO 1.74—78; pp. 8—9). Similar statements are found, for example, in the Mahābhārata (3.177.20f.), "The marks of the *śūdra* are not found in a brahmin; but a *śūdra* is not necessarily a *śūdra*, nor a brahmin a brahmin. In whomever the brahmin's marks are found, ... he is known as a brahmin; and in whom they are not found, him they designate as a *śūdra*" (VAN BUITENEN, 1975: 564; see also MUIR, 1879: 60—73, 256—65). It would be unwarranted, however, to assume that Hara. also recognized the possibility of brahminization of *śūdras*.

[137] *Vide* Manu 1.93—95, especially 94: "For the self-existent (Svayambhū), having performed austerities, produced brahmins first from his own mouth, in order that the offerings might be conveyed to the gods and manes and that this universe might be preserved" (BÜHLER, 1969: 24—25). The relation between gods and their

activity out of regard for the [world]. Moreover, since their ritual activity gives rise to purity of mind, there is fitness for knowledge as a result. Ritual activity, therefore, is also necessary... All living beings experience various fruits in a subsequent birth by reason of good and bad deeds committed in previous births. But some are blind, others deaf or lame; some are good-looking, strong, well-to-do, and intelligent; some are discriminating and calm; some are witless and impatient. Thus, in various ways one sees the fruit of *karman* arise. By the same token, living beings enter the brahmin caste, etc., by reason of previous *karman*. Yet this is perceived by scripture — not in another manner. Brahmins would not be at all equal to or less than others because they have the same inherent nature or because they lack good qualities. Kingly status can never be enjoyed even by a subject endowed with many good qualities or even by a subject whose good qualities are equivalent [to the king's]. This brahminical status, too, is acquired by meritorious deeds [previously] done; because of instruction [from them who have it], one can perform sacrifices, etc., to God."[138]

Modes of Worship (MP 5.70; p. 78, *supra*)

Soma.: "As a knowledge of letters would come to a child by means of metalic [objects in the shape of] letters, so do those who are wise make an image of mud and stone for the sake of knowledge of God's form."[139]

---

devotees is reciprocal. "The worshipper by his offerings and his hymns strengthens the god, and thus enables him to afford the help which the suppliant requires" (MUIR, 1879: 61; see also MUIR, 1870: 88—91).

[138] *Jagaccakrapravṛttyartham ājñaptā brāhmaṇā yataḥ / tato 'pīśājñayā kāryā avaśyaṃ brāmaṇaiḥ kriyāḥ // yajñāyattaṃ jagaccakram ata īśo 'sṛjad dvijān / atas tatprītaye kāryaṃ karmāvaśyaṃ dvijātibhiḥ // kiṃ ca svakarmabhiḥ sattvaśuddhiḥ saṃjāyate yataḥ / tataś ca jñānayogyatvaṃ karmāvaśyakatāpy ataḥ //* (ŚTV 6a.95—97; p. 55) *pūrvajanmakṛtaiḥ puṇyapāpair uttarajanmani / nānāphalāni bhujyante prāṇibhiḥ sakalair api // kecit tu netravikalā badhirā paṅgavo 'pare / kecit surūpa balino dhanino buddhiśālinaḥ // kecid vivekinaḥ śāntāḥ kecin mūḍhā amarṣiṇaḥ / evaṃ hi dṛśyate nānāvidhaḥ karmaphalodayaḥ // tathaiva karmaṇā prācā brāhmaṇādyāś ca jātayaḥ / labhyante prāṇibhis tv etac chāstradṛṣṭaṃ na cānyathā //* (6a.188—91; p. 65) *na hi tulyasvabhāvatvān nyūnatvād vā guṇair api / viprāḥ syur itarais tulyā nyūnā vāpi kathañ ca na // api bhūriguṇair yukto bhṛtyas tulyo 'pi vā guṇaiḥ / na jātu dharaṇīpālapadavīṃ bhoktum arhati // eṣaiva padavī brāhmī kṛtapuṇyair upārjitā / yadādeśāt pareśasya yajñādīn kartum arhati //* (6a.193—95; p. 65).

[139] *Yathā dhātumayair varṇair varṇabodhaḥ śiśor bhavet / tatheśarūpabodhāya mṛcchilārcā kṛtā budhaiḥ //* (MPŚ 3.28). The tutorial function of image worship, whereby those who are incompetent to grasp abstruse metaphysical truths are brought into contact with the sacred, is a well-known defense within Hinduism for this practice. Unwittingly, it seems, Muir left himself open to this rejoinder by citing Śātātapasmṛti (see n. 56, p. 78, *supra*; cf. *agnau kriyāvatāṃ devo divi devo manīṣiṇāṃ / pratimāsv alpabuddhīnāṃ yogināṃ hṛdaye hariḥ //* Nṛsiṃhapurāṇa 62.5, quoted in KANE, 1962: 973). Even Roy, who was not a friend of image worship, approvingly cited the following verse (GHOSE, 1978: 162) from the Mahānirvāṇatantra (13.13) in support of the use of *mūrtis* ("images") by certain types of people: "It is for the benefit of such worshippers as are of little understanding that the different forms are imagined according to the attributes [of the Divinity]" (WOODROFFE, 1971: 317).

Hara.: "Those who always delight in virtuous deeds, their minds completely purified, take a bath in the Ganges when, by accident, they commit a bad deed. Their perseverence in doing good deeds would thereby definitely not diminish. On the contrary, bathing in the Ganges is reserved for those who, conscience-stricken, do not delight in sin, for the sake of their purification."[140]

Nīla.: "Images are never worshipped with the mind [focused] on either clay or wood — only with the mind on God, who is all-pervasive. Say what defect there is in that! God is declared to be all-pervasive, indeed, and spotless like the sky. He accepts homage when worshipped with the mind on that [idea]... Likewise, by repeating the names of Bhagavān incessently, consciousness enters into God time and again. What harm is there in that either? Now, it is false to say that [repetition] of the name of God is tantamount to a son making his father weary, saying 'Father! Father!'... Likewise, those who know the purport of the proscription, which is found in places, of bathing in the Ganges, pilgrimages, paying homage to images, etc., know that, although these things are said to cause merit, surely this [proscription], too, aims at commending knowledge of God, patience of mind, purification of consciousness, etc.... But worship of the sun and so forth in the form of an indicator of God is stipulated also for images, etc., with the imagination [fixed] squarely on God."[141]

---

[140] *Ye sadā dharmakāryeṣu ratāḥ saṃśuddhamānasāḥ / daivāt kṛte kukārye tair gaṅgāsnānaṃ vidhīyate // utsāhabhaṅgo naiva syāt teṣāṃ satkarmakāriṇāṃ / na tu ye pāpakāryeṣu ratā ninditacetasaḥ // teṣāṃ śuddhividhānārthaṃ gaṅgāsnānaṃ niyantritaṃ //* (MPO 1.59—61; p. 7).

[141] *Na loṣṭhakāṣṭhabuddhyā hi pūjyante mūrtayaḥ kvacit / vyāpakeśvarabuddhyaiva ko doṣas tatra bhaṇyatāṃ // vyāpako hi smṛto devo nirlepaś ca viyad yathā / tadbuddhyā pūjyate yatra tatra svīkurute 'rcanaṃ //* (STV 3.43—44, p. 28) *tathaiva bhagavannāmakīrtanena nirantaraṃ / īśe muhurmuhuś ceto yāti tatrāpi kā kṣatiḥ // atha svapitaraṃ putraḥ pitaḥ pitar iti bruvan / khedaṃ karoti vai tadvad īśanāmnety asadvacaḥ //* (3.46—47; p. 29) *tathaiva gaṅgāsnānāder yātrāmūrtyarcanādinaḥ / ukte 'pi puṇyahetutve niṣedho yaḥ kvacit sthitaḥ // tasyāpi khalu tātparyaṃ vidus tātparyavedinaḥ / cittaśuddhimanodāntīśvarajñānādisaṃstave //* (6a.62—63; p. 52) *īśapratīkarūpeṇa yā tu sūryādyupāsanā / mūrtyāder api saṃdiṣṭā seśabhāvanayaiva hi //* (6a.117, p. 57). As a word preferred by Śaṅkara to *mūrti*, *pratīka* ("indicator" or "pointer") occurs frequently in his commentary on the Vedāntasūtras, especially 4.1.4—7 and 4.3.15—16 where its function and limitations are discussed. According to his interpretation, *pratīkas* belong to the realm of *aparā vidyā*; their object is the conditioned Brahman; and they yield a less than satisfying result for people in search of *mokṣa*. In meditation, the lower Brahman is superimposed on them, not vice versa. Moreover, Brahman can be contemplated in them only insofar as their individuality is effaced; as long as they are meditated upon in and of themselves as objects, the meditator remains trapped in transmigratory existence. Instead of attaining *mokṣa*, worshippers of *pratīkas* are recompensed according to formulas enumerated in the Chāndogya-Upaniṣad (7.1—14). Unlike those who contemplate Brahman without the mediation of *pratīkas*, those who fix their attention on images do not tread the *devayāna* to the *aparabrahman* (Thibaut, 1896: 340—50, 402—04). Clearly, *pratīka* does not fit into Judeo-Christian categories of thought concerning images, according to which their worship amounts to crass idolatry.

Behavior of the Gods (MP 5.53—64; p. 77, *supra*)

Soma.: "In regard to evil in the description of the erotic passions of the gods, to which you object, the Purāṇas, which do indeed have a diversity of figurative allusions, were made so that those attached to desire, etc., will understand the meaning of the Vedas. People do not incur sin by repeating Acyuta's [Kṛṣṇa's] erotic-like deeds. There is, on the contrary, only complete purification of mind, since he who is devoid of existence in birth and so forth simulates this illusory act of birth, etc., for the sake of liberating people from sin."[142]

Hara.: "I said earlier that God has no body. He resorts to a body only for the sake of mankind's emancipation. Since those who have bodies are naturally incapable of restraining the senses, he created [a body] in order to teach people a lesson. When one is occupied with an object of sense, the divine voice is by no means [heard]. The mind, therefore, is to be assiduously established in restraint of the senses. Thus, there is no doubt that, with whichever frame of mind one reveres God, God would exist for him in just such a shape. As all the *gopīs* ("cowherdesses") revered God as a husband, so did he, too, fulfill their desire. But he does not advise men to imitate this."[143]

Nīla.: "Now, it is improper for those who are extremely unintelligent to have criticized Kṛṣṇa's *līlās* with their own intellects. How great the difference between God, whose *līlās* are infinitely difficult to understand and who knows numerous reasons [to explain them], and unintelligent *jīvas*! Oh, this is rash! This is amazing that, of this specific [weak-minded] kind of man

---

[142] *Asatvaṃ śaṃkase yac ca devaśṛṃgāravarṇane // tatra kāmādisaktānāṃ vaidikārthāvabuddhaye / nirmitāni purāṇāni dhvanivaicitryavaṃti hi // śṛṃgāravaccaritakīrtanato 'cyutasya naino nṛṇāṃ kimuta buddhiviśuddhir eva / janmadibhāvarahito 'nukaroti janmakarmādimāyikaṃ ayaṃ nraghamuktaye yat //* (MPŚ 3.6b—8). This passage is in accordance with Śrīdhara Svāmin's claim that Kṛṣṇa's *līlā* ("play," "sport") was intended to woo those who are inclined toward erotics: "The purport is, that he seeks to incline to himself even such persons as are attracted to sensual love, and greatly devoted to external things" (on Bhāgavatapurāṇa 10.33.37; MUIR, 1873: 53).

[143] *Īśvarasya na deho 'sti pūrvam uktam idaṃ mayā / kevalaṃ lokasiddhyarthaṃ dehas tena samāśritaḥ // na dehadhāriṇāṃ śakyaḥ kartum indriyanigrahaḥ / sahajeneti lokānāṃ śikṣārthaṃ vidadhe tathā // na jātu devavāṇy asti pravṛttāv indriyārthake / tasmān manaḥ prayatnena sthāpyam indriyanigrahe // tathā yo yena bhavena bhajate parameśvaraṃ / taṃ pratīśas tathāmūrtir bhaved eva na saṃśayaḥ // yato vrajāṃganāḥ sarvāḥ svāmibhāvena bhejire / parameśaṃ tathā so 'pi tāsāṃ kāmam apūrayat / na tu tena samadiṣṭam evaṃ kāryaṃ narair iti //* (MPO 1.47—51; pp. 5—6). Hara.'s precedent for discouraging those who might want to imitate Kṛṣṇa's dalliance with the *gopīs* was the Bhāgavatapurāṇa itself, in which this story is found. The principle behind this prohibition was elaborated by the narrator, Śuka (10.33.31—32): "Let no one other than a superior being ever even in thought practise the same: any one who, through folly, does so, perishes, like any one not a Rudra [drinking] the poison produced from the ocean. The word of superior beings is true, and so also their conduct is sometimes [correct]: let a wise man observe their command, which is right" (MUIR, 1873: 50). It has been observed that the Sahajiyās, a Bengali Vaiṣṇava sect, did in fact take Kṛṣṇa's conduct with Rādhā and other *gopīs* as a model for their own orgiastic rituals (ELIADE, 1959: pp. 100, 104).

and woman, each one suspects him of adultery and so forth. But who knows the reason for the creator's *līlās*? Was it because he was desired by the *gopīs* that he enjoyed them, or was there another reason, and so on? It is also false to say that his *līlā* incites sin. God's *līlā* is never seen to incite sin. On the contrary, those who heartily delight in God's *līlās* are seen to be detached from *saṃsāra* (the "transmigratory world") and sin as well. Behold this power in God's *līlās*! As a man's love toward them increases, his mind becomes purified... Since the divine function is just this, to act in accordance with the right path, it is not to be acquired by his good conduct nor to be forfeited by bad conduct. He clearly reveals his glory, showing favor to the *gopīs*, who rejected attachment to all objects because their minds were fixed on God alone. Hari, becoming manifest in the hearts of those who sing his heroic deeds, removes impurity and grants peace of mind. This is the experience of good people, believers who sing holy songs about Bhagavān, that consciousness becomes purified. Since our love increases while singing 'Yadunandana! Govinda! Rāma! Kṛṣṇa!' what, in your presence, do we say? Bhagavān, undergoing incarnation, makes people good-hearted by means of his *līlās*. What else, indeed, must he do? With our meagre intelligence, we do not have the aptitude to criticize God's deeds. Who knows his ultimate intention ... Moreover, those very *līlās* done by Bhagavān Hari in Gokula were done during boyhood — not after investiture. However, in the scriptures it is seen that, before acquiring knowledge and immediately after investiture, Kṛṣṇa only performed his duty.[144] ... Now, where it is heard that

[144] Within the Hindu tradition itself, critics have accused the gods of hypocrisy for disporting themselves in ways for which ordinary men are consigned to hell. In the Naiṣadhacarita (7.122—23), for example, Kali lodges this complaint against the *devas*: "Let Brahmā sport with any girl, and you amuse yourselves with celestial nymphs, but Kali must live in celibacy. You preach *dharma* and yet you do things that one can hardly bear to hear about" (O'FLAHERTY, 1976: 290). With regard to the subject at hand, Kṛṣṇa's dalliance with the *gopīs*, even the Bhāgavatapurāṇa, which relates this story, records the offended sensibilities of King Parīkṣit, to whom it was told (10.33.27—29). The questions raised by him about the propriety of these events elicited Śuka's warning (*supra*, n. 143) against taking Kṛṣṇa's *līlā* as license for adultery. This admonishment was not considered adequate by commentators, in view of Kṛṣṇa's own reference to himself as an example to all men in all things (Bhagavad-Gītā 3.21): "Whatever the noblest does, that too will others do: the standard that he sets all the world will follow" (ZAEHNER, 1969: 169). According to Śrīdhara, the reason why no sin accrued to Kṛṣṇa, whereas mortals imitating him would incur guilt, is that he is the *antaryāmin*, the internal witness, whose ontological fullness renders him incapable of desire: "In the case of the divine, all-pervading, Being there is no such thing as an attachment to other men's wives [since he pervades, and is one with, everything]. It is 'he who moves within, the ruler,' the witness of the understanding, etc., who in sport takes a body; but he does not resemble such persons as ourselves, so that he should be in fault" (on Bhāgavatapurāṇa 10.33.36; MUIR, 1873: 51—52). Along this line of reasoning, the metaphysical disparity between Kṛṣṇa and his devotees precludes imitation; there is room only to recite and admire his *līlā*. The position taken by Nīla. on the spiritual efficacy of Kṛṣṇa's dalliance was the viewpoint of the Bhāgavata also, stated in its concluding *śloka* (10.33.40): *vikrīḍitaṃ vrajavadhūbhir idaṃ ca viṣṇoḥ śraddhānvito 'nuśṛṇuyād*

deities acted sinfully, there one hears nonetheless about purification, because of seeing their sin punished. What person, indeed, is there in this world who is free from sin? This is, however, God's justice, that one is purified by punishment. Where it is heard, for example, that Biḍaujas [Indra] had sexual intercourse with Ahalyā, one hears there, too, that his sin was punished on account of her husband's curse. Because of [his] punishment by God, worship of that pure-minded Śatakratu [Indra], whose ardor was stilled by good merit, is not, therefore, at fault."[145]

---

atha varṇayed yaḥ / bhaktim parāṃ bhagavati pratilabhya kāmaṃ hṛdrogam āśv apahinoty acireṇa dhīraḥ // (MUIR, 1873: 51). The idea that listening to and repeating Kṛṣṇa's *līlā* could eradicate desire, the disease of the heart, was one that Muir was never able to dignify with objective treatment. In his discussion of the verse just cited in Original Sanskrit Texts, he could not resist sarcasm, slipping into the MP mentality: "A remarkable instance of homeopathic cure, certainly!" (1873: 51). For details on the general problem of human imitation of apparently immoral gods, see O'FLAHERTY, 1976: 286—91. At no time did Muir, it must be noted, allude to phenomena in the life of Kṛṣṇa to which the Hindu tradition was not already sensitive and to which it did not have ready answers, those, in general, applied by Soma., Hara., and Nīla.

[145] *Atha ye kṛṣṇalīlāsu doṣam āhuḥ svayā dhiyā / na tat samucitaṃ teṣām atisvalpadhiyāṃ kila // kveśvaro 'nantadurjñeyalīlaś cānekahetuvit / kva jīvāḥ kṣudradhiṣaṇā aho sāhasam asty adaḥ // sarvāḥ striyaś ca puruṣā yadīyā eva kevalaṃ / tasmiṃs tu vyabhicārādīn śaṅkante yad tad adbhutaṃ // gopībhiḥ prārthito 'raṃsta tāsu kiṃ vānyakāraṇāt / ityādi dhātuḥ ko veda līlānāṃ kāraṇaṃ tu yat // uttejikāsti tallīlā pāpasyety api vāg vṛthā / na kvāpy uttejanaṃ dṛṣṭaṃ pāpānām iśalīlayā // pratyuteśvaralīlāsu ye ratāś cittapūrvakaṃ / teṣāṃ viraktiḥ saṃsārāt pāpād api ca dṛśyate // imaṃ paśyata līlānāṃ prabhāvaṃ paramātmanaḥ / yāsu premodbhave puṃso jāyate śuddhamānasaṃ //* (ŚTV 6a.136—42; pp. 59—60) *idam evaiśvaraṃ kṛtyaṃ yat sanmārge pravartanaṃ / na tasya dharmair āptavyaṃ heyaṃ vāpy asty adharmataḥ // tyaktasarvārtharāgābhyo gopībhyo diśatā śivaṃ / īśaikatānatāyās tu mahimā sampradarśitaḥ //* (6a.144—45; p. 60) *pragāyatāṃ svavīryāṇi svānta āvirbhavan hariḥ / apākaroti mālinyaṃ manaḥśāntiṃ ca yacchati // gāyatāṃ śraddadhānānāṃ pāvanīr bhagavatkathāḥ / śuddhim eti yathā cittaṃ tat satām ānubhāvikaṃ // yadunandana govinda rāma kṛṣṇeti valgatāṃ / yad udbhavati naḥ prema kiṃ brūmo bhavataṃ puraḥ // dhṛtvāvatāraṃ svīyābhir līlābhir bhagavān janān / kurute sādhuhṛdayān kim anyad dhi karotu saḥ // nāsmākam adhikāro 'sti cariteṣu parātmanaḥ / doṣān alpadhiyā dhātuṃ ko vedāsyāśayaṃ paraṃ //* (6a.148—52; p. 61) *kiṃ ca yā akarol līlā bhagavān gokule hariḥ / tā hi paugaṇḍavayasi na tūpanayanāt paraṃ // anantaraṃ tūpanīter vidyāgrahaṇapūrvakaṃ / dharma eva hi kṛṣṇena kṛtaḥ śāstreṣu dṛśyate //* (6a.165—66; pp. 62—63) *atha yatra tu devānāṃ pātakācaraṇaṃ śrutaṃ / śuddhiś ca śrūyate tatra tadaṃhodaṇḍadarśanāt // ko nāma vidyate loke dehī pāpavivarjitaḥ / kiṃ tu śudhyati daṇḍena nyāyo 'sau paramātmanaḥ // tathā hy ahalyāgāmitvaṃ śrutaṃ yatra biḍaujasaḥ / tatraiva śāpāt tadbhartuḥ śruto daṇḍas tadaṃhasaḥ // tataḥ śuddhātmanas tasya puṇyāsāditatejasaḥ / śatakrator na doṣāya saparyeśānuśāsanāt //* (6a.111—14; p. 57). The story of Indra's rape of Ahalyā and the substance of the curse are contained in the Rāmāyaṇa (Uttarakāṇḍa 30.19ff.; MUIR, 1868a: 120—22). Gautama himself, who cursed Indra, contradicts Nīla., saying that this incident would lead to more rather than less adultery among mankind: "This vile passion that thou hast manifested, O Perverse Wretch, will undoubtedly spread among men and women and whosoever shall be guilty of it shall bear half the responsibility, whilst the other half shall be thine..." (H. P. SHASTRI, 1959: 477). As a case in point, one might cite Nahuṣa, who lusted for Indra's wife, Indrāṇī, and, when encountering resistance from the gods, complained

Stages of Sanskrit (MP 5.17—26; p. 76, *supra*; n. 51, p. 76, *supra*)

Hara.: "That scripture which conforms to the Vedas the wise would have to accept, but all who are wise reject that which goes contrary to the sense of the Vedas. Because the sense of the Veda is difficult to understand, the great *ṛṣis* made the Śruti, Smṛti and Purāṇas as commentaries upon it. It is said, therefore, that they possess authority because of the authoritativeness of the Vedas. Respect is due to [their] composition, even though a very long time had passed [since creation]."[146]

Nīla.: "Now, I don't understand that defect, based on differences in language, which other people suspect there to be in the four Vedas. Likewise, the hymns belonging to the four Vedas and the Brāhmaṇas and the Upaniṣads as well are understood to have one single language. Now, so what if one would say that the language in certain Upaniṣads belonging to the Atharva-Veda is seen to be popular and of a kind different than the Śrūtis?[147] Does injury befall the Veda's glory? And does also a *sādhu*, assaulted by thieves, become impure? There are various kinds of people in this variegated world; who, indeed, is there who knows this: 'Who will do what?' What woman, to a paramour, should be avoided? And what, to the covetous, is not

---

as follows: "Indra once violated Ahalyā, the glorious consort of a seer, while her husband was alive: why did you not stop him?" (Mahābhārata 5.12.6; VAN BUITENEN, 1978: 208). It is noteworthy that Nīla. did not follow Kumārila Bhaṭṭa's precedent for explaining the rape of Ahalyā allegorically. According to this Mīmāṃsaka, she was the night and Indra the sun (MUIR, 1868a: 122; MÜLLER, 1860: 529f.; KANE, 1946: 845—48).

146 *Vedānuyāyi yac chāstraṃ tad grāhyaṃ viduṣāṃ bhavet | vedārthaviparītaṃ yat sarvais tat tyajyate budhaiḥ || vedārthasya durūhatvāt tasya ṭīkāsvarūpataḥ | śrutismṛtipurāṇāni nirmitāni maharṣibhiḥ || ato vedaprāmāṇatvāt teṣāṃ prāmāṇyam ucyate | gate 'pi sucire kāle nirmitāv api mānyatā ||* (MPO 1.26—28; p. 3). Hara.'s statements do not mean that Smṛtis and Purāṇas are on an equal footing with the Vedas. Whatever authority the former varieties of scripture possess is derivative, not primary. For example, Manusmṛti, recognized to be of human origin (*pauruṣeya*), nonetheless possesses unimpeachable orthodoxy in view of its Vedic foundation (*vide* KULLŪKA BHAṬṬA on Manu 1.1; MUIR, 1868b: 180—81). The principle behind the demarcation between primary and secondary authority, not very clearly stated in this passage from the MPO, is more systematically expressed in extracts from the Nyāyamālāvistara and Śaṅkara's Brahmasūtrabhāṣya (quoted in MUIR, 1868b: 179—91).

147 The reason why Nīla. singled out Upaniṣads belonging to the Atharva Veda (numbering thirty-one in the list enumerated by the Muktikā-Upaniṣad) as possibly spurious is not altogether clear. Perhaps it was because the 1840 edition of the MP mentioned two Atharvan Upaniṣads, the Rāmapūrvatāpanīya and Gopālatāpanīya (n. 52, p. 77, *supra*); but there the context was the Kṛṣṇa cult, not stages of language. Possibly this tentative admission occurred to him independently of Muir. In any event, this was hardly a significant concession on Nīla.'s part, since certain Hindus had always held the Atharva in suspicion: "All these Upaniṣads which are, properly speaking, non-Vedic, are generally called 'Upaniṣads of the Atharvaveda.' They were associated with the Atharvaveda, because the authority of this Veda as sacred tradition was always dubious and it was therefore no difficult matter to associate all kinds of apocryphal texts with the literature belonging to the Atharvaveda" (WINTERNITZ, 1972, 1: 242—43).

to be taken? Who, to those who are blinded by arrogance, is not insignificant? What, to the wicked, is not to be done? Never would that [difference in language] diminish the Veda's glory; a jewel surrounded by hundreds of glass beads does not, indeed, diminish in value. Now, on account of the difference in subject-matter, the language of Mantras, Brāhmaṇas, and the Upaniṣads is somewhat mutually distinct. Just as, for example, the language in a grammar-book would not be found in a book devoted to logic, made for one purpose, so must one consider the case to be here also. It is taught that the origin of the Vedas is from God, like breath; of his own accord, he had the Vedas explain himself, whose nature is like the precepts [in them]. Then the *ṛṣis* saw those hymns on account of their own respective austerities, and because of seeing various hymns they thus became the *ṛṣis* [associated with] them.[148] ... The language in the Mahābhārata, etc., is seen to be clearer than the Vedas; language of that sort, somewhat different than the Purāṇas, is also found in Smṛtis, etc. The language of the Purāṇas is recognized to be much more perspicuous than those [other texts].[149] Gradation [of language] is for the welfare, indeed, of those who are slow-minded in different degrees."[150]

---

[148] See Nirukta 2.11 (MUIR, 1871: 195) for a similar definition of *ṛṣi*.

[149] This oversimplification of problems presented by the obsolete language of the Vedas to latter-day interpreters hardly does justice to etymological treatises, such as the Nirukta, which attempted to throw light on the obscurities of the former texts. The Nirukta itself says (1.15): "Now without this work the meaning of the hymns cannot be understood..." (MUIR, 1871: 169). Therefore, to say that Vedas and Purāṇas differ from each other only in respect to the degree of clarity in which they were written, or that they provide scholars with opportunities to exhibit their erudition, is to ignore the fact, admitted by Hindu grammarians, that aspects of the Vedic language had fallen out of currency. It would seem that a more realistic and candid discussion of this problem would not have jeopardized Nīla.'s defense of the scripture's *pramāṇatva*. A more rigorous critique of Orientalist arguments, exemplified by Muir and later propagated by MONIER—WILLIAMS against the eternity of the Vedas, can be found in two essays by the Ārya Samājist Pandit GURU DATTA VIDYĀRTHĪ, "The Terminology of the Vedas and European Scholars," and "Criticism on Monier Williams' 'Indian wisdom'" (L. DAS, 1897: pp. 15—55, 56—84). The line of defense Muir had predicted (see p. 100, *supra*) was, in fact, the very one taken by GURU DATTA: "The first canon for the interpretation of Vedic terms, which is laid down by Yaska... is that the Vedic terms are all *yaugika*... This principle the European scholars have entirely ignored, and hence have flooded their interpretations of the Vedas with forged or borrowed tales of mythology, with stories of historic or pre-historic personages" (the author was here criticizing MUIR's Original Sanskrit Texts; L. DAS, 1897: 21—22). For details on GURU DATTA's career, see JONES, 1976: *passim*.

[150] *Atho caturṣu vedeṣu śaṅkante yat pare janāḥ / bhāṣābhedakṛtaṃ doṣaṃ taṃ tu nopalabhāmahe // caturvedīyamantrāṇāṃ brāhmaṇānāṃ tathaiva ca / vedāntānām api tathā bhāṣaikaivopalabhyate // athātharvaṇavedīyopaniṣatsu tu kāsucit / bhāṣā śrutivijātīyā dṛśyate laukikīti cet // āstāṃ kiṃ tāvatā vedamahimā kṣatim ṛcchati / api coraiḥ samākrāntaḥ kiṃ sādhur api dūṣyate // vicitre hi jagaty asmiñ janā nānāvidhāḥ sthitāḥ / kaḥ kiṃ kariṣyatīty asya jñātā ko nāma vidyate // kā strī tyājyā bhujaṅgānāṃ kiṃ agrāhyaṃ ca lobhinām / ko na tuccho madāndhānāṃ kiṃ akāryaṃ durātmanāṃ // na tāvatā tu vedānāṃ hīyeta mahimā kvacit / na hi kācaśatair vyāptaṃ ratnaṃ maulyena hīyate // atha mantrabrāhmaṇānāṃ vedāntānāṃ ca vai mithaḥ / kiñcit prabhidyate vāk sā viṣayasya bhidāvaśāt // yathā hy ekakṛte granthe yā vāk nyāyamaye*

Vedic Historicity (MP 2nd ed., 6.51—62; pp. 54—56; see n. 60, p. 79, *supra*)[151]

Nīla.: "A defect is said to result from tellung about recent events [in the scriptures]; but what defect would that be in Śrūti, the word of God who knows past, present, and future? Scriptures connected with factual happenings are by no means defective, since careful deliberation proves that *saṃsāra* is beginningless."[152]

Purāṇic Cosmography (MP 5.73—77; p. 78, *supra*)

Nīla.: "Now, the measurement of sky, earth, and so forth in the Purāṇas is said to be for the purpose of worshipping God in an all-encompassing form.

---

bhavet / na sā vyākaraṇagranthe tathaivāpi manyatāṃ // niśvāsavat pareśāc ca śrutas teṣāṃ samudbhavaḥ / svātmānaṃ vidhirūpaṃ sa svayaṃ vedān ajigrahat // tatas te ṛṣibhir dṛṣṭā mantrāḥ svasvatapobalāt / tattaddarśanatas tattanmantrarṣitvam athāpnuvan // (ŚTV 6a.72—82; pp. 53—54) *vedebhyo hi sphuṭā bhāṣā bhāratādiṣu dṛśyate / kiñcid bhinnā purāṇebhyaḥ smṛtyādiṣv api tādṛśī // tebhyo 'tiviśadā vāṇī purāṇeṣv anulakṣyate / uttarottaramandānāṃ hitārthaṃ hy uttarottaraṃ //* (6a.130—31; p. 59).

[151] In the background of Nīla.'s rejoinder were Muir's comments on developments in the Kṛṣṇa cult and the Veda's panegyrics upon kings who lived after creation. In his view, these features prove conclusively that the Vedas postdate the origin of the world.

[152] *Yas tv ādhunikavṛttāntakathanād doṣa ucyate / traikālikajñeśavāci ko doṣaḥ sa bhavec chrutau // vicāreṇa yataḥ siddham anāditvaṃ ca saṃsṛteḥ / bhūtārthakaprayogāś ca naiva duṣyanti sarvathā //* (ŚTV 6a.84—85, p. 54). The brevity of Nīla.'s response to Muir on this point indicates that this type of criticism did not have originality and that Hindu thought had already reached a settled opinion with regard to it. Muir's objections, in fact, were merely another facet of a larger problem already satisfactorily dealt with by Śaṅkara in the Vedāntasūtrabhāṣya (1.3.30). The question there is whether or not there can be an eternal connection between the words of the Veda and the objects, specifically deities, to which they refer, in view of the doctrine of periodic annihilation and recreation of the universe. Śaṅkara made a negative answer impossible by quoting scriptures to the effect that "name and form" (*nāmarūpa*) have unbroken continuity throughout each successive *kalpa*. One such citation was Viṣṇupurāṇa 1.5.60—61 (cf. Manu 1.30): "Just as, in each season of the year, all the various characteristics of that season are perceived, on its recurrence, to be the very same as they had been before; so too are the beings produced at the beginnings of the ages. Possessing both the will and the ability to create, and impelled by the powers inherent in the things to be created, the deity produces again and again a creation of the very same description at the beginning of every Kalpa" (MUIR, 1868a: 60). On this basis the cases of kings panegyrized in the Veda do not differ from references to deities; all have an identity substantially the same as in former *kalpas*. The foundation of Śaṅkara's argument is the doctrine of beginningless *saṃsāra*, explicated in 2.1.36 and quoted at the outset of 1.3.30: "The eternity of the world is agreeable to reason" (*upapadyate ca saṃsārasya anādityam*; MUIR, 1868b: 308). So obvious was the apologetic conclusion to be drawn from this that Nīla. was content merely to paraphrase this proposition in order to contradict Muir. Muir's argument against the eternity of the Vedas was partly of Indian origin, viz., the criticisms advanced by the *pūrvapakṣin* in verses 28 to 30 of the Pūrvamīmāṃsāsūtras. A translation of the scholiast Śabara Svāmin's defense may be found in MUIR, 1868b: 77—80.

Its only aim is to describe God's glory; it is not said there that the measurement of earth, etc., is real. But now, if one asks in this regard how a scripture could be divine if it says something untrue, then calm down! If the measurement of the earth, etc., was meant to be taken literally, then the Purāṇas would have the defect mentioned by you. But their aim is definitely not that; on the contrary, its [aim] is only to glorify God. This glory is to be expressed in many ways in order to worship God, whose body is all-encompassing. They don't call a man a liar, who says, when describing the wealth of a wealthy man, 'This wealthy man has hundreds of thousands of rings.' Certainly, people do not understand the possession of hundreds of thousands of [rings] as strictly factual. On the contrary, his remark is not faulty because the number is not literal. In like manner, careful deliberation does not detect a defect in the mass of Purāṇas either, which give priority to describing God's glory. It is not a defect, therefore, for the Purāṇas to depict the glory of God in many ways, even though they are mutually inconsistent. But one must not suppose on this basis that they are ignorant of the Siddhāntas; subjects belonging to all scriptures are to be seen in a Purāṇa. In your religion there is also a conflict between religion and science. In science it is acknowledged that the earth moves, but in [your] scripture, the sun moves."[153]

---

[153] *Athākāśapṛthivyāder mānaṃ yat pañcalakṣaṇe / procyate tad upāsārthaṃ virāḍrūpe parātmanaḥ // kevalaṃ tasya tātparyam īśamāhātmyavarṇane / na tu tatrocyate mānaṃ pṛthivyādes tu tāttvikaṃ // nanv atāttvikam arthaṃ ced vakti śāstraṃ tad aiśvaraṃ / kathaṃ syād iti ced atra procyate tan niśāmaya // tātparyeṇa pṛthivyāder yadi mānaṃ vivakṣitaṃ / purāṇānām bhavet tarhi syād doṣo bhavadīritaḥ // tat tu nāsty eva kiṃ tv eṣāṃ māhātmyaṃ kevalaṃ vibhoḥ / vaktavyam asti bahudhopāsanārthaṃ virāṭtanoḥ // yathaiṣa lakṣamudrāvān dhaniko 'stīti bhāṣiṇaṃ / na mithyāvādinaṃ prāhur dhanino dhanavarṇane // na hi tathyaiva vijñātā janais tallakṣaśālitā / atātparyāt tu saṃkhyāyās tadvaco nāsti doṣabhāk // tathaiva devamāhātmyavarṇanaikapare 'pi ca / doṣaḥ purāṇasaṃdohe na vicāreṇa lakṣyate // ata eva purāṇānāṃ vaimatye 'pi parasparaṃ / bahudheśvaramāhātmyaṃ doṣo varṇayatāṃ na hi // na tāvatā tu siddhāntājñānaṃ teṣāṃ prakalpyatāṃ / viṣayāḥ sarvaśāstrāṇāṃ dṛśyante pañcalakṣaṇe // bhavatāṃ ca mate 'py asti śāstravidyāviparyayaḥ / śāstre tu bhānor vidyāyāṃ pṛthivyā gatir iṣyate //* (ŚTV 6a.175—85; pp. 63—64). Cf. the remarks of Subājī on this subject (pp. 85—86, *supra*). Although neither pandit used the term *arthavāda*, it is clear that this is what they had in mind when defending the Purāṇas against Muir's allegation of scientific naivety. *Arthavādas* are commendatory passages often interpreted as devices to enhance *vidhis* ("prescriptions"), but in this context the greatness of *īśvara*. It is understood that, by their very nature, *arthavādas* may contradict passages also considered authoritative in the same or other texts. But the two pandits disagreed in their conception of what constitutes a Purāṇa. Whereas Subājī considered its sphere of authority to be limited to *parā vidyā* and *aparā vidyā* to be the rightful domain of the Siddhāntas, Nīla. believed the Purāṇas to be authoritative in both fields of knowledge. The final verse cited above (6a.185) refers back to 3.6 where Nīla. had indicted the Bible's apparent lack of knowledge regarding the sun's immobility: *kvacid viruddhā vidyāyāḥ sūrye gatir udīryate / tato 'pi matakartṝṇām ajñatvam iva bhāsate //*. The entire quotation above should be compared with Nīla.'s postconversion remarks on the Purāṇas' scientific reliability, which are recorded in the Epilogue (p. 170, *infra*).

Observations on Hindu Apologetics in the MP Controversy

Pertinent passages in the MPŚ, MPO, and ŚTV indicate that, within the MP Controversy context, Hindu apologetics accented resistance to rather than accommodation of Christianity. With respect to its doctrinal content and Hinduism's, these extracts show that Soma., Hara., and Nīla. were disinclined to admit either concord between their religion and Muir's or to assimilate discordant features into the Sanātana Dharma. Only the doctrine of the triune God qualified as a possible analogue to something already present in Hinduism: the ultimate indistinctness of a plural number of deities from the one absolute Brahman. And although the three critics failed to realize that this supposed analogue was based on a dubious interpretation of the Trinity, the total context of their apologetics leaves no doubt that they were not overly excited about this apparent convergence. God the Father, Son, and Holy Spirit were, after all, implicated in a whole series of unsound ideas, including creation, redemption, and sanctification (or probation). Thus, the thrust of Hindu apologetics in the period under review was to deny common ground, emphasize the *sui generis* character of Hinduism, expose Christianity as erroneous, and dissuade fellow Hindus from regarding the Khṛṣṭadharma as a serious claimant to their religious allegiance.

Basic to any explanation of the uniformly negative assessment of Christianity made by the pandits are two factors. First, wherever the epistemological basis of Hindu apologetics was the Veda itself, rather than religious experience or some other locus, the tendency among Hindus has been (at least in the period from Ziegenbalg to Muir) to dismiss Christianity as deficient in all that appertains to matters of religion. Whether the Veda was the bedrock of judgment upon other religions simply because of its antiquity and centrality in Hinduism or because of sophisticated reasoning about *pramāṇatva* ("authoritativeness"), the result was the same: all other competing interpretations of God, the world, man, and salvation are false. The striking continuity between criticisms made by the Malabarian brahmins and the arguments of Soma., Hara., and Nīla. support this observation.

The MP Controversy has been portrayed here as unique in the annals of Hindu apologetics — little known though they be. To be sure, the encounter between Muir and the pandits was unparalleled in terms of refinement of issues and the length and breadth to which they were discussed. Unlike Ziegenbalg's Malabarian informants, the later critics distinguished between specifically social and religious aspects of the clash between the two religions. Soma., Hara., and Nīla. never accused Christianity of being unfit for Hindus because, for example, missionaries spit and allow their wives to leave home during menstruation (see p. 25, *supra*). These differences notwithstanding, the basic content of the anti-Christian critiques of the Malabarian brahmins and the MP Controversy pandits is identical. Unqualified adherence to the revealed teaching of the Veda is the thread that held their apologetics together in spite of differences in space and time.

In this frame of reference, the Hindu apologists of the MP period were repeating themes already advanced and making judgments previously applied, only with more precision than had theretofore been possible. The fact that, with almost absolute certainty, one can say that the three pandits were not indebted to their Malabarian predecessors or even the two apologists (Morabhaṭṭa Dāndekara and Nārāyaṇa Rāo) who clashed with John Wilson in Bombay, strongly suggests that fidelity to the Vedas, as alone revelatory, coincides with a defiant posture toward Christianity. All of this points to the existence of a strongly conservative element, uncongenial to heterodox doctrines, within eighteenth and nineteenth-century Hinduism.

The second factor accounting for the uniformly negative critique of the Khṛṣṭadharma by the MP Controversy apologists is that, insofar as their interpretations of Christianity enabled them to apprehend it accurately, Muir's exposition of that religion propounded little or nothing that had not already been discussed at some time in Hinduism and rejected by the mainstream of orthodoxy. Notes to the translation pointed out repeatedly where either Soma., Hara., or Nīla. are likely to have been guided by precedents in selecting their lines of attack upon and defense against the MP. For example, long before Muir, Hindus had reached settled conclusions about the nature of creation and the deity's role in it. All these precluded a favorable response to the Christian belief in an *ex nihilo* creative act, since that would implicate God in a tangle of ethical dilemmas. Most Hindus had already rejected retributive punishment in favor of remedial penalties within the scheme of rebirth. They had, by and large, found in *mokṣa* a religious value superior to *svarga*. Hindus arguing among themselves (heterodox versus orthodox and even orthodox versus orthodox), from a multitude of contrasting viewpoints, had over a period of many centuries provided Hinduism with an arsenal of arguments and counterarguments at the disposal of the three pandits in the MP Controversy.

One cannot say, of course, that anything in the Hindu tradition had prepared the pandits for Paleyan Evidential Apologetics; yet they deftly safeguarded Vedic authority by employing *tarka* in the manner approved by Manu, countering Muir with his own arguments. They did not fare so well against the MP's Orientalist critique of Vedic *pramāṇatva*, which viewed Sanskrit as the product of historical development. The terms of this argument were unfamiliar and time was necessary for their weight to be felt.[154] Except for *śuddhi*, the overlap between what Muir meant and what the pandits understood by his terms was adequate to prevent serious breakdowns in communication. Wisely chosen though it may have been, the dominant meaning, "purification," overwhelmed the Pauline connotation of

[154] By way of contrast to n. 149 above, which pointed to the attempt of Pandit GURU DATTA VIDYĀRTHĪ later in the century to neutralize the "stages of Sanskrit" argument against the eternity of the Vedas, it is useful to note that by mid-century the Orientalist-inspired critique had already found an advocate in ĪŚVAR CANDRA VIDYĀSĀGAR, Principal of the Calcutta Sanskrit College. In his Sanskrit anthology, Ṛjupāṭha, an argument similar to Muir's appeared: "It is commonly said that all the Purāṇas were composed by Vedavyāsa. But the style of the different Purāṇas is so various that they cannot be conceived to be the work of one person" (quoted in MUIR, 1871: 162).

justification that Muir wished to infuse into it. The pandits' rejection of the *śuddhi* offered by Christ followed a definite logic: *śuddhi* obviates adverse karmic repercussions; Christians continue to suffer for their sins; Christianity's claim that it offers true *śuddhi* is consequently false. In spite of these terminological obstacles, one can say that the major facets of Christianity, if not its fine points, were largely comprehended, judged, and found lacking in a way that was entirely consistent with Hinduism's own treatment of dissident viewpoints within itself.

Perhaps the most remarkable feature of Hindu apologetics within the MP context is not so much what it contained but what it lacked. A most curious absence is Jesus Christ, the figure at the very center of Christianity. This lack of interest is especially surprising in view of the awe in which he was held even during the time of the MP Controversy by Hindus such as Rammohun Roy and Keshub Chandra Sen in Calcutta and the reverential fascination of contemporary Hindus. To Soma., Hara., and Nīla., Jesus was mostly a *deus ex machina* introduced by Christians to extricate their creator God from the dilemma he had brought upon himself by his *ex nihilo* creative act. They were not interested in his beatitudes — if they even knew about them — neither did they wish to adopt him as an *avatāra* (with the exception of Soma.; see p. 92, *supra*) or identify his name with Kṛṣṇa.[155] This absence is only partly accounted for by the fact that Christ did not have an especially central role in the MP. Nīla. heard much about the character of Jesus in conversations with his partner-in-dialogue, but nonetheless portrayed him simply as a remote savior-god in the ŚTV. It was symptomatic of Hindu-Christian encounter at this stage that Christ's salvific function was at the forefront of discussion rather than his moral character. The reciprocal relation between his saviorhood and his personal attributes was either misunderstood or rejected. Moreover, his participation in a plan of salvation that contravened accepted standards of justice, precluded overt admiration for other ethical qualities he may have possessed.

Yet there was something remotely attractive and unsettling to Nīla. about the person of Christ, and there is indirect evidence of this in his comments on Kṛṣṇa's *līlā*. For the most part Nīla. followed others in the Hindu tradition who testify that Kṛṣṇa's mischievious frolics in Vṛndāvana with the *gopīs* were merely ways in which to woo worldly-minded devotees to

---

[155] Identifying the names Kṛṣṇa and Christ, thoroughly unsound from the etymological standpoint, has recently become a key element in the apologetics of the International Society of Kṛṣṇa Consciousness (ISKON), which places great emphasis upon chanting the names of God. In the record of a dialogue held in 1974 between A. C. BHAKTIVEDĀNTA SWAMI PRABHUPĀDA and a German Benedictine monk, one finds the Hindu scholar completely at ease with this apologetic tactic. "'Christos' ist die griechische Version des Wortes 'Kṛṣṇa'... 'Christus' ist eine andere Weise, 'Kischto' anzurufen, und 'Krischto' ist eine andere Form der Aussprache des Wortes 'Kṛṣṇa', Gottes Namen... Jesus Christus bedeutet Jesus, der Sohn des Christus oder Kṛṣṇas. Er selbst hat sich als Sohn Gottes bezeichnet. Deshalb, ob Sie Gott 'Krischto' oder 'Kṛṣṇa' oder 'Christus' nennen — es bleibt sich letztlich gleich" (Christus-Krischto-Kṛṣṇa, n. d.: 49—50, *passim*).

himself. Along this line of reasoning, the Bhāgavatapurāṇa's account of Kṛṣṇa's *līlā* has the same function for a Hindu that the Song of Solomon has for a Christian. But, one senses that, at the end of his spirited defense, Nīla. was groping nervously for further justification for Kṛṣṇa's behavior, and, therefore, added — somewhat lamely — that he always behaved circumspectly after his brahminical initiation. This urge to defend Kṛṣṇa by going beyond the limits of the traditional defense in the Bhāgavatapurāṇa may well have been caused by Nīla.'s repeated dialogues with Smith, who often juxtaposed the conduct of Christ and Kṛṣṇa. Be that as it may, the subject of Kṛṣṇa was a delicate one for each pandit possibly because it easily lends itself to sarcastic misinterpretation. Consequently, this was the point at which the pandits, particularly Nīla., came closest to accommodating the ethical spirit of Christianity.

If the pandits said very little directly about Christ, who is at the center of Christianity, they expended considerable effort discussing an issue of negligible concern in that religion: nonhuman life and the ethics of *ahiṃsā* (even though only its negative form, *hiṃsā*, was used by Soma.). This subject, along with Kṛṣṇa, raised the pandits' emotional pitch and provoked Nīla. to protest against abuse of animals. From their perspective, the Christian proclivity to regard cattle as beef to be consumed was contemptible and heinous. Moreover, eating these creatures signaled the impending chaos of the Kali Yuga. Positively speaking, restraint of violence toward animal life was an integral element in a larger complex of ideas, including the concept of remedial punishment. One might say that the pandits' heated declamations on this topic point to a belief that a compassionate stance toward nonhuman life is the natural outcome of sound ideas in other areas. For Christians to be unconcerned about animals is to graphically demonstrate that their beliefs about God, the world, man, and salvation are unsound. Soma., Hara., and Nīla. thereby reveal an especially significant insight into Hindu apologetics: it was not what Christianity did say about Christ but what it did not say about nonhuman life that astounded and appalled them.

Having covered some major facets of the pandits' resistance to Christianity, these will be recapitulated below along with more minor points in relation to the Malabarian brahmins' and Bombay apologists' critiques noted above in chapter two. From these observations as a whole, several general principles about Hindu apologetics will be extrapolated.

(1) Christianity lacks the prestige of antiquity that characterizes the Sanātana Dharma. (*vide* Malabarians, p. 23, *supra*).[156]

(2) An *ex nihilo* act of creation implicates God in all that is wrong with man and the universe, exposing the Bible to the accusation that it propounds a concept of divinity repugnant to morality.

---

[156] Hindu critics of Jainism also regarded that religion as an upstart, and Jain apologists expended much effort arguing that an early origin was on their side as well as Hinduism's (HANDIQUI, 1949: 326).

(3) Christianity fosters contempt for and abuse of nonhuman life by failing to recognize its legitimate claim to the benefits of rebirth (Malabarians, p. 24, *supra*).
(4) The Christian idea of union with God in heaven is tantamount to the *svargas* of Hinduism. Heaven is, therefore, inferior to the permanence of *mokṣa*.
(5) In his earthly life, Jesus Christ brought more grief than enlightenment to mankind, and, in his capacity as savior, he contravened recognized standards of justice (Malabarians, p. 24, *supra*; Nārāyaṇa Rāo, p. 30, *supra*).
(6) Forensic justification (δικαιοσύνη, *śuddhi*) violates all norms of logic and justice, leads to antinomianism, and discourages genuine repentence (Malabarians, p. 24, *supra*; Morabhaṭṭa Dāndekara, p. 28, *supra*).
(7) Original sin is illogical, unjust, and contradicted by empirical observation, physiology, and psychology.
(8) *Karman* and rebirth are logically more satisfying explanations of suffering than the Christian notion of probation or sanctification.
(9) Punishment, as understood in Hinduism, is remedial rather than retributive, as believed in Christianity (Malabarians, p. 24, *supra*).
(10) According to Hindu concepts of causality, originated souls are impermanent. The metaphysical basis of the Christian hope of eternity is, therefore, erroneous.
(11) Hinduism is not crass polytheism but the doctrine of one God or Absolute adapted variously in order to lead all types of people from the conditioned and relative to the supreme and absolute (Malabarians, p. 24, *supra*).
(12) Intrareligious rivalry does not upset Hinduism's equilibrium; rather, it stems from *karman* and can be excused as a by-product of religious fervor.
(13) The six *darśanas* are each designed to attract a certain kind of person, and all of them lead to the same end, but some more directly than others.
(14) Mankind's basic defect is epistemological rather than moral, as asserted by Christians.
(15) Brahminhood is rooted in *karman*; it cannot be acquired outside of the process of rebirth, but can, according to one view, be forfeited through immorality.
(16) Image worship is not idolatry but a means to purify the mind by withdrawing the senses from the world and concentrating thought upon God.
(17) Divine deportment is beyond comprehension and criticism; it subdues rather than stimulates the senses (Malabarians, p. 24, *supra*; Morabhaṭṭa Dāndekara, p. 26, *supra*).
(18) Vedic authority is intact and beyond question; variations in Sanskrit are due to differences in content rather than the passage of time and linguistic mutation.
(19) When not purposely hyperbolic, Purāṇic cosmography is true to the nature of the universe, whereas the Bible is scientifically uninformed, especially regarding basic astronomy (Nārāyaṇa Rāo, p. 30, *supra*).

Two principles stand out conspicuously in this overview of the issues dealt with by pandits in the MP Controversy; both are basically restatements of observations made in paragraphs two and three of this section. First, it is beyond question that the pandits derived their ideas of God, man, the universe, and salvation from the Vedas, their standard of truth and comparison in all matters pertaining to religion and ethics, but were not averse to speculative reasoning in order to contradict their opponent and uphold the integrity of their scripture and tradition. Second, allegiance to the Vedas obviated accommodation to Christianity and dialectical movement toward a truth beyond both religions. This unremitting resistance was facilitated by Hinduism's own record of rejecting dissident beliefs tantamount to those professed in Christianity.

These principles account for the stiff resistance of Soma., Hara., and Nīla.; they explain why the MPŚ, MPO, and ŚTV are genuinely apologetical and why they precluded scholarly objectivity. Therefore, one may say that, although not a creedal religion in the same sense as Christianity, the pandits (especially Hara. and Nīla.) nonetheless understood Hinduism to have a doctrinal core, deviation from which would mean ceasing, at least intellectually, to be a Hindu.

These observations have only the apologetics of the MP Controversy within their purview, although some points of convergence between the three pandits and their near contemporaries in Hinduism have been traced in notes along the way. It would be quite a different matter to contrast the dogmatic stances of Soma., Hara., and Nīla. with representatives of neo-Hinduism, the apologetical patterns of which developed in quite a different direction. Of course, limitations of time and space prevent such a comparison from being made here.[157] This reservation notwithstanding, the materials presented above may be regarded as representative of a strain of resistant Hinduism that found expression throughout the early nineteenth century in Indian-language mediums, which have been too often neglected when scholars comment upon Hindu-Christian relations in that period.

---

[157] Perusal of the bibliography will acquaint the reader with a number of publications useful in making comparisons of this type. Especially recommended are A. KRÄMER's Christus und Christentum im Denken des modernen Hinduismus (1958), and P. HACKER's "Aspects of Neo-Hinduism Contrasted with Surviving Traditional Hinduism" (1978).

VI. CHRISTIANITY IN THE GENERAL SCHEME OF DHARMA

Chapter one of this study in Hindu apologetics drew attention to a silence on the part of Hindu authors towards Christianity, a silence especially conspicuous in view of incursions upon Indian soil by European colonists accompanied by zealous missionaries. As far as the Sanskrit language is concerned, this silence remained unbroken until the outbreak of the MP Controversy early in the nineteenth century (and not much earlier even when regional languages are taken into consideration).

Silence, in the sense of deliberately ignoring other views, was of course a long-standing defensive tactic practiced during periods of sectarian strife within Hinduism itself. J. Gonda notes that devotees sometimes demonstrated contempt for deities other than their own simply by omitting to mention them by name (1970: 198, n. 87). But a distinction must be made between silence in intra- and interreligious contexts, and here we are primarily concerned with the latter. Without imposing modern terminology upon an era that did not yet think in such hermetic categories, it would be even more exact to say that Hindus were silent toward, or did not reflect upon, religions qua religions because they did not, or were unable to, recognize them as fully-accredited Dharmas alongside of, or in opposition to, their own.

Mention was also made of certain factors militating against recognition of non-Hindu religions as authentic Dharmas: prohibition of social intercourse with *mlecchas* and study of their languages, to cite only two examples (*vide* p. 47, *supra*). The consequence of these restrictions in later times was that Hindu apologists were afflicted with a myopia that turned their attention inward toward familiar adversaries, Buddhists, Jains, and materialists, who had long ceased to pose an actual threat to Hindu dominance, instead of outward toward immediate dangers posed by Islam and Christianity.

Hindu apologetics could not, under these inhibiting conditions, develop into new phases because the science of resisting competing religions presupposes that they are recognized to exist vis-à-vis one's own. Awareness of religious plurality stimulates apologetics into action; without it this branch of Hindu intellectual activity clearly became antiquarian and scholastic. It is conceivable that Hindu apologists could have expended all their efforts in denying to competitor religions their full status as Dharmas with legitimate claims to teach alternative forms of ethics, metaphysics, and soteriology. But this is not what one finds in the literature of the MP Controversy. Soma., Hara., and Nīla. did not dispute Muir's claim that the *khṛṣṭadharma* is an alternative to their own. Rather, by mustering all the criticisms translated in the previous chapter, they insisted that it is an inadequate alternative, deficient in truth, which would lead only to grief if it replaced the Vedic Dharma.

The MPŚ, MPO, and ŚTV reflect, therefore, a crucial juncture in Hindu apologetics: recognition of religious plurality. Of course, this transition began to take place at some earlier point in the latter-day history of Hinduism. One cannot say exactly where or when this occurred, although some tentative remarks have already been made with respect to "religion" as an approximate meaning of Dharma in Jain, Tantric and Gauḍīya Vaiṣṇava literature (*vide* pp. 66—69, *supra*). Whether or not these sources predisposed the three pandits to admit that other Dharmas exist, it is clear that their conception of religion allowed for plurality.

Having accorded to Christianity its status as a Dharma, albeit a bad one, the MP apologists were faced with the task of fitting it into an interpretive framework. In other words, having once admitted that Christianity exists, they had to explain why. Consequently, one finds in their respective treatises general schemes of Dharma tantamount to theologies of religions. For the most part, these schemes were not novel; they drew upon preexisting patterns for interpreting intrareligious plurality. Just as the religious history of Hinduism afforded ample scope for applying to Christianity criticism that had already circulated and become standardized, the pandits (Hara. and Nīla. more than Soma.) found a place for Christianity in their schemes of Dharma in much the same way that Hindus were used to accounting for differences among themselves.

When analyzing the pandits' resolutions of religious plurality, one should bear in mind the third *lakṣaṇa*, universality (*sāmānyatā*), which Muir proposed as a characteristic of the Satya Dharma. Whereas the pandits conceded to Christianity its status as a Dharma, they could by no means acquiesce to this claim. The idea that all people, wherever and whenever they live, are duty-bound to accept one religion, whether Muir's or another, was the pivot on which the pandits' schemes of Dharma turned. Of course, Muir's insistence upon Christianity's universality was, in a reverse sense, analogous to Hinduism's particularity, or its traditional reluctance to accredit other religions as genuine Dharmas, but it nonetheless struck the pandits as audacious. Both positions denied that other religions are salvific, but only Christians boasted — or so it seemed to the pandits — that they were eager to make other people shift their allegiance from one Dharma to another.

Therefore, although the main purpose of this chapter is to inquire into ways in which the pandits resolved the issue of religious plurality, it is also worthwhile to assess their schemes of Dharma with respect to the subject of tolerance. To say how one should relate oneself to another Dharma is closely connected to one's answer to why that other Dharma exists. The pandits had much to say about proper conduct and attitudes towards differing doctrines and individuals who subscribe to them. One should not, however, expect to find consistency in their remarks, either with regard to the subject of tolerance or their schemes of Dharma. These were not systematic treatises on the theology of religions as Hindu and Christian authors now write them. Each pandit approached these subjects from a different angle; only after examining them individually is it possible to extrapolate some general principles which they shared in common.

To repeat, it is to be observed in all of the following that, in the context of the MP Controversy, there was neither a uniform scheme of Dharma into which Christianity was placed nor a uniform concept of tolerance and its opposite.[158]

MPŚ: The Unity and Compatibility of Religions

Soma.'s approach to religious plurality was rooted in twin concepts, the unity of religions (*mataikya*) and their noncontradictoriness (*matāvirodha*), ideas which he expounded at length in the first two chapters of the MPŚ bearing those titles respectively (see p. 92, *supra*). These concepts are

[158] With reference to the subject of tolerance and intolerance, terminology will be utilized from two sources: P. Hacker's "Religiöse Toleranz und Intoleranz im Hinduismus" (1957) and G. Mensching's Tolerance and Truth in Religion (1971). Hacker distinguishes between practical and doctrinal tolerance. By the former he means "die menschliche Duldung von Angehörigen fremder Religionen, die darin besteht, daß diese nicht wegen ihrer Religion schlechter behandelt werden als Glieder der eigenen Religionsgemeinschaft." Practical tolerance is further divided into noninterference in matters of religion accorded by the state ("staatliche Toleranz") and tolerance of individuals towards members of other religions ("private Toleranz"). Doctrinal Tolerance is defined as "das Geltenlassen der Lehren einer fremden Religion" (Hacker, 1957: 168). Intolerance, of course, is simply the antithesis of each category but can also be either active or passive (1957:171). Mensching's terminology is similar to Hacker's but more elaborate. Hacker's "staatliche Toleranz" corresponds to Mensching's "formal tolerance"; "doktrinäre Toleranz" to tolerance toward the content of other religions, which Mensching expressed as "positive acknowledgement of a foreign religion as a genuine and legitimate religious possibility of encounter with the sacred." Intolerance toward the content rather than the form of other religions occurs when they are "repudiated or even attacked and persecuted because they are regarded as untrue and misleading in content." Formal tolerance may, of course, occur as part of a policy of political expedience. Mensching, therefore, refers to tolerance toward another religion's content as "intrinsic." These terms combine in various concatenations: "formal intolerance together with intrinsic intolerance; formal tolerance in connection with intrinsic intolerance; formal intolerance bound up with intrinsic tolerance" (Mensching, 1971: 11—12, *passim*). Mensching may have improved upon Hacker's terminology, but sophisticated classifications cannot compensate for inadequate attention to the religious history of Hinduism. Suspicion is strong that Mensching was able to conclude that Hinduism has tolerance "in [its] blood" (1971: 64) only by means of a highly selective discussion of Ṛg Vedic passages (e. g., 1.164.46), the Bhagavad-Gītā (9.23), and S. Radhakrishnan, in whom the "spirit" of these passages had "remained alive right into contemporary Hinduism" (1971: 67). In between these references is a great deal of Purāṇic literature bearing on the subject of tolerance which Hacker wisely took into consideration, coming to the conclusion that it is impossible to speak, as Mensching did, of Hinduism as a whole simply in terms of tolerance or intolerance (Hacker, 1957: 179). For this reason, Hacker spoke at length also about "inclusivism," which is neither adaptation nor syncretism but a tendency to see the beliefs of others as stages on the way to one's own doctrine (see, e. g., his discussion of this in relation to the Pāñcarātrins and others, 1957: 177ff.; also Gonda, 1970: 94—95).

deceptively similar to certain formulations often heard nowadays as definitions of the Hindu attitude toward other religions, among them the following: all religions are equal; all religions are one; all religions are true; all religions are the same.[159] So prevalent are these formulations that the liklihood is considerable that they will interfere with a proper interpretation of the most irenic passage to be found in the MPŚ, which was translated earlier (p. 92, *supra*). "Worship him, the universal *ātman*, true lord, who is honored as the 'Buddha' in the Buddhist *darśana*, 'Jina' in the Jain scripture, known by the name 'Christ' in the Christian religion and as 'Allah' in the Mohammadan religion, and by the names 'Arka,' 'Prathameśa,' 'Śakti,' 'Girīśā,' 'Śrīśa' and so forth in the three-fold [science], various Tantras, and Purāṇas." Did Soma. intend by this to say — to repeat the formulations above — that Buddhism, Jainism, Christianity, Islam, and Hinduism in its various subgroups are equal as religions? That they are all one, true, and the same? Without extensive qualifications, each of these adjectives ("equal," "one," "true," "same") reinforces unwarranted simplification and misunderstanding. The procedure here is to take each of these formulations alternately, assessing their strengths and weaknesses in connection with five other clarifying passages from the MPŚ, which are presented below in their textual order.

A) "Since in everyone's religion there is some world-creator, all people worship him and consequently attain [him]. And everywhere scriptures are spoken by God for the sake of the human intellect; no one, [however], who has not understood them in due order by means of a guru, is released... Now, by no means does he attain *mukti* in any path, whose whole knowledge of the heart's misery is merely verbal, whose consciousness is injured and destroyed by the flood of poison in sense-objects, who is indifferent to worshipping Hari and intent upon his own business."[160]

B) "In the Kali Age, whosoever spurn their respective scriptures are sinners, even though they be brahmins, etc., because everyone's own religion is always conducive to felicity."[161]

---

[159] For these specific formulations and aspects of the subsequent analysis, the present writer is indebted to an article by A. SHARMA (1979), but differs from his conclusions with respect to tolerance in Hinduism.

[160] *Asti kaścij jagatkartā sarveṣām api yan mate / sarve 'pi taṃ niṣevaṃte taraṃty eva tataś ca te // sarvatra ceśvaroktāni saṃti śāstrāṇi buddhaye / gurvānupūrvyāvijñāya tāni ko vā na mucyate //* (MPŚ 1.6—7) *atha yadi mukhamātreṇa rtitāśeṣavidyo hṛdi viṣayaviṣaughadhvastaśastaprabodhaḥ / haribhajanaviraktaḥ svīyakāryaprasaktaḥ katham api pathi kutrāpy eṣāṃ muktiṃ na yāti //* (MPŚ 1.9).

[161] *Viprādayo 'pi ye kecit svasvaśāstratyajaḥ kalau / pāpāḥ svadharmaḥ sarveṣāṃ yataḥ śreyaskaraḥ sadā //* (MPŚ 2.43). Cf. Mṛtyuñjaya Vidyālaṅkāra's defense of traditional Hinduism against the aspersions of Rammohun Roy: "If anyone among you wishes to attain the exhalted mansion of God, ... will he renounce the absolute authority contained in his peculiar Scriptures [the Vedas, Bible and Koran are mentioned]; will he desert the path prepared and pursued by ancient sages, scatter thorns and mud in the way, or tread in a new path prepared by himself? He who pursues the path which his own religion points out, shall surely be recompensed" (1817: 34—35).

C) "Men who travel on other roads are not said to be competent for the Vedic *mārga.* It is for this reason that Hari would be displeased when someone spurns his own religion."[162]

D) "When men who dwell in various quarters are going to a certain city, in no way whatsoever would they ever reach it by [travelling] only on one path. Likewise, those men, whom the all-creator made to possess different qualifications (*adhikāra*) and [put into] different situations, would be unable to attain God by means of any single path."[163]

E) "You should never revile people who are satisfied with their own religion! ... Oh, oh! Listen you disciples of Christ! I, solicitous of [your] welfare, tell you this truthfully: it is absolutely true that one should not revile the religion of another. One should not, moreover, spurn one's own religion... Diminution of Hari's religion, anger, cruelty, subversion of authority, and dissension among the populace would result from reviling the religion of others. Increase of God's religion, contentment, gentleness, harmony between the ranks [of society], and friendship among the populace would result from praising all religions. For each person his own religion is best; the same religion would be perilous for another person. Now, therefore, praise be to those who worship Hari according to their religion without reviling other [paths]."[164]

If one takes the first formulation, all religions are equal, in the sense that all religions are equally valid irrespective of individual differences (A. Sharma, 1979: 59), does this mean Soma. was an advocate of interfaith prayer or multiple religious-allegiance, as M. Chatterjee has phrased it (1976: 123)? The MPŚ, in its entire context, cannot be taken as support for either form of catholicity; indeed, to exchange one's religion for another was identified by this pandit as a grave sin occurring in the Kali Yuga (extract B).[165] To call prayerfully upon God as Hari is not the same as to call upon

---

[162] *Vedamārgārhatā noktā nṛṇāṃ anyādhvagāmināṃ / ataḥ svamatasaṃtyāgo neṣṭaḥ syāt kasyacid dhareḥ //* (MPŚ 3.10).

[163] *Nānādigvinivāsino 'tra manujā yāṃto yadaikaṃ puraṃ hy aikenaiva pathā kathaṃ cana yathā na prāpnuyuḥ sarvathā / tadvad viśvakṛtā kṛtāḥ sthitibhidā bhinnādhikārā narās te taṃ naikatamena kenacid api prāptuṃ prabhuṃ śaknuyuḥ //* (MPŚ 3.35).

[164] *Svadharmaniratān lokān mā niṃdiṣṭa kadā cana //* (MPŚ 3.38b) *bho bho khṛṣṭānuśiṣṭāḥ śṛṇuta hitarato vacmi vas tathyam etad dharmo nānyasya niṃdyaḥ punar atha na nijas tyājya ityeva tattvaṃ //* (3.39b) *dharmahānir hareḥ kopaḥ krūratvaṃ rājyavicyutiḥ / janabhedaś ca jāyeta paradharmasya niṃdanāt // dharmavṛddhir vibhos toṣaḥ saumyatā padasaṃgamaḥ / janamaitrī ca jayeta sarvadharmapraśaṃsanāt // śreyān svadharmaḥ sakalasya jaṃtoḥ sa eva cānyasya bhayāvahaḥ syāt / ataḥ svadharmeṇa hariṃ bhajadbhyaḥ parān aniṃdadbhya idaṃ namo 'stu //* (MPŚ 3.42—44).

[165] The Viṣṇupurāṇa (6.1.44—47) e. g., describes the increased tempo of the Kali Yuga (*kalivṛddhi*) as follows: "Whenever there is noticed an increase [in the number] of the heretics, then, oh Maitreya, should the full swing of Kali be estimated by the wise. Whenever there is a decrease in the number of the good who follow the path of the Vedas, and the efforts of those who cultivate Dharma relax, then, Maitreya, the

him as Christ or Buddha, etc., because each name is only one part of a complex of religious ideas and practices designed for a particular kind of person or nation of like-minded individuals.

In this connection, it is useful to recall what Subājī said earlier in the LṬ with respect to *mlecchas*. It was noted there (*vide* p. 91, *supra*) that non-Hindu cultures are unable, because of their geographic location in northerly climates, to observe the *varṇāśrama* system. The weather is too severe and nights too long for brahmins to maintain their purity by ritual observances. "Since those who live [in *mleccha* countries] are powerless to perform ritual activities, Bhagavān, having undertaken to become an *avatāra*, bestowed on them a theistic-scripture, in their very language, so that they may attain contentment — but only by good behavior other than this [e. g., *snāna* and *saṃdhyā*]" (*vide* p. 91, n. 80, *supra*). Religious plurality, therefore, is a reflection of geographical realities and the breakdown of the system of caste and stages of life. Extract A reinforces this point: the same God gives to all men their respective scriptures, but not all of them have brahmins or gurus who can explicate those sacred books in such a way that their full salvific potential is realized. Corresponding to geographical differences are racial or ethnic pecularities showing that mankind has various needs, tastes, abilities, etc. "Since God made men with particular natures, those belonging to a specific race must follow a particular scripture uttered by God. If only one scripture is agreeable to God, why did he, lord of the world, not make mankind single-natured? For this very reason, that he made spatial, temporal, and other differences, it would be perfectly certain that differences between scriptures would also be quite pleasing to him" (*vide* p. 92, n. 81, *supra*). The corollary, of course, is that God looks unfavorably upon conversion because converts act contrary to the grain of their nature as God made it. Therefore, according to Soma.'s position, one must add to the formulation, all religions are equal, the qualification that they are equally valid only for particular groups of individuals; there can be no crossing over (A. Sharma, 1979: 59); and prayer addressed to Viṣṇu does not have the same value for a Christian that it has for a Hindu or, to be more exact, a Vaiṣṇava.

A more promising sense in which one could say that, from the standpoint of the MPŚ, all religions are equal, is the formulation that they are equal as paths, ways, approaches, or *mārgas*. All lead upward, albeit some more directly than others because they have trained guides (gurus and brahmins) to point the way (extract A). This aspect of equivalency brings out two facets of Soma.'s apologetics. First, it countered Muir's claim to *sāmānyatā* by making each religion purposeful, but only with reference to its

---

predominance of Kali should be guessed by the learned... When the people do not show respect to the sayings of the Vedas but are inclined towards the heretics, then, oh best of the twice-born, the augmented influence of the Kali age should be inferred" (Hazra, 1975: 207).

own adherents. Second, it illustrates the process of inclusivism: Hari, who condescends to meet the diverse needs of human beings in their respective cultural and geographical settings, is identical with the deity in each religion. Soma. thereby reduced Christianity to an upstart religion making extravagant claims about universality.

With reference to the second formulation, all religions are one, if by this one means that their content is identical (A. SHARMA, 1979: 61), then this cannot lead to a proper understanding of the MPŚ. It was not the case that Soma. found in the *khṛṣṭadharma* what he knew, as a Hindu, to be truth. A less outspoken critic of Christianity than either Hara. or Nīla., Soma. nonetheless dismissed its beliefs concerning justification and nonhuman life as false. On these grounds he saw the two religions as mutually contradictory. Likewise, he did not concede that Muir's positions were identical, in part or in whole, with his own. In his view Christianity is not only different from Hinduism but false as well.

A more exact formulation would be to say religions are identical with respect to purpose: each one is "conducive to felicity" (*śreyaskāra*; extract B). Though fit only for certain types of travellers, they are all roads leading to the same goal from sometimes diametrically opposed directions. The purpose of calling upon Hari — finding felicity, especially in *mokṣa* — is the same as prayer to any other deity. Therefore, the identity between religions is one of function and purpose instead of content. The "noncontradictoriness" (*matāvirodha*) to which Soma. referred must not be understood as denial of doctrinal differences between religions, but rather that Dharmas do not work at cross-purposes with each other, except when one attempts to eliminate others.

To say that Soma.'s position was that all religions are true is, without further qualification, also a misunderstanding. The previous paragraphs have already made clear that his resolution of religious plurality did not reduce differences between religions to mere appearance. But even though Christianity and Hinduism are not both true with respect to doctrine, both are, paradoxically, paths to truth. There is a sense, therefore, in which Viṣṇu who gives to all men their scriptures, speaks contradictorily. The conclusion, which shows the tendency of inclusivism, is somewhat self-serving: if Christianity, even though false, leads to Hari anyway, how much more directly must Hinduism. The novelty in the MPŚ is that this process of subordination was applied to a religion of non-Indian origin, as it had not been as a rule in the past. The Yogavāsiṣṭharāmāyaṇa, for instance, contains the following passages: "Oh Rāma! The ideas of creation consisting of *ahaṅkāra*, *manas*, *buddhi*, etc., which have been described by me as modifications of one, are differently described by the students of Nyāya, Sāṅkhya, and Materialism. The followers of Jaimini, Ārhats, Buddhists, adherents of Vaiśeṣika and various others such as the Pāñcarātras have done the same in a different manner. All of them, however, will go to the same eternal goal as passengers from different places travelling at different times reach a particular city".[166] With such precedents as this available, one can see that the most insightful formulation of Soma.'s standpoint is that all religions are true only in the sense of being paths to truth. To invert this order would be, as A. SHARMA observes, "identifying the path with the truth, the means with the end" (1979: 63).

With respect to the formulation, all religions are the same, one can already rule out the possibility that Soma. meant they are identical either in terms of content, value, or truth. Again, it is their function, purpose, or goal that does not differ. But in this connection attention must be drawn to the lesson (*vide* extract E) that Soma. wanted, on the basis of this kind of sameness, to teach his readers. The didactic tone of this passage distinguishes it from others, for there he was scolding a blasphemer, or so Muir seemed to him. To claim universality for one's own religion is indirectly to impugn others. The reason for praising instead of reviling other religions goes beyond the mere fact of their function as paths; it includes also the idea that each person has an *adhikāra*, i.e., eligibility, fitness, competence, aptitude for, even a right or entitlement bordering on obligation to, one particular Dharma. A religion is meant to be observed throughout one's life, because one's birth as a Christian or Hindu is not accidental but in accordance with *karman* acquired in previous lives.

With these ideas in the background, Soma.'s admonition in extract E can now be rephrased as follows: "You started life on one particular path, follow it to the end!" As a modern illustration of this message, a quotation from an article by Swami B. H. BON MAHARAJ is useful (1965: 2—3), for it has many resonances in the foregoing MPŚ extracts. "An individual in its state of self-forgetfulness and bondage cannot unfold his or her cognitional faculty of the pure self. It is, therefore, said that a fallen soul... must approach a spiritual master [extract A] in order to know the real truth. This means that an individual must have developed through practises in various births a given degree of intellectual and moral maturity before he or she can aspire to understand, practise, follow and realize absolute knowledge... It is because of this that [Hinduism] had never been proselytizing or converting others into its fold. One has got to go through many births... in religions of partial or relative truths before one is born with the requisite intellectual and moral eligibility [*adhikāra*] to practice [Hinduism]." This corresponds well with Soma.'s position, although the phraseology is distinctly Advaitic: the worth or purpose of any Dharma should never be denied absolutely (A. SHARMA, 1979: 67), a mistake which Muir had made with regard to Hinduism. Everyone is on an upward path, yet for some travellers the paths are steeper and more arduous climbing.

---

[166] *Ahaṃkāramanobuddhidṛṣṭayaḥ sṛṣṭikalpanāḥ / ekarūpatayā proktā yā mayā raghunandana // naiyāyikair itarathā tādṛśaiḥ parikalpitāḥ / anyathā kalpitāḥ sāṃkhyaiś cārvākair api cānyathā // jaiminīyaiś cārhataiś ca bauddhair vaiseṣikais tathā / anyair api vicitrais taiḥ pāñcarātrādibhis tathā // sarvair api ca gantavyaṃ taiḥ padaṃ pāramārthikaṃ / vicitraṃ deśakālotthaiḥ puram ekam ivādhvagaiḥ //* (Utpattiprakaraṇa 96.48—51).

The final line of extract E is crucial in discerning a certain barb in Soma.'s otherwise irenic resolution of religious plurality: "Now, therefore, praise be to those who worship Hari according to their religion without reviling other [paths]!" The superiority of Hindu Dharma, then, is not so much its insight into the nature of truth as its profound grasp of the unity (*aikya*) and compatibility (*avirodha*) of mankind's diverse religions. One is reminded of GEORGE ORWELL's maxim that all men are equal, but some more than others.

To recapitulate in a phrase, Soma.'s scheme of Dharma, into which he placed Christianity, is path-oriented. It is a case of unity in diversity, the unity especially of all deities in Viṣṇu, and a clear instance of inclusivism. In HACKER's terms, the tolerance generated by this scheme was doctrinal, practical, and private. In MENSCHING's terms, it was both formal and intrinsic.

MPO: *extra Vedos nulla salus*

Hara.'s theological animus toward Christianity has already been noted with respect to its severity. But his pugilistic stance and unabashed rumor-mongering must not obscure the thoroughly orthodox conception of revelation underlying his apologetics: the eternal preexistence of the Vedas. Since these sacred books are coeval with creation, Hara. dismissed the Khṛṣṭadharma as juvenile, bereft of the prestige of antiquity: "Only that religion is true which has prevailed on earth since the time of creation, and not one which arose subsequently" (p. 94, n. 85, *supra*). "If there is to be faith in a book, let it be in the Veda, since it has prevailed on earth from the time of creation onward!" (p. 99, n. 95, *supra*). "Why would learned people trust in [Muir's] religion, which was propounded by Christ when much time had passed?"[167] The message of these passages is clearly a warning that one must not settle for anything less than the most ancient of all scriptures, the Vedas, which Brahmā preserves throughout each successive *kalpa*. In this connection, the question of access to the Vedas comes to the forefront of Hara.'s resolution of religious plurality.

Who, then, has access to the Vedas? What kind of people are they? Attention has already focused upon Soma.'s moderate attitude toward *mlecchas*, their social disabilities due to the climatic adversities of their locales, and Viṣṇu's condescension to equip them with *śāstras* substituting for the Vedas. Like the LṬ, the MPO also related the question of access to divine truth to the *varṇāśrama* system, but without offering as much in the way of alternatives as the former treatise did. In order to understand Hara.'s place for Christianity in the general scheme of Dharma, it must be seen in the context of the following passage: "At the time of creation, only four *varṇas*

---

[167] *Yāte bahutare kāle khṛṣṭadvārā svakaṃ mataṃ / jñāpayām āsa kenātra viśvāso viduṣāṃ bhavet* // (MPO 1.15; p. 2).

could be created. Brahmā made for them the character of good *dharma*. How could the eternal Vedic religion be observed by *yavanas* and others, who have fallen from their *dharma* on account of corrupt conduct? The character of *dharma* consists of ten elements: constancy, patience, self-control, avoidance of thievery, purity, restraint of senses, devout thought, knowledge, truth, and suppression of anger. Thus, their entire lives lived in accordance with these general *dharmas*, they [become] eligible [*adhikārins*] for [Vedic] *dharma*, having become Hindus [*hindutvaṃ prāpya*] in a subsequent birth."[168] Throughout this extract are a number of assumptions directly bearing upon the subject of access to the Vedas or, to be more precise, the Vedic or Sanātana Dharma. All of these are connected with the term *yavana*, which may here be taken as a comprehensive term for non-Hindus rather than specifically Western, Grecian, or Islamic people, to whom the word has been applied at various points in the record of its usage. *Yavana* in this context is nearly synonymous with *mleccha*, although it may be less slanderous.[169] If they are, mutatis mutandis, substantially the same, then whatever light Hindu literature throws upon them will be useful for knowing how Hara. approached the matter of religious plurality.

The first of these assumptions is that *yavanas* have fallen (*bhraṣṭa*) from Vedic *dharma*. A status which they once had they have no longer. The reason why *yavanas*, in Hara.'s view, have fallen from grace, in the sense of losing certain soteriological privileges, is probably the very one from which Soma., as already noted, deviated: they are the offspring of *pratiloma* marriages between, according to the usual combination, a *kṣatriya* father and *śūdra* mother (Halbfass, 1980: 190). Another possibility is that they were formerly *kṣatriyas* who became *śūdras* because they failed to perform sacred rites in consultation with brahmins (*vide* Manu 10.43—44). As they are off to a bad start due to conduct contrary to the grain of *dharma*, *yavanas* experience the malaise of degeneration. They do not speak Sanskrit, a characteristic feature of Āryan civilization, and this disability is intrinsic to *mlecchas* (Halbfass, 1980: 193).[170] They are outside of the *varṇāśrama* system, excluded from initiation (*upanayana*), and, therefore, from the Veda itself. Manu 12.33—43 relegates them to *tamas*, the condition of darkness, implying ignorance, sensuality, covetousness, sleepiness, pusillanimity, cruelty, atheism, and

---

[168] *Catvāra eva varṇāḥ syuḥ sṛṣṭikāle vinirmitāḥ / teṣāṃ kṛte sudharmasya lakṣaṇaṃ brahmaṇā kṛtaṃ // duṣṭācāreṇa ye bhraṣṭāḥ svadharmād yavanādayaḥ / kathaṃ taiḥ sevyamāno 'stu vedadharmaḥ sanātanaḥ // dhṛtiḥ kṣama damo 'steyaṃ śaucam indriyanigrahaḥ / dhīr vidyā satyam akrodho daśakaṃ dharmalakṣaṇaṃ / evaṃ sādhāraṇair dharmair yāpitāśeṣajīvanāḥ / parajanmani hindutvaṃ prāpya dharmādhikāriṇaḥ //* (MPO 1.68—71; p. 8).

[169] For information on the development of and variations in these terms, see Halbfass, 1981: 195ff.

[170] Of course, the MP, a Sanskrit treatise, worked against this aspect of the word *mleccha*. But the idea that *mlecchas* are, according to tradition, ignorant of Sanskrit may be the reason why Hara. felt compelled to accuse Muir of writing that language poorly (*yādṛśaṃ saṃskṛtaṃ tena likhitaṃ tat tu nottamaṃ / nipuṇāḥ paṇḍitā yasmān na bhāvārthāvabodhane / samarthāḥ kevalaṃ*, etc., MPO 3.2; p. 16).

inattentiveness: "Elephants, horses, *śūdras*, and despicable barbarians [*mlecchas*], lions, tigers, and boars [are] the middling states, caused by [the quality of] darkness" (12.43; BÜHLER, 1969: 493). One can sink lower, but not much.

Yet another assumption on Hara.'s part is that, despite these severe handicaps, *yavanas* have acquired a modicum of *dharma*. They are not entirely bereft of order-enforcing virtues, but the few that they have learned are extremely general and ordinary: constancy (*dhṛti*), patience (*kṣamā*), self-control (*dama*), avoidance of thievery (*asteya*), purity (*śauca*), restraint of senses (*indriyanigraha*), devout thought (*dhī*), knowledge (*vidyā*), truth (*satya*), suppression of anger (*akrodha*). It may not be a coincidence that these duties correspond to a similar list of *dharmas* in the Mahābhārata (12.65.17—22), where Indra explained to King Māndhātṛ, an Āryan, the behavior to which his *yavana*, *śaka*, and other non-Āryan subjects must conform (*vide* KANE, 1941: 384).[171] Both the Śāntiparva and the MPO are evidence of a willingness on the part of some Hindu authorities to allot to *mlecchas* a small measure of dignity and hope. They may be corrupt and low-bred, their conduct mean and despicable (*duṣṭācāra*) in contrast to the well-bred and enlightened living (*śiṣṭācāra*) of twice-born Hindus, but at least they can improve their lot by observance of these ordinary duties, which are the minimum for all mankind. One can say that, by practicing these *dharmas* throughout their entire lives, the *yavanas* are, according to Hara., debarbarized.

However, more than merely moral improvement is at stake. *Yavanas* live a life that is a kind of purgatory for acquiring merit in order to reenter the state of grace from which they have fallen. By refraining from the behavior to which their status predisposes them, they acquire a fitness, aptitude, competence for, and right to (*adhikāra*) the Hindu Dharma, which is specific and exclusive instead of general. This transition to a higher plane of religion cannot occur within the space of a single lifetime; death must intervene, followed by rebirth as a Hindu.

One can see that the scheme of Dharma into which Hara. accommodated Christianity was Hinducentric, revolving around the concept of *hindutva*, or existence as a Hindu. This term may be a neologism,[172] but its connections with earlier conceptions about Bhārata, or India, as *karmabhūmi* are secure. In the religious cosmography of the Hindus, Bhārata, or Āryāvarta, is the land of the Āryas or *dvijas*, the boundaries of which are mentioned in Manu 2.22—23. Encompassing this region are countries inhabited by *mlecchas*.

---

[171] Cf. especially verse 20: *ahiṃsā satyam akrodho vṛttidāyānupālanaṃ / bharaṇaṃ putradārāṇāṃ śaucam adroha eva ca //*.

[172] Subsequently *hindutva*, in consonance with its current usage, became a codeword in the Indian nationalist movement, as in V. D. SAVARKAR's Marathi treatise Hindutva (Bombay, 1923; for analysis see D. SMITH, 1963: 458—60, and KLIMKEIT, 1978: 311ff.). There is, however, a Bengali tract by the same title published in 1892 by an author named CANDRANĀTHA VĀSU in Calcutta, in which the concept does not connect with nationalistic aspirations.

Obtaining birth as a Hindu in *karmabhūmi* is a rare soteriological privilege, because only there can one hope to forestall adverse karmic repercussions, undergo *upanayana*, and acquire the *tattvajñāna* necessary for breaking out of *saṃsāra* and the round of rebirth. This is not a privilege for man in general; it is for Hindus only. "Es ist als *karmabhūmi* ausgezeichnet, als Land, in dem das *karman*, die Macht früherer Taten, aktiv gesteuert oder auch aufgehoben werden kann, in dem der Weg zur Erlösung aus dem Kreislauf der Geburten und Tode (*saṃsāra*) eingeschlagen werden kann. Hier herrscht der *dharma* und gibt dem Lande einen religiös-sittlichen und soteriologischen Sonderstatus" (HALBFASS, 1981: 197; *vide* also 1977: 228—29).[173] In view of this religious cosmography, one can see that, in Hara.'s approach to plurality in religion, Christianity's soteriological value is merely provisional; it is both a step downwards from Hinduism and a step upward towards it. Although one may fall into this religion because of adverse *karman*, one may at least observe its *dharma* and thereby recover lost ground in a subsequent birth.

This Hinducentric scheme of Dharma also accounts for the MPO's ambivalence toward Christian doctrine. Of course, Hara. made an effort to answer Muir on several points, but the impression is strong that he was debunking and ridiculing rather than reasoning seriously with Christianity. After all, the Bible, according to his presuppositions, was post-Vedic, and, therefore, excluded from close attention and fit mostly for sarcasm. Such perfunctory dismissal of non-Vedic *śāstras* was not unknown in the religious history of Hinduism. For example, Madhūsudana Sarasvatī's harmonization of Hindu *darśanas*, the Prasthānabheda, defends its omission of philosophical and religious ways and methods (*prasthāna*) used by *mlecchas* by noting that they exist outside of the Vedas (*vedabāhyatva*) and are inefficacious with respect to the goals of human endeavor (*puruṣārthānupayogatva*).[174] In his translation of this treatise, P. DEUSSEN was prompted to remark editorially, *extra Vedos nulla salus*, emending the well-known Roman Catholic maxim (1906: 46). For Hara. as well as for the author of the Prasthānabheda, *mlecchaśāstras* have no authoritativeness (*pramāṇatva*) and can either be ignored or ridiculed by Hindus.

---

[173] In later times, *karmabhūmi* was reinterpreted, in accordance with modern Hindu universalism, to mean the whole earth instead of Bhārata only. In VIVEKANANDA's view, "This earth is called the *karma-bhūmi*, the sphere of *karma*. Here alone man makes his good or bad *karma*" (quoted in HALBFASS, 1981: 389). At other times the swami reverted to the traditional idea: "If there is any land on this earth that can lay claim to be blessed Punya-bhumi, to be the land to which souls on this earth must come to account for Karma, the land to which every soul that is wending its way Godward must come to attain its last home, ... it is INDIA" (quoted in NAIPAUL, 1977: 149). Even M. K. GANDHI sometimes spoke about salvation with an Indocentric bias: "For me there can be no deliverance from this earthly life except in India. Anyone who seeks such deliverance ... must go to the sacred soil of India" (NAIPAUL, 1977: 156).

[174] *Evaṃ militvā nāstikānāṃ ṣaṭprasthānāni / tāni kasmān nocyante / satyaṃ / vedavāhyatvāt teṣāṃ mlechādiprasthānavat paramparyāpi puruṣārthānupayogitvād upekṣaṇīyam eva /* (WEBER, 1850: 13—14; see also HALBFASS, 1981: 210).

However, even though salvation apart from the Veda is impossible, in Hara.'s scheme of Dharma, Christianity has at least a tutelary function. Hierarchically, it is strictly subordinate to Hinduism. It is a purgatory in which fallen beings acquire the aptitude and fitness to become eligible for the Hindu Dharma in *karmabhūmi*. As with the MPŚ, humankind is segregated into groups having greater and lesser soteriological privileges.

With respect to the subject of tolerance, it is clear that Hara.'s case is unlike Soma.'s. To use HACKER's terminology, the MPO advocated both practical and doctrinal intolerance. As practical intolerance, it was active instead of merely passive. According to MENSCHING's categories it was intrinsic intolerance of Christianity's content. One would even speculate, on the basis of the stridently militant passages of the MPO translated in the previous chapter (see pp. 93—94), that Hara. would have recommended to the reigning monarch, had he been Hindu instead of British, "staatliche Intoleranz" and the banishment of converts to the Khr̥ṣṭadharma (*vide* Manu 9.225).

ŚTV: Christianity as a Dharma of Delusion

The apologetics of the ŚTV was based upon yet a third scheme of Dharma, which brings this study into contact with Purāṇic interpretations of intrareligious plurality within Hinduism itself. Evidently Nīla. was influenced by a stream of thought inclined toward active intolerance, involving not only the idea that worshippers of gods other than one's own are heretics (e.g., Padmapurāṇa 6.234.27: *avaiṣṇavas tu yo vipraḥ sa pāṣaṇḍaḥ prakīrtitaḥ*; ABS, 1926: 387), but also the notion that the heresies or heterodoxies (*nāstikya, vedabāhyatva, pākhaṇḍa, pāṣaṇḍa*)[175] which those devotees follow are delusions (*moha*)[176] brought upon them intentionally by one deity or another. In other connections one finds the analogous ideas of false *avatāras* and delusive scriptures (*moha-* or *tāmasaśāstras*) as factors accounting for the delusive Dharma (*mohadharma*). With these precedents to account for intrareligious diversities within Nīla.'s religion, it will be seen that, either by direct or indirect implication, he equated the *khr̥ṣṭadharma* with other *mohadharmas*, Christ with false *avatāras*, and the Bible with *mohaśāstras*. But this scheme of Dharma, or anti-Dharma, was not thoroughly consistent or unambiguous, and attention will need to be drawn to several, perhaps only apparent rather than real, contradictions.

The preponderance of ŚTV passages translated in the previous chapter show that, among the three pandits, Nīla. was the one who took the content of Christianity most seriously. This fact is probably to be attributed to his regular encounters with the Reverend William Smith, his partner-in-dia-

---

[175] According to J. GONDA, *pāṣaṇḍa* "denotes any person who, or doctrine which, is hypocritical, or heretical and falsely assumes the characteristics of 'orthodoxy'" (1970: 201, n. 167). Other definitions may be found in W. O'FLAHERTY, 1971: 272—73.

[176] For philological analysis of *moha*, derived from the causative form of the root *muh* (to be confused, bewildered, etc.), see A. GAIL, 1969: 918.

logue, before whom he needed to defend Hinduism vis-à-vis Christianity with reference to specific doctrines. But this should not obscure the other fact that Christianity was basically objectionable to Nīla., as it had been to Hara., on two points: its rejection of the Vedas and *varṇāsramas*.[177] In terms of content, it is not only false (*asat*, 2.14, p. 6), child's play (*bāladhīgamya-*, *bāladhīkalpita-*, 3.51, p. 29), and uttered by and for fools (*mugdhoditārthaka-*, *baliśokta-*, 2.29, 77, 138, pp. 8, 13, 19), it is also meant to thoroughly delude simpletons (*bāliśānāṃ vimohāya*, 2.103, 127, pp. 15, 18). Verses 3.39—40 (p. 28) repeat the idea that there is in Christianity an element of perverse dishonesty under the guise of its doctrines: "All these and other things in your religion seem as though contrived in order to totally delude simpletons: [the doctrine that] the nature of *mokṣa* is enjoyment of sense-objects; lack of a way to salvation for animals; omitting to talk about multiple births; the opinion that only one existence is observed; the messenger who corrupts the mind [i. e., Satan], etc."[178] According to this analysis of Christianity's content, its falsehood is more than epistemological error; it is not merely excluded from the *varṇāśrama* system and Vedas, as Soma. and Hara. would have it; it is also a punitive disability for those "simpletons" who embrace it or who are born into it.

In 6a.196—201 (p. 66), Nīla. shed more light on who these unfortunate people are, the cause of their low aptitude, and the reason why this religion is foisted upon them. "Now, whichever Smṛtis should be reviled and shunned by the orthodox, God created so that sinners will be punished... These bad ways are made for their punishment. Only sinful people, for instance, take pleasure in them. Again and again into a foul hell God flings filthy-minded rogues who delight in depraved behavior, longing to commit deeds yielding much misfortune but little that is desirable. This, for example, God plainly teaches through the scripture: those Smṛtis are made in order to give punishment to wicked people. For this very reason, those who acquiesce to God's instruction, performing meritorious deeds faithfully, do not believe in those Smṛtis."[179] By observing the *khṛṣṭadharma*, Christians are therefore

---

177 In this connection, it is worthwhile to note that Śrīdhara, in the Nyāyakandalī, said that "the Veda is known to be the work of a Superior Being (*puruṣaviśeṣa*), because its message is unquestionably accepted by all who belong to the *varṇāśrama* order of society," whereas Buddhist and Jain scriptures are not (HANDIQUI, 1949: 390).

178 *Mokṣo viṣayabhogātmā gatyabhāvas tathā paśoḥ / anekajanmākathanaṃ dṛṣṭaikabhavasammatiḥ // cittadūṣakadūtādyā ye 'rthāś cānye bhavanmate / saṃmohanāya bālānāṃ kalpitā iva bhānti te //.*

179 *Atha yāḥ smṛtayaḥ kāścin nindyās tyaktāś ca vaidikaiḥ / pāpināṃ daṇḍabhogārtham īśas tā udapādayat // avaśyaṃ pāpināṃ daṇḍo bhavatām api saṃmataḥ / tathaiva teṣāṃ daṇḍārthaṃ kadadhvānaḥ kṛtā ime // tathā hi ye narāḥ pāpā rocayante ta eva tāḥ / bahvanarthāvahālpeṣṭadāyikarmasu lolupāḥ // dhūrtā doṣayutācāraratā malinabuddhayaḥ / punaḥ punar bhagavatā pātyante narake 'śucau // tathā hi śāstradvāraitad vyaktaṃ bodhayatīśvaraḥ / duṣṭānāṃ daṇḍadānārthaṃ smṛtayas tāḥ kṛtā iti // ata eva hi ye puṇyakarmāṇaḥ śraddhayā yutāḥ / na tāḥ smṛtīs te manyante saṃmateśānuśāsanāḥ //.*

paying the penalty for transgressions against their *dharma* in previous existences. All of the depravities associated with *mlecchas*, (sensuality, etc.), which were noted earlier in the context of the MPO (*vide* pp. 150—51, *supra*), may be the sins alluded to here. With this background, Nīla.'s scheme of Dharma involves a conflict between transgressors and a retributive God.

At first sight, this passage appears to contradict everything that Nīla. said about remedial punishment in opposition to Muir. Moreover, in Hinduism it is the exception rather than the rule that torment brought on by transgressions is endless.[180] A whole complex of ideas, including *prāyaścitta*, *saṃsāra*, and rebirth exempts Hindus from the horror of everlasting damnation. But having progressed from the MPŚ's path-oriented scheme of Dharma to the MPO's recognition of Christianity as at least preparatory for Hinduism, the ŚTV's severity toward the *khṛṣṭadharma* is clearly of a greater magnitude. "Again and again" is a phrase that suggests unceasing repetition and even intensification from worse to worse, without hope of release. The language is so strong that one wonders how, in this scheme of Dharma, Christians can ever acquire a fitness and eligibility (*adhikāra*) for *mokṣa*. A precedent for this hopelessness may be found in the Bhagavad-Gītā (16.18—21), wherein the "devilish" destiny of certain sinners is luridly described. "Selfishness, force, and pride, desire and anger — [these do] they rely on, envying and hating Me who dwell in their bodies as I dwell in all. Birth after birth in this revolving round, these vilest among men, strangers to [all] good, obsessed with hate and cruel, I ever hurl into devilish wombs. Caught up in devilish wombs, birth after birth deluded, they never attain to Me: and so they tread the lowest way. Desire — anger — greed: this is the triple gate of hell, destruction of the self: therefore avoid these three" (ZAEHNER, 1969: 372—74). This passage has been interpreted to mean that, only "as long as" one is subject to desire, anger, and greed, one cannot realistically expect to enter *mokṣa* (EDGERTON, 1972: 184); and that those who tread the "lowest way" will never be redeemed (ZAEHNER, 1969: 23—24). Clearly, the second reading is close to Nīla.'s position: each religion yields a result commensurate with the qualities that it inculcates in its adherents. Christians are condemned to their religion, and to the fate to which it inevitably leads, as a consequence of their enmity to *dharma* and God.

Harsh though this scheme of Dharma may be, it does not actually contradict what Nīla. said earlier about remedial and retributive punishment.

---

[180] One prominent exception is the dualistic school of Vedānta associated with the thirteenth-century philosopher Madhvācārya, which posits an actual and eternal distinction between *jīvas* and the Supreme Being. Among these *jīvas* are three classes, the first of which is destined for *mokṣa*, the second to perpetual transmigration, and the third, consisting of demons, sinners, and adherents of the *māyā* doctrine (Advaita Vedānta), to an eternal hell (GRIERSON, 1916: 234). The Bṛhannāradīyapurāṇa, a sectarian Vaiṣṇava Purāṇa with an intolerant brahminical standpoint, describes sinners for whom there is no atonement, who are irrevocably condemned to hell: e. g., people who venerate *liṅgas* or images worshipped by *śūdras* or women, and brahmins who visit Buddhist temples (WINTERNITZ, 1972, 1: 557—59).

In the Hindu view, a closed system of creation, brought into being by an *ex nihilo* creative act on the part of an omnipotent and omniscient God, implicates the deity in the transgressions of his creatures and makes his punishment of them appear sadistic. From Nīla.'s standpoint, however, God is not responsible for whatever enmity creatures show to him; after all, he does not create them but merely guarantees the process of karmic compensation. The idea that punishment is endless may be a seldom-chosen alternative to the prevailing notion of temporary and remedial punishment, but it does at least exist and does not fundamentally contradict other doctrines in Hinduism.[181]

Turning now to the question of precedents within Hinduism for the concept of Dharmas as delusions fraudulently imposed upon certain segments of mankind, one encounters a plethora of Purāṇic myths to this effect, a fact which necessitates highly selective treatment here. Numerous myth-cycles, first occurring in the Vedas and continuing into Epic and especially Purāṇic literature, use the delusion (*moha*) motif prominently. Later versions graft the heresies of Buddhism and Jainism (not always carefully distinguished) onto earlier myths concerning legerdemains played by gods upon demons. This motif, then, is tantamount to an *ad hominem* argument, for it slurs those religions by identifying them with demonic beings (O'FLAHERTY, 1976: 174ff.).

Questions concerning chronology and interpolation are immaterial here; these myths were, after all, established as Smṛti texts long before Nīla. came into contact with them. Their sheer quantity is the reason why they were likely to have been precedents for him.[182] Among myths containing clear allusions to Viṣṇu as responsible for the delusive Jain and Buddhist Dharmas, one related in the Viṣṇupurāṇa (3.17.9—45 and 3.18.1—34) is especially illustrative of assumptions implicit in the above-translated extract from the ŚTV. R. C. HAZRA's summary of this passage is as follows[183]: "In ancient times the gods, being defeated by the demons (Asuras) in a war which was continued for a divine year, went to the northern side of the ocean of milk and eulogized Viṣṇu who, consequently, produced Māyāmoha [i. e., delusion brought about by *māyā*] from his own body and gave him to the gods. This Māyāmoha, with his body stripped of all garments, his head

[181] Of course, it is possible that Nīla. was influenced by the Christian doctrine of eternal damnation, which was introduced to him by his partner-in-dialogue. However, there is no explicit evidence to make this supposition more than speculative.

[182] Even a brief summary of these myth-cycles is not feasible here. Among the articles and books listed in the bibliography referring to heresy in Hinduism, see especially ABS (1926), CHOUDHARY (1956), and O'FLAHERTY (1971 and 1976: 174—211).

[183] The principal variations of this myth are found in the Padmapurāṇa (Sṛṣṭikhaṇḍa 13), Matsyapurāṇa (24.43—49), and Devībhāgavata (4.13). R. C. HAZRA argues that the Māyāmoha myth is an interpolation in the Viṣṇupurāṇa, originating not earlier than 500 A.D. (1975: 24—25; see also S. N. ROY, 1965: 276ff.). O'FLAHERTY regards this particular version of the myth as the seventh and final step in its development-cycle (1976: 199—200); but GAIL's analysis differs (1969: 921).

shaved and a peacock feather in hand, went to the banks of the Narmadā where the demons were living, preached to them the religion of 'the naked' (i. e., Jainism) and turned them [into] 'Arhatas.' Next, Māyāmoha put on red clothes, painted his eyes with collyrium and preached Ahiṃsā (i. e., Buddhism) to the remaining demons. As a consequence of this preaching the demons soon gave up the Vedic religion and got weakened. Consequently they were attacked by the gods, defeated, and massacred" (HAZRA, 1975: 24).

It should be noted that this myth differs from Nīla.'s explanation of Christianity's origin in one significant respect: whereas jealous gods deluded the demons in the Viṣṇupurāṇa despite their adherence to *dharma*, the ŚTV attributes the cause of delusion specifically to the wickedness of Christians themselves in previous existences. However, two supporting bits of disparate evidence reinforce the impression that myths of this type — if not this very one — were precedents for Nīla.'s attitude toward the *khṛṣṭadharma.*

The first evidence relates to the more elaborate version of the Māyāmoha story in the Padmapurāṇa (5.13.316ff.). Among the cavils raised by Māyāmoha against the Vedic Dharma was the matter of Indra's seduction of Ahalyā (*vide* WINTERNITZ, 1972, 1: 538), a point to which Muir also addressed himself moralistically, thereby earning a homiletical reprimand from Nīla. (*vide* p. 130, *supra*).

The second piece of evidence is provided by a hardly reliable but nonetheless interesting source. Hindu-Vishva, a monthly magazine of the Vishva Hindu Parishad (an organization originally founded to counteract missionary activity in India[184]), recently published an article which interprets the Viṣṇupurāṇa myth in such a way that it includes, besides the references to Jainism and Buddhism, a veiled prophecy concerning the advent of Islam and Christianity (RAJAN, 1972: 29). As exegesis such a reading of the text is hopelessly speculative, yet it indicates that contemporary Hindus, confronted with religions inimical to their own, still find in the concept of delusion a useful scheme for interpreting religious plurality.

Corresponding to the idea of delusive Dharmas is the notion of false *avatāras*, whose mission is to propound *mohadharmas*, thereby leading certain persons or groups away from the path of true Dharma. Incarnation for this purpose appears to contradict the often quoted Bhagavad-Gītā passage (4.7), which declares that Kṛṣṇa becomes incarnate periodically in order to bring *dharma* and *adharma* into equilibrium; but it may — paradoxically — serve exactly that function. The most conspicuous example of this kind is the Buddha *avatāra* of Viṣṇu. At a later point than the sixth-century

---

[184] The Vishva Hindu Parishad ("Hindu World Fellowship") was specifically founded (September 1964) to oppose the 38th International Eucharistic Congress in Bombay (December 1964), which Pope Paul VI attended. Among the founding members were M. S. Golwalkar of the Rashtriya Svayamsevak Sangh and Swami Chinmayananda. Its first nationwide conference was the Vishva Hindu Sammelan at the Kumbha Melā (January 1966) in Allahabad. Many speechs denouncing missionary activity and the Eucharistic Congress were then delivered (ZEITLER, 1965: 115ff.).

date of the Viṣṇupurāṇa myth cited above, this *avatāra* became identified with the nebulous figure of Māyāmoha. The Bhāgavatapurāṇa (10.40.22a), for example, refers to the founder of Buddhism as follows: "Glory be to the Buddha, the pure, the deluder of the Daityas and Dānavas [the demons who became Jains and Buddhists]!" (*Namo buddhāya śuddhāya daityadānavamohine*). Oddly enough, among the heresies attributed to this false *avatāra* and his votaries was a kind of materialism favoring only perception as a *pramāṇa* (*pratyakṣavāda*) and the idea that the *ātman* is the body (*dehātmavāda*; Kalkipurāṇa 2.6.42, 2.7.17; ABS, 1926: 395). Had Nīla. been aware of these verses, their connection with a false *avatāra* may well have entered his mind and influenced his assessment of Muir's assertion that *pratyakṣa* ("perception") invalidates the *māyā* doctrine (MP 5.122—26, p. 79, and p. 79, n. 59 and 60, *supra*). If, therefore, God spreads a lie through one religion, he may as well do it by means of another also.

Of course, the Buddha *avatāra* later acquired positive aspects, beginning in the ninth century A. D., especially as a deity conferring beauty upon his supplicants. But from the fifth century A. D., by which time the Buddha's name began to appear in Purāṇic lists of incarnations (CHOUDHARY, 1956: 239),[185] to the ninth century A. D., his mission was only to delude demons, etc., and to prepare the way for Kalki, the last *avatāra*, to destroy *pāṣaṇḍins* and *mlecchas* (HAZRA, 1975: 88). The contrast between earlier and later references to the Buddha *avatāra* — the delusion-motif becoming muted or even lost entirely as time passed [186] — is evidence that only with great reluctance, and probably only after Buddhism ceased to pose a serious threat, did Hindu orthodoxy begin to tolerate this Dharma. By the same token, the respect now accorded to Jesus Christ by Hindus may well have been preceded by a period, exemplified by the ŚTV, in which he was, by association with a *mohadharma*, a false *avatāra*.

In the previously translated ŚTV extract, Nīla. singled out non-Vedic Smṛtis, the Bible and possibly the Koran as well, as vehicles of delusion used by Viṣṇu for punishing transgressors of *dharma*. This idea connects with the subject of *tāmasaśāstras*, or scriptures in which the quality of darkness is predominant. Manu 12.95—96 details the characteristics of, and dangers in, such Smṛtis. "All those traditions (*smṛti*) and all those despicable systems of philosophy, which are not based on the Veda, produce no reward after death; for they are declared to be founded on darkness. All those [doctrines], differing from the [Veda], which spring up and [soon] perish, are worthless and false, because they are of modern date" (BÜHLER, 1969: 505). The Bible, of course, matches this definition of *tāmasaśāstras* as well as Nīla.'s and Hara.'s declaration that it contradicts Śruti and leads away from *mokṣa*. But

---

[185] Details on the chronology of and deviations in these lists may be found in CHOUDHARY, 1956: 238—46; HAZRA, 1975: 88—90; and KANE, 1941: 720—23.

[186] Comments on the positive interpretation of the Buddha *avatāra* by the eleventh-century Jain writer Kṣemendra in the Daśāvatāracarita and by the twelfth-century Vaiṣṇava Jayadeva in the Gītāgovinda will be found in O'FLAHERTY, 1976: 204—11.

the ŚTV departs from this passage in Manu by making Viṣṇu directly responsible for inventing the Bible as a delusive device. For this idea there is also ample precedent in Hinduism. Among the many instances of *mohaśāstras* mentioned in Hindu literature,[187] only one is selected here, Padmapurāṇa 6.263.66—70. Indra there tells Parvati how he propounded, at Viṣṇu's behest, various *tāmasaśāstras* (the list includes all *darśanas* except Vedānta and Yoga).

"Listen, goddess, while I declare to you the Tāmasa works in order; works by the mere hearing of which even wise men become fallen. First of all, the Śaiva systems, called Pāśupata, etc., were delivered by myself. Then the following were uttered by Brāhmans penetrated by my power, viz. the great Vaiśeshika system by Kaṇāda, and the Nyāya, and Sānkhya, by Gotama and Kapila respectively. Then the great system, the Pūrva-[mīmānsā], was composed by the Brāhman Jaimini on Vedic subjects, but on atheistic principles. So too the abominable Chārvāka doctrine was declared by Dhishaṇa, while Vishṇu, in the form of Buddha, with a view to the destruction of the Daityas, promulgated the false system of the Bauddhas, who go about naked, or wear blue garments" (MUIR, 1868b: 202).[188]

Keeping in mind this scheme of Dharma, which connects the plurality of religions with false *avatāras* bearing *tāmasaśāstras* generating *mohadharmas*, some ambiguities and inconsistencies in the ŚTV can now be approached more effectively. A major uncertainty occurs in the first verse of the prologue, addressed to Viṣṇu: "Lord Śrīnivāsa do I worship, whose *līlā* is beyond reason, whom people with diverse competencies worship in various ways" (*bhinnādhikāraiḥ puruṣair bahudhā samupāsitaṃ / atarkyalīlam īśānam śrīnivāsam upāsmahe //*). At first glance this opening remark, deceptively hospitable in a text so censorious toward non-Vedic religions, is reminiscent of Bhagavad -Gītā 9.23. "[Yet] even those who lovingly devote themselves to other gods and sacrifice to them, full filled with faith, do really worship Me though the rite may differ from the norm." But the often neglected twenty-fourth verse comes closer to the meaning of the ŚTV passage. "For it is I who of all sacrifices am recipient and Lord, but they do not know Me as I really am, so they fall [back into the world of men]" (ZAEHNER, 1969: 282). Having an *adhikāra*, or eligibility, competence, and aptitude only for the *khṛṣṭadharma* as a result of previous transgressions, Christians nonetheless, and in a very strained and indirect sense, actually

---

[187] Other examples and discussions of *mohaśāstras* will be found in GONDA, 1970: 92ff.; ABS, 1926: 387ff.; CHOUDHARY, 1956: 234ff.; LORENZEN, 1972: 11; KANE, 1941: 975—77.

[188] *Śṛṇu devi pravakṣyāmi tāmasāni yathākramaṃ / yeṣāṃ śravaṇamātreṇa pātityaṃ jñāninām api // prathamaṃ hi mayaivoktaṃ śaivam pāśupatādikaṃ / macchaktyāveśitair vipraiḥ samproktāni tataḥ paraṃ // kaṇādena tu samproktaṃ śāstraṃ vaiśeṣikam mahat / gautamena tathā nyāyaṃ sāṃkhyaṃ tu kapilena vai // dvijanmanā jaimininā pūrvaṃ vedamayārthataḥ / nirīśvareṇa vādena kṛtaṃ śāstram mahattaraṃ // dhiṣaṇena tatha proktaṃ cārvākam atigarhitaṃ / daityānāṃ nāśanārthāya viṣṇunā buddharūpiṇā / bauddhaśāstram asat proktaṃ nagnanīlapaṭādikaṃ //* (GARBE, 1895: 4).

worship the same God as Nīla., for he is not only responsible for, but is at the center of, their misguided worship. Viṣṇu is, as it were, an unknown God whom Christians worship with what little *adhikāra* they possess.

However, another set of ŚTV passages makes a consistent interpretation of this scheme of Dharma problematic.

"Indeed, God's blessing upon all men is exactly the same: felicity (*śreyas*). We are all allowed, therefore, to worship our own religion. Rather should you put faith in your own scriptures than find fault thoughtlessly with ours."[189]

"Assuredly, in this sacred land endowed with brahmins, God has made his entire purpose manifest. Now, in your Western countries (*yāvanadeśeṣu*) also, somehow or other God taught [the way to] worship himself for the sake of human welfare. For instance, the content of your scripture and likewise of Muslims and others appears to be thoroughly within the ken of the intellect of simpletons. But our [scripture] is seen to be deeply profound; proclaimed in the divine speech of the Vedas; possessed of many ways [to God]; its truths recondite."[190]

Clearly, these passages are difficult to reconcile with the previously translated extract containing references to Smṛtis intended for sinners whom God will consign to hell repeatedly. Whether or not Nīla. was actually of two minds about religious pluralism, at least one can see a greater leniency in these verses towards Christianity and Islam, the latter of which was named only here in the ŚTV. There is, then, a form of common grace, albeit not a specific grace, *mokṣa*, which Viṣṇu bestows upon adherents of other religions. Much depends on the meaning of *śreyas* in this passage, which may be either "happiness" or "salvation", but a consistent interpretation of the text favors the former. Nīla.'s last and most thorough statement on his scheme of Dharma (6a.196—201), after all, states clearly that Christians are on a downward rather than upward path. If *śreyas* means felicity of a general sort, then these passages may suggest that a little *dharma* is better than none in Viṣṇu's attempt to strike a balance between order and chaos.[191] Along this line of reasoning, Nīla.'s admonition that Muir ought to concentrate on his own Dharma rather than interfere with others concides with Soma.'s path-oriented scheme. Once a *mārga* is undertaken, it must be followed, even downward, because one's eligibility for it is not fortuitous; it is a repercussion predestined by one's own *karman*. Yet even those unfortunate people

---

189 *Tulyaiva khalu sarveṣāṃ śreya āśīr nṛṇāṃ prabhoḥ / tasmāt svaṃ svaṃ mataṃ sarve 'py arhāmaḥ samupāsituṃ // yuṣmābhiḥ svīyaśāstreṣu kāmaṃ śraddhā vidhīyatāṃ / na punar dūṣyatām śāstram asmākaṃ svalpayā dhiyā //* (ŚTV 3.16—17; p. 26).

190 *Athavā parameśena deśe 'smin brāmaṇānvite / pavitre sakalo nūnaṃ svābhiprāyaḥ sphuṭīkṛtaḥ // atho yāvanadeśeṣu bhavadīyeṣu ceśvaraḥ / kathañcin nṛhitārthāya svām upāsām upādiśat // tathā hi bhavatāṃ śāstraṃ bāladhigocarārthakaṃ / tathaiva yavanādīnām api bhāti samantataḥ // asmākaṃ tv atigambhīraṃ vedavācā ca divyayā / proktaṃ bahvadhvabhir yuktaṃ gūḍhatattvaṃ ca dṛśyate //* (ŚTV 3.54—57; pp. 29—30).

191 Bhagavad-Gītā 2.40: "Even a little of this duty [*dharma*] saves from great danger" (EDGERTON, 1972: 13).

who face eternity in foul hells (*aśaucanaraka*) must order their lives with a degree of *dharma*, otherwise chaos engulfs the world.

Nīla.'s scheme of Dharma and anti-Dharma made religious plurality play a largely negative and punitive role. On this basis, the *khṛṣṭadharma* can hardly have legitimate claims to *sāmānyatā*; rather than being universal, it is a religion only for hardened transgressors. In HACKER's terms, the ŚTV is both practically and doctrinally intolerant; by MENSCHING's standards, Nīla.'s attitude was intrinsically intolerant. Yet this false *avatāra*, *moha-dharma*, and *tāmasaśāstra* obviously intrigued him, as his subsequent conversion proves. The caprioles in his career were remarkable, for in terms of his own scheme of Dharma, he took the downward path (*vide* pp. 169—72, *infra*).

THE BASIS OF RELIGIOUS PLURALITY

It is clear at this juncture that the MP Controversy pandits did not propound one single and consistent scheme of Dharma or agree in assessing Christianity's salvific potential. The only common factors were their unanimous rejection of Muir's contention that only the *khṛṣṭadharma* has an authentic claim to universality (*sāmānyatā*), and their reluctance to make counterclaims to this same effect on behalf of Hinduism. One may even say that they were more concerned about emphasizing the limitations and particularity of all religions, including their own, than about proving the falsehood of any vis-à-vis the Vedas. Discrepancies between Christianity and Hinduism were unreconciled because they viewed biblical doctrines as fundamentally antagonistic to Śrūti and — what is more important here — because they understood them to be purposeful, in one way or another, for a specific class of people. If, then, religions have any common basis, it is, according to their schemes of Dharma, an identity of purpose rather than content. Due to basic differences in mankind, there is plurality instead of singularity of religion. Each Dharma corresponds to a particular kind of person, who may suffer from lack of competent instructors (MPŚ), or who may be acquiring merit in order to become a Hindu (MPO), or who may be destined, on account of transgressions, to a succession of hells (ŚTV). In each case the religion yields a result commensurate with the characteristics of a particular class of individuals. The universal quality in religions is that they all lead somewhere, and the quality that distinguishes them permanently and ultimately from each other is their suitability for the people who are born into,[192] believe in, and observe them.

[192] Readmission to the fold is sometimes possible for Hindus who abandon or forfeit their caste, and *śuddhi* or *patitaparāvartana* ceremonies occur frequently (*vide* KANE, 1941: 391—93). Bhāgavatas have been more open than other Hindus to admission of foreigners (*vide* Bhāgavatapurāṇa 2.4.18). A certain Heliodoros, a second-century A. D. ambassador of a Greek king, is said to have been a Bhāgavata (HAZRA, 1975: 199). Some Tantric texts also claim to admit casteless foreigners into their communion, e. g., the Mahānirvāṇatantra (14.177, 187, 189). J. D. M. DERRETT is of the opinion that relaxation of caste restrictions in that text was due to influence from Christianity (1968a: 146). The general trend of Hinduism is certainly inimical to such practices, and the MP Controversy pandits strongly opposed it.

In order to further elucidate the principle that plurality in religions is intrinsic and purposeful, it will be useful to examine a complex of ideas associated with the term *adhikāra*, the underlying unifying factor in the three schemes of Dharma previously investigated. The many facets of this word have only been partially exhausted by translating it in the foregoing as "aptitude" (e. g., in the section on incompatible *darśanas* in chapter five) or as "competence" or "eligibility". *Adhikāra* is a protean word and must be approached from other angles as well. As with so many other technical terms, it brings this study into contact with a larger constellation of ideas which provided precedents for the pandits in their encounter with Christianity.

It is symptomatic of *adhikāra* that it occurs almost invariably wherever Hindu authorities discuss the issue of access to the Vedas and their saving knowledge with reference to certain classes of people, whether they be brahmins or women or *śūdras* or, by extension to an interreligious context, Christians, Muslims, and others. An exhaustive survey of this term is, of course, not feasible within the scope of this chapter. Particular reference will be made to its function in the context of Advaita Vedānta, in view of the prevalent tendency to regard that system of philosophy as the basis of Hindu universalism and tolerance.[193]

Adhikāra is not to be limited to the idea of aptitude, as if it means IQ and can be tested and gauged according to modern methods of measuring intelligence. But on one facet it is exactly that, and could be supplemented with other words in a similar vein, such as competence or ability or capacity or qualification. That *adhikāra* is not limited to intelligence alone can be seen by referring to the qualifications necessary for persons wishing to study the Vedas, as Śaṅkara enumerated them in the Brahmasūtrabhāṣya: (1) discernment between eternal and non-eternal substances (*nityānityavastuviveka*); (2) renunciation of enjoyment of rewards here and in the next world (*ihāmutraphalabhogavirāga*); (3) attainment of six qualities of mind, tranquility (*śama*), restraint (*dama*), renunciation (*uparati*), resignation (*titikṣā*), concentration (*samādhi*), and belief (*śraddhā*); (4) longing for *mokṣa* (*mumukṣutva*).[194] Clearly, a psychological predisposition, as well as bare intellectual talent, is presupposed here.

An equally important facet of *adhikāra* is implied by words such as prerogative, privilege, right, entitlement, and eligibility, all of which connect with the scheme of caste, *karman*, and rebirth. These, too, are integers in the *adhikāra* equation because birth is never accidental; it is a karmic repercussion for better or worse. Birth as one of the twice-born, *brahmins*, *kṣatriyas*, and *vaiśyas*, is surely better than birth as one of the once-born, *śūdras*. The former have special rights, prerogatives and duties which the latter do not,

---

[193] E. g., MENSCHING, 1971: 64—69; D. E. SMITH, 1966: 6; PUHAKKA, 1976: 52ff. A. SHARMA's critique of this assumption (1978: 134—37) is highly relevant, but differs from the present one.

[194] Following the lists and terminology of DEUSSEN, 1973: 77—82, and ZIMMER, 1951: 51—56.

and vice versa. But with reference to the question of access to the Vedas, the twice-born have not earned their eligibility for *brahmavidyā*, except in the sense of having accumulated merit in previous existences. In their present life they undergo *upanayana*, an initiation which allows them to begin Vedic studies. *Śūdras* do not participate in this kind of ceremony, however, and consequently they are permitted only to listen to recitations of the Itihāsas and Purāṇas. They are, in short, disqualified by their caste-status from access to liberating knowledge.

Aptitude and eligibility are in reciprocal relation with one another; each determines and is determined by the other member of the equation. Absence of aptitude accompanies ineligibility; disqualification implies incompetence. Injustice is excluded, de facto, on account of inequality, from this scheme of Dharma. Just as ability and inability are opposite forms of *adhikāra*, so is exclusion the counterpart to participation — without inequity arising. The integers cannot be rearranged so that their sum is different; nor do *śūdras* get the benefit of the doubt. Their caste-status cannot be compensated by other factors, such as intelligence, because eligibility and competence are always commensurate. Even *śūdras* who desire *brahmavidyā*, and Śaṅkara at least admitted this to be a possibility, were faced with an insurmountable handicap — their caste (see Brahmasūtrabhāṣya 1.3.34). "The *śūdra*, so long as he has not been raised on the path of transmigration to a higher caste, remains entirely excluded from all share in the teaching of salvation" (Deussen, 1973: 64). For reasons such as these, Śaṅkara insisted that *śūdras* must be prevented from hearing, reading, and learning the Veda, and from practicing its injunctions. Severe punishments were prescribed for violators (Brahmasūtrabhāṣya 1.3.38).[195] Far from being unjust from Śaṅkara's viewpoint, these penalties reflect his recognition of fundamental human differences, which alter only through a series of existences instead of within the span of a single life.[196]

If *śudras* are excluded from saving knowledge, *mlecchas* (Christians, Muslims, etc.), a fortiori, are also. Especially in Hara.'s scheme of Dharma are the two classes of persons underprivileged with respect to salvific opportunities, yet both may look forward to future improvement and enhanced *adhikāra*. Compared with *śūdras*, however, *mlecchas* in Nīla.'s scheme are even more disadvantaged, for they are forever debarred even from acquiring enough *adhikāra* for access to the few prerogatives that once-

---

[195] Śaṅkara's entire argument spans 1.3.34 to 1.3.38. See either Muir, 1868b: 292—300, or Thibaut, 1890: 223—29. For analysis refer to Halbfass, 1975: 35—37.

[196] The Bhaktisūtras of Śāṇḍilya are an interesting contrast to Śaṅkara's position on *śūdras*. According to this text, *bhakti* is more important than *jñāna* in attaining *mokṣa*. The only prerequisite is desire for release from rebirth, and even *śūdras* want that. What is more, although the Vedas are the highest source of knowledge, and only the three higher castes have access to them, *śūdras* may attain a derivative knowledge from the Purāṇas and Itihāsas (Muir, 1868b: 177—78). This option, too, existed in Hindu thought, but the MP Controversy pandits were more in debt to the same presuppositions as Śaṅkara.

born Hindus have. Soma., of course, was the exceptional thinker, for only he believed that *mlecchas* have their own extra-Vedic revelation. But his scheme of Dharma, too, was based upon human differences corresponding to variations in *adhikāra*.

Religious plurality, therefore, is the counterpart of *adhikāra*. The one proves the other, according to Nīla., because "just as God made various distinct *mārgas*, so is it certain, consequently, that people have different *adhikāras*" (*kiṃ ca yasmāj jagannāthaś cakre mārgān pṛthagvidhān / bhinnādhikārāḥ puruṣā ity asmād api niścitaṃ* // ŚTV 6a.29; p. 48). By the same token, he defines one's *adhikāra* by the attraction (*ruci*) one feels toward a certain *mārga*.[197] This means that one is drawn toward the religion that one acquires at birth, and within that religion, to a particular *darśana* or *mārga*. Thus, the concept functions equally well in inter- or intrareligious frameworks. Hindus are Hindus rather than Christians because they have aptitude and eligibility only for their Dharma and not for Christianity. Moreover, a Vedāntin subscribes to Vedānta because he is competent to understand its truth and is entitled to its benefits instead of to the fruits of Nyāya, Vaiśeṣika, Sāṅkhya, Yoga, etc. Accordingly, to transfer from one Dharma or *darśana* to another would be a retrograde step for some persons and inordinately rapid progress for others. Standing faithfully by one's own religion, therefore, is one of the few principles that unified the pandits in opposition to Muir.

To recapitulate, religious plurality, according to these three schemes of Dharma, is intrinsic and purposeful. Universality in religions is only a unity of purpose and not of content. Any religion's claim to *sāmānyatā* is nullified by the realities of human differences; for all such assertions fail to take into account variations in ability and caste-regulated prerogatives. Advaita Vedānta itself is compatible with the idea of soteriological privileges. On this basis, then, Christianity's claim to be suitable for all people, irrespective of their psychological, religious, and social backgrounds, could only strike orthodox Hindus as a presumptuous contradiction of divinely ordained human differences.

It would, of course, be an interesting — but altogether different — question to inquire into transformations in the meaning of *adhikāra*, a word which has been reinterpreted by neo-Hindus since the time of the MP Controversy.[198]

---

[197] *Yasmin yasya bhaven mārge ruciḥ śāstreṇa bodhite / tasmiṃs tasyādhikāro 'stīty adhikārasya bodhakaṃ* // (ŚTV 6a.31; p. 49).

[198] The writings of AUROBINDO GHOSE, who psychologized the term almost to the complete exclusion of other elements in the traditional concept, would be especially useful in this regard. "All stages of spiritual evolution are there in man and each has to be allowed or provided with its means of approach to the spirit, an approach suited to its capacity, *adhikāra*" (AUROBINDO, 1940: 776). The egalitarian VIVEKANANDA was an outspoken critic of *adhikāra* as a basis for excluding certain kinds of people from *brahmavidyā*. "For all my respect for the Rishis of yore, I cannot but denounce in the strongest terms their method which they always followed in

The foregoing presentation of the pandits' three schemes of Dharma and the varieties of tolerance and intolerance generated by them was undertaken in order to bring the study of Hindu attitudes to other religions into closer relation to the history of encounter between Hindus, Christians, and others. Too little is yet known about Hindu apologetics to warrant the generalization that Hinduism has "tolerance in [its] blood" (MENSCHING, 1971 : 64), and such poetic hyperbole as the following: "The Hindu tolerance of [religious] plurality is not an iridescence arising from the photic interplay of some of its facets; it is not an aspect but an ingredient of the 'substance' itself" (A. SHARMA, 1978: 145). Without attention to the actual context of dialogue between Hindus and men of other faiths, some writers have been apt to concentrate on Śrūti and Smṛti passages interpreted in such a way as to preclude the possibility of intolerance and less than hospitable schemes of Dharma occurring in Hinduism's historical record.

One cannot begin to discuss this subject by referring to Ṛg Veda 1.164.46 ("Truth is one, sages call it by various names"), a verse which A. BHARATI aptly says has been "milked for all it's worth" (1970: 282), then proceed to quote carefully selected passages from the Bhagavad-Gītā and the books of S. RADHAKRISHNAN.[199] As important as these scriptural and other passages may be, selection of materials must be as comprehensive as the scope of the subject itself. Additional attention to literature in Indian languages reflecting the realities of interreligious encounter during its period of greatest intensity, the early and mid-nineteenth century, is a matter of primary concern. More consideration should also be given to intrareligious relations within Hinduism, since history provides Hindus with patterns for understanding the existence of other religions vis-à-vis their own. It is hoped that this study of the MP Controversy contributes to clarification of this subject by adhering closely to these methodological principles.

---

instructing the people... They said they kept the end hidden from the view of the people because they could not understand its real meaning, because they were not worthy recipients of such high instructions. This *adhikārivāda*... is the result of pure selfishness... Those who were so eager to support the *adhikārivāda* ignored the tremendous fact of the infinite possibilities of the human soul" (BURKE, 1973: 11—12). The Ramakrishna school has made *adhikārin* a term for a *jīvanmukta* who condescends to remain in the world in order to lead others toward *mokṣa*. This idea seems to be an amalgamation with the *bodhisattva* ideal (*vide* SARADANANDA, 1953: *passim*).

[199] Examples of this selective textual approach to Hindu attitudes to other religions will be found in K. L. S. RAO, 1972: 38ff., and G. MENSCHING, 1971 : 64—69.

VII. EPILOGUE: THE AFTERMATH

Although the MP Controversy did not alter the character of interreligious dialogue in India on a broad scale, it had a definite and curious impact on the subsequent careers of two disputants, Muir and Nīla. Unfortunately, there is nothing to indicate whether or not the affair was of continuing interest to the other two Hindu participants, Subājī and Hara. The following sections trace these repercussions in the lives of Muir and Nīla. and show that these unforeseen effects were not wholly distinct and separable from the pivotal events that brought them into conflict with each other in the first place.

Muir and Modern Biblical Criticism

After revising the MP for the third time (between 1852 and 1854), Muir stopped composing Sanskrit *ślokas* and turned instead to academic study of Indian literature, Christian theology, and furtherance of higher education in his native Scotland. Upon returning to Edinburgh, he undertook his monumental five-volume project, Original Sanskrit Texts, which required almost twelve years to complete. The materials in these still-standard books never betray the author's original purpose in amassing them: to demonstrate that Christianity is rationally superior to Hinduism. In addition to his own Indological contributions, Muir endowed the "Chair of Sanskrit Language, Literature, Philosophy, and Comparative Philology" at the University of Edinburgh in 1862. (The first two professors appointed to this chair were T. Aufrecht and J. Eggling.) Muir left apologetics behind in India and thereafter eschewed interreligious conflict during his retirement as a Sanskritist, theologian, and philanthropist.

The dichotomy between Muir's Indian and British careers is more conspicuous in his role in late nineteenth-century disputes concerning biblical inspiration than in his academic pursuits. Always a scholar, it was as a Christian that he changed most. By looking at this lesser-known aspect of his life, one sees that he began to view the MP as captious, dogmatic, and repugnant to his mature conception of religion as basically a nonsupernatural system of morality. With this change of mind, Muir became embroiled in intra- instead of interreligious controversy, and to comprehend this reversal, the rise of biblical criticism in the mid-Victorian Church of England must be considered.

Muir had written the MP as a quasi-Evangelical. He combined the idea that the mind has an innate capacity to verify religious truths with concern for the destiny of non-Christians, some of whom, he feared, could be damned. Back in Britain, however, he ceased to sympathize with this viewpoint, preferring instead the ideology of the so-called Broad Church movement led by Thomas Arnold of Rugby and, on the continent, by Baron Bunsen. Muir had begun to think, as did this group, that Christian doctrine was sorely out of alignment with the modern mind. This implied primarily that faith must agree with reason, a position he already advocated in the MP. The change was that he no longer believed Paley's Evidential Theology, based upon miracles, could satisfy a reasoning mind with regard to the issue of biblical inspiration. The truth of revelation, he began to claim, is proven by its moral loftiness, not by citing miracles and prophecies. Moreover, he saw that the historical veracity of Christianity could not be asserted on the basis of an unbroken literary tradition, an assumption explicit in the MP but shown to be dubious by German critics (CHADWICK, 1970: 76—77). According to these ideas, antisupernaturalistic in their presuppositions, the Bible became an "expression of devout reason" (CHADWICK, 1970: 81), rather than a repository of divine truths authenticated by miracles. The real difference between religions, then, is in their ethical principles.

This change in theological orientation, which implied that Muir had thoroughly renounced the MP, was related to his encounter with Hindu apologists. It had occurred to him that the Bible could not be exempted from the rigorous philological and historical analysis to which he had subjected the Vedas. Therefore, casting aside all scruples for the *khṛṣṭīyaśāstra*, he began to practise biblical criticism according to modern, German principles. Moreover, Hinduism and Christianity became to him examples of human responses to God; but he did not cease at that time to be a professed Christian.[200]

Whether in India or Britain, Muir was not one who shirked controversy. He became active in propagating German biblical criticism during the 1860s, a turbulent period for the Church of England. Many clergymen were then strongly opposed to the growing consensus that the "Word of God is in the Bible" rather than the "Word of God is the Bible" (CHADWICK, 1970: 110). Attracted to the new viewpoint, Muir published his Brief Examination of Prevalent Opinions on the Inspiration of the Scriptures of the Old and New Testaments in 1861, identifying himself not by name but only as "a layman of the Church of England." He denied inerrancy on the following grounds: mutual discrepancies in the Gospels; the unfulfilled Second Advent of Christ in the Apostolic Age; illogical and inconclusive reasoning in the Epistles; and events posterior to Moses included in the Pentateuch. This was not by

[200] Muir was a generous supporter of scholarship, and one instance of his charity during this period also speaks for his frame of mind. In 1857 he awarded a substantial prize to Rowland Williams, a leading Broad Churchman, who wrote a dissertation comparing Christianity and Hinduism, Paramēswara-jnyāna-gōsthī (1856). According to Williams, "It seemed illogical... that the miracles of the Vedas should be rejected by Christians when equally incredible happenings in the Bible were accepted without question. He wondered why scholarly tests which applied to the religious books of the East should not be used on the Bible..." (CROWTHER, 1970: 84). In 1861 Williams was brought before a judicial committee of the Church of England and convicted of heresy for denying the supernatural origin of the Bible *in toto* (CHADWICK, 1970: 75—94).

any means an outstanding book; at best it was a lucid and carefully argued statement of thinking already done by others. The introduction, written by HENRY BRISTOW WILSON, a Broad Churchman convicted of heresy later the same year (CHADWICK, 1970: 75—94), is more apposite, for it clearly reveals the impact of the MP Controversy upon Muir's belief in the Bible.

"Can it be legitimate to demand of the Mahommedan and the Hindu to test, by their reason and their moral sense, the Scriptures which they hold to be inspired, and which contain many truths, to invite them to 'sift the chaff from the wheat' in that which their fathers and teachers tell them is a revelation, and not to allow the application of the same method to the Christian scriptures? We may be assured that, as Christianity comes into actual close contact with Orientals of acute intellects, and inheriting traditional faiths, it will be met with a style of controversy which will come upon some among us with surprise. Many things will be disputed, which we have been accustomed to take for granted, and proofs will be demanded, which those who have been brought up in the external evidence school of the last century, may not be prepared to supply. When we insist that the inspiration of the Vedas is merely a traditional claim which cannot shut out an examination of their contents and of the systems alleged to be founded on them, neither the pandits of Benares [Nīla.], nor the free-thinkers of Calcutta [Hara.], will admit our claim on behalf of our Bible, to have, in the outset of the argument, a greater presumption in its favour. Indeed by not at once appealing to the immeasurable superiority of the Christian religion generally taken in its moral purport, we should be keeping in the background the strongest part of our case" (Muir, 1861: lv—lvi).[201]

This was not an admission on Muir's part, relayed through Wilson, that he had conceded to Subājī, Hara., and Nīla.; rather, retaining confidence in Christianity's ethical values, he admitted that his method of reasoning about religion had been ill-chosen. Still searching for the ground of his faith, Muir's writing in this period indicates that he had shifted his attention from miraculous to moral evidences. One sees this, for instance, in his preface to Prophets and Prophecy in Israel (1877), written by a Dutch biblical scholar, ABRAHAM KEUNEN. "[In] those cases where the prophecies were fulfilled (and where it is shown that the prediction was committed to writing before the event), their accomplishment, if not accidental, must be attributed either to the prophets sagacity or to the influence of his words upon the conduct of those to whom they were addressed" (KEUNEN, 1877: xxxviii).

Two years later Muir abandoned even this position with respect to moral evidences, admitting that Christian virtues are neither superior to others nor *sui generis*. His last major project, Metrical Translations from Sanskrit Writers (1879), was symptomatic of this change because it belonged more to

---

201 The second (1862) edition of this book bore Muir's name. After that he was so unpopular among Evangelicals that they attributed to him another anonymous treatise, Supernatural Religion (1874—77), actually written by W. R. CASSELS, one of the most outspoken British atheists in that period.

John Muir
(1810—1882)
Courtesy of the University of Edinburgh

Nehemiah (Nīlakaṇṭha) Goreh, SSJE
(1825—1885)

comparative religion than either Indology or theology. Citing a profusion of morally didactic passages from Indian literature, juxtaposed with others from biblical and classical Greek authorities, Muir made a *prima facie* argument in favor of their equivalence. "These sentiments and observations are the natural expression of the feelings and experiences of universal humanity; and the higher and nobler portion of them cannot be regarded as peculiar to Christianity... And are not even the literatures, whether sacred or profane, of all countries, more or less, disfigured by something repugnant to the moral sense?" (Muir, 1879: xxxiii—xxxiv, xliv).

Given this reversal of each major position adopted in the MP — Christianity's miraculous evidences, its moral excellence (*śreṣṭhatā*) and universality (*sāmānyatā*) — one senses that Muir's renunciation of his role in the controversy was complete and that he believed neither religion emerged victorious from the conflict or gained any lasting benefit from it.

Nīlakaṇṭha as Nehemiah Goreh, SSJE

The preeminent role of *śraddhā* in the ŚTV did not mean that faith came easily to Nīla., either in the Vedas, Purāṇas, or, subsequently, the Bible. As a skilled logician, a master of *tarkavidyā*, he would settle for nothing less than full certitude, rationally based assurance about religious truths. Instead of social constraints, the obstacles impeding this conviction were largely cerebral. Consequently, the tension between faith and reason, so simply stated in the ŚTV, dogged him to the end of his career. One discerns in his caprioles that he was never quite at ease either in his disbelief of Hinduism or in his newfound Christian faith.

In one of their last conversations before his conversion, Nīla. informed Smith, his partner-in-dialogue, that, if he would become a Christian, he would want to be "*pakkaḥ*" ("pure," "mature"), "able to give a reason to all" who would ask why he had converted (W. Smith, 1850: 92). In a face-to-face encounter with Muir, who notably tempered his emphasis on objective verification of religious truths, he was counseled "not to dive too deep or you shall be drowned, nor seek to fathom things for which God has not given man the line" (Smith, 1850: 106). Nonetheless, Nīla. clearly thought he had thoroughly investigated the religion of his birth and the religion of his choice and that reason dictated conversion to the latter.

The earliest indication of this rationalistic stance came after the following news item appeared in an Urdu language newspaper published in Benares: "The son of a most respectable man, Nīlakaṇṭha, went from here on the 12th to Jaunpur, and there through error wandered into a ruinous path, and has come to eat and drink with the Christians!" (Smith, 1850: 142). In reply to this insinuation that he had been mesmerized, Nīla. wrote the following: "Now, as to my having renounced Hinduism, let it be known that I have not done this without enquiry; but having by incontrovertible arguments seen its falsehood, I have renounced it. Thousands of your so-called divine teachers have described God in a thousand contradictory ways:

from which it is clear that they knew nothing at all about him... As to the Purans, they are full of nonsensical stories about the sun and the moon and the earth. If anyone, renouncing prejudice and a party spirit, will examine the matter, he will be convinced that Hinduism is the invention of men" (SMITH, 1850: 143—44). Thereafter, one finds that Nīla.'s judgment of his hereditary religion was, in the same vein as the above, unsparingly harsh. In a letter to Muir he stressed one point in particular: "The Nyāya and other systems of the Hindus are so replete with false reasonings, that, for depraving the human intellect, they are a manifest poison" (MUIR, 1856: 112).

After his baptism, traces of Nīla. the Hindu are lost in the figure of Nehemiah the Christian. His first major contribution to anti-Hindu apologetics was a revised version of a vernacular treatise by his partner-in-dialogue, Sat Mat Nirūpaṇ (1848), which he enhanced by adding many apposite quotations from the Purāṇas (GARDNER, 1900: 86—87). An original work was next, Vedānt Mat kā Bicār aur Khṛṣṭīyamat kā Sār (1853), in which he was identified only as a "Benares pandit" (*kāśī ke ek paṇḍit se banāyā gayā*). This was a preparatory version of his 1860 magnum opus, Ṣaḍdarśanadarpaṇa (A Mirror of the Six Philosophical Systems), written while he was a scholar-in-residence at Bishop's College, Calcutta.[202] Characteristic of the author's way of reasoning about religion was the awesome title of the English translation, A Rational Refutation of the Hindu Philosophical Systems (1861). This text, counterpoint to the ŚTV, concluded with advice identical to that which he gave prior to his conversion (see p. 107, *supra*). "Reason, as we now find it, is... inadequate to lead us to the way of salvation, or to purify our corrupt nature. For these ends we must have recourse to the Word of God. And as regards this Word, when presented, reason, once more, is of great use in enabling us to test it, and to recognize it for what it professes to be. But the result will not be thus, unless [one] applies [oneself] to the search of Holy Writ in the way I have specified. For there are many truths which, though at first blush they revolt the mind, are seen, after patient investigation, to be quite in accord with all that is reasonable and right" (Goreh, 1897: 202).

Nīla.'s career changed abruptly in 1854, before which time he had been employed as J. R. Ballantyne's pandit in the Benares Sanskrit College (GARDNER, 1900: 107). In that year he was appointed tutor to the dispossessed ruler of Lahore, Dhulip Singh, a Sikh who had become a Presbyterian. In the retinue of the king, he visited Britain and was even favored with an audience before Queen Victoria (GARDNER, 1900: 90—95; LOGIN, 1970: 106—09). More significant was an encounter with MAX MÜLLER at Oxford, to whom he was introduced by Muir.[203] MÜLLER's account of their initial

---

[202] For contemporary reviews of this work, see SAINT-HILAIRE, 1864: 173ff. and GOLDSTÜCKER, 1862: 245ff.

[203] At the same time, Nīla. became acquainted with Professor M. MONIER-WILLIAMS, whose books credit him for much information on brahminical rituals (e. g., MONIER-WILLIAMS, 1891: 373, 422).

meeting reads as follows: "While I was sitting in my room at Oxford copying Sanskrit mss., a gentleman was shown in... and addressed me in a language of which I did not understand a single word. I spoke to him in English, and asked him what language he was speaking, and he replied with great surprise, 'Do you not understand Sanskrit?' 'No', I said, 'I have never heard it spoken, but here are some mss. of the Veda which will interest you.' He was delighted to see them, and began to read, but he had soon to confess that he was unable to translate a single word" (MÜLLER, 1899a: 51). Thus began MÜLLER's interest in Nīla., about whom he always spoke with "reverential affection" (Life and Letters, 1902: 167), and his observations contrast sharply with what one finds in hagiographical writings about the converted pandit.

MÜLLER's first impression of Nīla.'s piety and mental gifts was summed up in these words: "All I can say is that in the whole of my life I have never seen so true a Christian, so true a martyr, as Nehemiah Goreh... I doubt whether, if left to itself, the Indian mind could reach a higher degree of intellectual vigour than it did in Nehemiah Goreh" (MÜLLER, 1899a: 58, 71). However, MÜLLER's impression altered drastically when they met again after many years.

During the long interval, Nīla. became enamored of Anglo-Catholicism and joined the Society of St. John the Evangelist (Oxford), which had branches in India, as a novice. MÜLLER had correctly predicted that an "innate tendency of the Indian mind" would develop in Nīla.: "He became a Christian *sannyāsin*" (MÜLLER, 1899a: 59; see also LOGIN, 1970: 106, and GARDNER, 1900: 134). Although his enthusiasm for Church Sanskrit and critical studies of the *darśanas* never subsided,[204] he became equally absorbed in the recondite theological controversies of the late nineteenth century, especially the Tractarian Dispute (GARDNER, 1900: 110—15).

To MÜLLER, who met Nīla. again in 1877, it seemed as if he had been completely transformed: "Now and then the old spirit seemed to move in him, but he soon relapsed into formulas which he had learnt, and which seemed to satisfy him, ... but it was sad to see the eagle with broken wings!" (Life and Letters, 1902: 37; see also CHAUDHURI, 1974: 292—93). One must bear in mind that MÜLLER's jaundiced view of Nīla.'s reliance on creedal language was a reflection of his own distinction between "the Christianity of the Church and the Christianity of Christ." This reservation notwithstanding, his diagnosis of Nīla.'s depressed state of mind had some basis, for he recorded that the pandit had remarked, in reference to his conversion, that he often "felt like a man who has taken poison" (MÜLLER, 1899a: 62).

The hagiological literature on Nīla. dismissed MÜLLER's account as fanciful (e.g., GARDNER, 1900: 98). The authenticity of his turnabout in relation to Hinduism cannot be denied, but by the same token, one must

---

[204] Even at the end of his life Nīla. continued to read W. H. Mill's Śrīkhṛṣṭasaṃgītā "in that peculiar intonation which is adopted by pandits in reading their shastras" (GOPAL, 1896: 57).

admit that he was plagued with life-long struggles with doubt. Near the end of his life, Nīla. himself acknowledged that he had not found an equilibrium between faith and reason. "One who is born and brought up in another religion must first be convinced by reason, that that religion is not true. He believes in his own religion, and if he is simply to exercise faith he will exercise it in his own religion. But if he is to use his reason in order to see whether his religion is true or not, he will also first wish to see whether Christianity really is what it claims to be. However, I have begun to think that it is not by going through a regular process of reason that men renounce one religion and embrace another, though such was certainly the case with me, and that is the very reason why my faith in Christianity is so poor" (Goreh, 1888).

Thus, the MP Controversy, itself of short duration, had serious repercussions in the lives of two disputants. The irony is striking: whereas the challenger became less and less orthodox in his Christian faith, the convert became more and more so in his. 1861 saw the publication of Muir's Brief Examination of Prevalent Opinions on the Inspiration of the Scriptures of the Old and New Testaments and Nīla.'s Ṣaḍdarśanadarpaṇa, undercutting each other just as the MP and ŚTV had done earlier, although on entirely different grounds. Moreover, as Muir became engrossed in comparative religion, Nīla. continued to face the existential challenge of Hinduism and Christianity, a confrontation which compelled him, as he saw it, to choose between the two religions — but not without regrets.

VIII. SUMMARY

As reconstructed in the foregoing chapters, the MP Controversy is proof that, whatever may be said to the contrary, at least some nineteenth-century pandits viewed Christianity vis-à-vis their own religion from the perspective of a theological animus rather than simply in terms of benign tolerance, as is sometimes supposed to have been the case. Exactly how widespread this *odium theologicum* may have been is moot, and probably shall remain so; yet it should be borne in mind that one and the same text, Muir's MP, elicited not only Soma's irenic MPŚ but also Hara.'s blustering philippic, the MPO, and Nīla.'s systematically severe ŚTV.

One can also be sure that stiff Hindu resistance, especially insofar as Christianity's doctrinal content and salvific potential is concerned, was not an ephemeral outburst restricted only to the MP Controversy era. Opposition of this sort can be traced to the early eighteenth century, when Malabarian brahmins recorded their impressions of the *khṛṣṭadharma* at the behest of Bartolomaeus Ziegenbalg, before whose time nothing committed to writing is known to survive. The staunchly Hindu but sedate tone of this correspondence contrasts sharply with anti-Christian intellectual hostility vented in Bombay during the 1830s in debates and tract-battles between the erudite but pugilistic John Wilson, Morabhaṭṭa Dāndekara, and Nārāyaṇa Rāo. Much remains to be known about the literary activities of the Hindu movement resisting Christianity, but there is no doubt that opposition was deeply rooted and expressed itself sporadically in anti-Christian treatises.

Throughout this period of confrontation, it is also clear that the participants engaged in genuinely theological and philosophical dialogue, however rudimentarily they defined and querulously discussed the issues. Indicative of this was the trend away from dismissing Christianity on purely cultural grounds. Whereas the Malabarian brahmins did not clearly differentiate between Christian cultic practices, personal habits, and customs on the one hand, and biblical teachings regarding God, the world, man, and salvation on the other, this was hardly an imprecision to which the Bombay and MP pandits were susceptible. The *khṛṣṭadharma* was an affront to them because its dogmas were regarded as false and its claims extravagant, rather than because Christians themselves were repugnant on account of their neglect of bodily cleanliness, consumption of meat, exotic rituals, and so forth. Bitter and strained though their dialogue was, it reflects a serious attempt to come to grips with the principal ideas at the center of both religions.

Apart from whatever mutual understanding or revitalization of Dharma to which it may have led, the creative aspect of this quarrel with Christianity was that an entirely new branch of Hindu apologetical literature flourished, albeit briefly. It was new in the sense that, although Christianity had existed in India since at least the third century, if not even earlier, fifteen centuries passed by before authors began to concentrate on the immediate threat posed by Christianity, instead of Buddhism, Jainism, and Materialism. In view of this belated rise of anti-Christian apologetics, it is useful here to recapitulate two factors, the intersection of which created conditions appropriate for the MP Controversy to occur.

First, Hindu authorities became increasingly aware that other Dharmas exist in addition to their own, even though they be fallacious and defective. Their transition from insularity to relative openness toward representatives of non-Vedic religions did not come about easily or suddenly, inhibited as they were by Dharmaśāstra passages warning against concourse with *mlecchas*, a prerequisite for interreligious dialogue. The Vedic Dharma had a monolothic presence in the minds of its adherents, eclipsing all contenders vying for status as alternatives. But contributing to a wider application of the word *dharma* were Hindu minority groups and extra-Vedic communities anxious to preserve and promote their separate identities, who used it (and *mata*) in a sense consistent with the notion of plurality. With varying degrees, the MP Controversy pandits surveyed Christianity from a Hinducentric point of reference. Nevertheless, their schemes of Dharma were open rather than closed, because, in all probability, a gradual shift in the religious consciousness of their predecessors had occurred. This change was nothing less than revolutionary, for it meant that Hindus, instead of Christians only, were in a position to grapple seriously with the claims and reality of other religions.

Second, Church Sanskrit reduced the reluctance of nineteenth-century pandits to engage in dialogue, because it obviated many objections against communicating with *mlecchas*. Writers such as Carey and Mill recognized that pandits would dismiss their evangelistic treatises as the fulminations of barbarians as long as they wrote them in regional Indian languages. In order to counteract this impression, they made a concerted effort to utilize technical Sanskrit terminology along with its allied conceptual framework in order, as they put it more often than once, to lead traditionally educated pandits from that which they knew already to that which they did not yet know. To a considerable extent, their attempts were successful, even if, from the statistical point of view, only a few Hindus became Christians. Church Sanskrit at least served to make the *khṛṣṭadharma* more accessible, acceptable, and intriguing to those who came into contact with, for example, the Śrīkhṛṣṭasaṃgītā, than would have otherwise been the case. Short-lived and immature though it was, the new hermeneutics communicated Christian thinking adequately. Except for the concepts expressed by *śuddhi* and *svarga*, the pandits seem to have largely understood what Muir, following precedents set by Carey, Mill, and Wilson, intended to convey. To avoid dialogue with Christianity in Sanskrit, therefore, would have been an abject failure so serious that Soma., Hara., and Nīla. were unwilling to countenance it.

Some Hindus having liberalized their approach to non-Vedic religions, and some Christian evangelists having found in Church Sanskrit a valuable vehicle for dialogue, the stage was set for sophisticated encounter between the two religions. Without reiterating each argument applied by the three pandits to Christianity, a summary of the basic features of their apologetics is in order. Grievances of a social nature, occurring in only one text, Hara.'s mordacious MPO, were strictly subordinate to theological and philosophical objections. The issues debated were, for the most part, ones that are found in textbooks describing the fundamental doctrines of either religion, with the curious absence of Jesus Christ, Christianity's central figure. In this connection it should be noted that the pandits approached the *khṛṣṭadharma* as a system, not as a way of moral or spiritual conduct to be lived according to patterns established by the *mahāmoktṛ*. Whatever attraction they may have felt toward this figure seems to have been dampened by his participation in a scheme of creation and salvation that raises more ethical ambiguities than it resolves.

If Christianity was unacceptable as a whole, it was also objectionable in each of its parts, except the Trinity, the apparent approval of which resulted from misunderstanding. Resistance, therefore, instead of accommodation, was the rule rather than the exception. But it would be incorrect to say that the pandits broke entirely new ground in their anti-Christian apologetics. The religious history of Hinduism itself, which mulled over, dismissed, and catalogued propositions tantamount to those put forth by Muir, provided an arsenal of ready-made retorts for the MPŚ, MPO, and ŚTV. Insight acquired from that religion's own internecine struggles is largely the reason why the pandits succeeded in responding to the MP as forcefully and uncompromisingly as they did.

Although Hindu recognition of religious plurality was long overdue, there is no reason to think that this delay resulted in decisional paralysis about which among the Dharmas is salvific. Whether it is the only way to *mokṣa* or at least the most direct route, Hinduism alone fulfilled the criteria for a *mokṣadharma*, however variously its features were defined. Pandits needed only to search their own scriptures to find patterns for explaining religious diversity. As was the case with their specifically apologetical arguments, Hinduism's record of intrareligious affairs offered model schemes of interpretation. It should be emphasized once again in this connection that various options were available for explaining the existence of other religions vis-à-vis their own. In point of fact, the trio selected three fundamentally different schemes of Dharma.

Therefore, whatever may be claimed to the contrary, it is misleading and historically inaccurate to speak of "the Hindu attitude to other religions" as if all Hindus have always conformed to a single interpretive scheme. Nor is it reliable to assume that the Hindu Dharma has invariably been tolerant of other religions. Neither Hindus nor Christians gain any advantage from this clarification, but writers who concentrate on classical Hindu documents for their assessment of tolerance in that religion will find much in the records of the MP Controversy to qualify their remarks. Whatever the actual proportion between Hindu tolerance and intolerance may be, one can at least be certain that both sets of mind existed. As with Gautama Buddha, so with Jesus Christ; both figures brought out the tendency in Hindus to be either exclusivistic or inclusivistic.

Whatever else might be said in its favor or disfavor, the MP Controversy was an authentic interreligious encounter. The participants were loyal to their own Dharmas and tried intelligently and honestly — if not sympathetically — to come to grips with each other. While at present these qualities may be thought to exclude each other, the historical record of dialogue between Hinduism and the Khr̥ṣṭadharma shows, on the contrary, that they did coexist.

APPENDIX

The third and final edition of the MP (1852—54) elicited yet another response from a fourth, unknown pandit. His critique of Muir's text is found in a collection of letters discussing the relative merits of Hinduism and Christianity. This correspondence, exchanged between an anonymous British missionary and Hindu partners-in-dialogue, was published in Hindi under the title Dharmādharmaparīkṣāpatra (1861).[205] About this informant nothing is known except that he was a Vaiṣṇava and probably a Bengali. Although his comments were brief, they are evidence that Nīla. was not alone in approaching non-Vedic religions as heresies, deviations from, and distortions of, truth. This unnamed pandit concentrated on Muir's personal heterodoxy and Christianity's negative role in a scheme of Dharma dependent on prevalent notions about chaotic religious and social conditions in the present Kali Age.

The pandit attacked Muir unsparingly: "The author is nothing but a *pākhaṇḍī*" (*kitāb banānevālā keval pākhaṇḍī hai*, p. 101). Whereas in an intrareligious context *pākhaṇḍī* would normally be translated as "heretic," in this interreligious setting it would be better rendered as "infidel," much in the same manner as Christians in the Middle Ages referred to non-Christians (e. g., Muslims). Following this accusation was a lurid quotation from the Bṛhannāradīyapurāṇa (14.105—06) instructing Vaiṣṇavas in the proper way to execute unbelievers and blasphemers.[206]

According to this mordacious correspondent, Muir was a *pākhaṇḍī* because, undeterred by warnings in the *śāstras* against blasphemy, he nonetheless reviled the Purāṇas and *avatāras*, without even summarizing their contents or deeds.[207] This hostility toward the author of the MP is especially noteworthy in view of the fact that Muir's third edition was far more moderate and conciliatory than either the first or second, the strident passages of which were excised.

The fourth pandit viewed Christianity as a contemptible nuisance disturbing the path of true Dharma and as a sign of the increased tempo of

---

[205] With the exception of the letter under consideration here, the correspondence was all originally composed in Bengali and published as Satyadharmaniścayārthapatra (1850). The letter concerning the MP appears first in the second edition, but it also, presumably, was the work of a Bengali.

[206] *Yaḥ śṛṇoti mahannindāṃ sādaraṃ tac chṛṇuśva me / teṣāṃ karṇeṣu pātyante taptāyaḥ kīlasaṃcayāḥ // tataś ca teṣu chidreṣu tailam atyuṣṇamulvaṇaṃ / pūryate ca tataś cāpi kumbhīpākaṃ prapadyate //.*

[207] *Ityādi purāṇavākyoṃ kā kimapi bhay na mān / śāstra purāṇa avatāroṃ kī jagah jagah nindā kī likhī aur un kā sārāṃś ek bhī na likhā / is se niśςay huā ki keval pākhaṇḍī hai //* (p. 103).

the Kali Yuga predicted by ancient sages. His confidence in the Purāṇas was unshaken because they had actually predicted this distressing state of affairs.[208] Among the authoritative passages cited was Bhāgavatapurāṇa 10.20—23: "While *Īśvara* poured down rain, dams were breached by floods, just as in the Kali Age the Vedic *mārgas* [are destroyed] by the false theories of heretics."[209] The pandit's declamations concluded with an extract from the Bṛhannāradīyapurāṇa, which has already been noted for its conception of sins for which no atonement can be made (*vide* p. 155, n. 180). Among the offenders listed there, who are condemned to hell either endlessly or for lengths of time stretching the mind's capacity to imagine, are Buddhists, those who neglect to offer sacrifices to deities and ancestors, and brahmins who live like *śūdras* and blaspheme against Śiva, Viṣṇu, the Vedas, *varnāśramas*, and Dharmaśāstras.[210] Being on a par with sinners of this sort, Christians are, *a fortiori*, consigned to a similar fate.

Once again, in accordance with intra-Hindu sectarianism, religious plurality was interpreted negatively, resulting in a scheme of Dharma that generated overt intolerance in the fourth pandit, just as it had previously in Hara. and Nīla.

---

[208] *Tattat purāṇoṃ meṃ trikālajña antaryāmī muniyoṃ ne sakalyuga dharmoṃ ke varṇan meṃ kaliyuga kā bhī varṇan kiyā / un ke likhne ke anusār sakal varṇit kaliyug ke dharm ṭhīk ṭhīk mil rahe haiṃ ham log anubhav kar rahe haiṃ / isī se to ham logoṃ ko apne purāṇādikoṃ meṃ atyant anaśvar dṛḍhatar viśvās hai / isī se to āp logoṃ kā likhnā keval mithyā hī samajh kar apne mat meṃ atyant viśvās kar rahe haiṃ //* (p. 106—07).

[209] *Jalaughair nirabhidyanta setavo varṣatīśvare / pākhaṇḍinām asadvādair vedamārgāḥ kalau yathā //*. Also cited was Harivaṃśa 177.7—8 and a verse from the Padmapurāṇa: *Kalinādharmamitreṇa dhareyaṃ bādhitā bhṛśaṃ / satyaṃ nāsti tapaḥ śaucaṃ dayā dānaṃ na vidyate //*.

[210] *Bauddhāḥ pākhaṇḍinaḥ proktā yato vedavinindakāḥ / tasmād dvijas tān nekṣyeta yato vedabahiṣkṛtāḥ //* (14.70) *yaḥ svakarmaparityāgī pākhaṇḍīty ucyate budhaiḥ / tatsaṅgakṛt tatsamaḥ syāt tāv ubhāv atipāpinau // kalpakoṭisahasrāṇi kalpakoṭiśatāni ca / sahasravaṃśasaṃyukto narake vāsam aśnute //* (14.133—34) *ucchinnapitṛdevajyā vedamārgabahiṣkṛtāḥ / pākhaṇḍā iti vikhyātā yātanā bahavaḥ smṛtāḥ //* (14.185) *eteṣāṃ pāpabāhulyān narakaṃ kalpakoṭiṣu / ete pākhaṇḍinaḥ proktās tasmād eṣāṃ na niṣkṛtiḥ //* (14.72) *śivanindāparāṇāṃ ca viṣṇunindāratātmanāṃ / satkathānindakānāṃ ca nehāmutra ca niṣkṛtiḥ //* (14.68) *vedaśraddhāvihīnatvaṃ gurutalpasamaṃ smṛtaṃ //* (14.49) *śāstranindāparaś caiva gurutalpasamaṃ smṛtaṃ //* (untraced) *yasmād dharmaṃ parijñāya tam eva dveṣṭi yo naraḥ / karoti cāpy udāsīnaṃ tam āhur brahmaghātakaṃ //* (18.27) *vedanindāparāś caiva dharmaśāstravinindakāḥ / śūdravṛttyeva jīvanti dvijā narakabhoginaḥ //* (18.79) *kuhakaiś ca janais tatra hetuvādaviśāradaiḥ / pākhaṇḍāś ca bhaviṣyanti cāturāśramyanindakāḥ //* (18.54) *vedanindāparāś caiva vipranindāparās tathā / viṣṇubhaktivihīnāś ca vedavidveṣinas tathā //* (untraced).

BIBLIOGRAPHY

ABBOTT, JUSTIN. 1921—23. The discovery of the original text of the Christian Purāṇa of Thomas Stephens. Bulletin of the School of Oriental and African Studies 2.679—83.

ABS, JOSEPH. 1926. Beiträge zur Kritik heterodoxer Philosophie-Systeme in der Purāṇa-Literatur, Beiträge zur Literaturwissenschaft und Geistesgeschichte Indiens (Festgabe Hermann Jacobi zum 75. Geburtstag), ed. Willibald Kirfel, 386—96. Bonn: Fritz Klopp.

AELEN, J. (ed.) 1931. Satyawedasaarasangraham: a short exposition of the essentials of the true religion. Nellore: St. John's Press.

ALI, MUHAMMAD MOHAR. 1965. The Bengali reaction to Christian missionary activities, 1831—1857. Chittagong: Mehrub Publications.

Answers to Hindoo objections against certain Christian doctrines. 1833. CCO 2.177—78.

ĀPṬE, NĀRĀYAṆA (ed.) 1905. Smṛtīnāṃ samuccayaḥ. (ĀSS, 48.) Poona: Ānandāśrama Press.

APTE, VAMAN SHIVARAM. 1978. The practical Sanskrit-English dictionary. Kyoto: Rinsen Book Company. (Reprint of the Poona edition of 1957.)

AUROBINDO, 1940. The life divine, 2. Calcutta: Arya Publishing House.

AVALON, ARTHUR (ed.) 1929. Mahānirvāna Tantra: with the commentary of Hariharananda Bharatī. (Tantrik Texts, 13.) Madras: Ganesh and Co. (Madras) Private Ltd.

— (trans.) 1953. The greatness of Śiva: Mahiṃnastava of Puṣpadanta with the commentary of Jagannātha Chakravartī. Madras: Ganesh and Co.

BAAGO, KAJ. 1969. Pioneers of indigenous Christianity. Bangalore: Christian Institute for the Study of Religion and Society.

BACH, JULIEN. 1868. Le Pére Calmette et les Missionaires Indianistes. Paris: Joseph Albanel.

BALLANTYNE, JAMES ROBERT. 1855a. Discourse on translation. Mirzapore: Orphan Press.

— 1855b. LGPGD (20 April—31 May). Range 215.43, no. 403.

— 1857. Candrabhramaṇavicāraḥ: does the moon rotate? The question argued in Sanskrit and English by pandits of the Benares Sanskrit College and James R. Ballantyne. Benares: Medical Hall Press.

— 1860a. Khṛṣṭadharmakaumudī: Christianity contrasted with Hindu philosophy. London and Benares: James Madden and Medical Hall Press. (Reviewed in CR, 1861, 35.81—109; Göttingische Gelehrte Anzeigen, 1860, 196—200.)

— 1860b. The Bible for pandits — the first three chapters of Genesis diffusely and unreservedly commented, in Sanskrit and English. London and Benares: James Madden and Medical Hall Press.

— (ed. and trans.) 1885. The Sānkhya aphorisms of Kapila, with... extracts from the commentaries. (3rd ed.) London: Trübner and Co.

BALLANTYNE, J. R. and GOVIND SASTRI DEVA (eds. and trans.) 1971. Yoga sutras of Patanjali. (2nd ed.) Delhi: Indological Book House. (1st pub. 1852.)

BANERJEA, KRISHNA MOHAN. 1839. The 'Mahimnastava,' or a hymn to Shiva: with an English translation. JASB 8.355—66.

— 1841. Truth defended, error exposed: strictures upon Hara Chandra Tarkapanchanan's answer to Mr. Muir's Mataparikshа. Calcutta: Ostell and Lepage, British Library.

— 1861. Dialogues on the Hindu philosophy, comprising the Nyaya, the Sankhya, the Vedant; to which is added a discussion of the authority of the Vedas. London and Edinburgh: Williams and Norgate.

BĀPU, SUBĀJĪ. N. d. Avirodhaprakāśa. N. p.

— N. d. Paraśurāmakṣetrasthā. N. p.

— 1836. Siddhāntaśiromaṇiprakāśa: a comparison of the pooranic, sidhāntic and Copernican systems of the world. Bombay: lithographed by R. Prera.

BASU, B. D. (ed.) 1974. The Mīmāṃsā sūtras of Jaiminī (SBH, 27.) New York: AMS Press, Inc. (1st pub. 1923—25.)

BHARATI, AGEHANANDA. 1970. The Hindu renaissance and its apologetic patterns. Journal of Asian Studies 29.267—87.

BHAṬṬA, OṂKARA [Onkar Bhut]. 1841. Bhūgolasāra, arthāt jyotiṣa candrikā. Agra: Agra School Book Society.

BHATTACHARYYA, JANAKI VALLABHA (trans.) 1978. Jayanta Bhaṭṭa's Nyāya-Mañjarī [the compendium of Indian speculative logic]. Delhi: Motilal Banarsidass.

Boden professorship of Sanskrit at Oxford. 1832. AJ, n. s., 7.246—48.

BON MAHARAJ, Swami B. H. 1965. Thirty-one questions and answers: relation between the religions. Indian Philosophy and Culture, 10.1—8.

BOXER, C. R. 1951. The Christian century in Japan 1549—1650. Berkeley and Los Angeles: University of California Press.

BOYD, ROBIN. 1969. An introduction to Indian Christian theology. Madras: Christian Literature Society for India.

— 1974. India and the Latin captivity of the church: the cultural context of the gospel. Cambridge: University Press.

Brief notice of the late Lancelot Wilkinson of the Bombay Civil Service, with his opinions on the education of natives of India and on the state of native society. 1853. London: printed for private circulation.

BÜHLER, GEORGE (trans.) 1969. The laws of Manu. (SBE, 25.) New York: Dover Publications, Inc. (1st pub. 1886.)

BURKE, MARIE LOUISE. 1973. Swami Vivekananda: his second visit to the West. San Francisco: Advaita Ashram.

CAREY, EUSTACE. 1836. Memoir of William Carey. London: Jackson and Walford.

CAREY, WILLIAM. 1795. BMS ms. Carey's ms. journal (unpaginated.)

— 1797. BMS ms. Carey to John Ryland, 6 July, Mudnabati.

— 1798. BMS ms. Carey to John Sutcliffe, 10 Oct., n. p.

— 1802. BMS ms. Carey to John Sutcliffe, 17 May, n. p.

— 1806. A grammar of the Sungskrit language, composed from the works of the most esteemed grammarians. Serampore: Mission Press.

— (trans.) 1808—16. Dharmapustakasya sarvavākyāṇi. Serampore: Mission Press.

— 1819. On the importance of Sungskrita to the future improvement of India. FI (monthly) 2.373—82, 426—42.

— 1822. On encouraging the cultivation of Sungskrit among the natives of India. FI (quarterly) 2.131—39.

CAREY, WILLIAM and JOSHUA MARSHMAN (eds. and trans.) 1806—10. The Ramayuna of Valmeeki. Serampore: Mission Press.

CAREY, WILLIAM, JOSHUA MARSHMAN and WILLIAM WARD. 1818. College for Asiatic Christian and other youth. Serampore: Mission Press.

CARMAN, JOHN B. 1968. Is Christian faith a form of bhakti? Visva-Bharati Journal of Philosophy 34.24—37.

CASTETS, J. 1931. Pioneers in European Sanskrit scholarship. Indian Review 32.345—51.

CASSELS, WALTER RICHARD. 1874—77. Supernatural religion: an inquiry into the reality of divine revelation. 3 vols. London: Watts and Co.

Catalogus codicum manuscriptorum Bibliothecae regiae, 1. 1739. Paris: n. pub.

CHADWICK, OWEN. 1970. The Victorian church, 2. (An ecclesiastical history of England, 5.) London: Adam and Charles Black.

CHATTERJEE, MARGARET. 1976. The concept of multiple allegiance: a hypothesis concerning the contemporary Indian religious spectrum. Man in India 56. 123—33.

CHATTERTON, EYRE. 1924. History of the Church of England in India. London: Society for the Propagation of Christian Knowledge.

CHAUDHURI, NIRAD C. 1974. Scholar extraordinary: the life of Professor the Rt. Honorable Friedrich Max Müller. London: Chatto and Windus.

CHOUDHARY, RADHAKRISHNA. 1956. Heretical sects in the purāṇas. ABORI 37.234—57.

Christus-Krischto-Kṛṣṇa: Gespräche mit Seiner Göttlichen Gnade A. C. Bhaktivedanta Swami Prabhupāda. N. d. Frankfurt: Bhaktivedanta Book Trust.

COLEBROOKE, HENRY THOMAS. 1858. Essays on the religion and philosophy of the Hindus. (new ed.) London: Williams and Norgate. (1st ed., 1837.)

COLLET, S. D. 1914. Life and letters of Raja Rammohun Roy. Calcutta: A. C. Sarkar.

CROWTHER, M. A. 1970. Church embattled: religious controversy in mid-Victorian England. Hamden, Connecticut: Archon Books.

DAS, LALA JIVAN (ed.) 1897. Works of late Pandit Guru Datta Vidyarthi, M. A., professor of physical science, Government College Lahore, 1. Lahore: "Panjab Economical" Press.

DAS, SISIR KUMAR. 1974. The shadow of the cross: Christianity and Hinduism in a colonial situation. New Delhi: Munshiram Manoharlal.

DASGUPTA, SURENDRANATH. 1932. A history of Indian philosophy, 2. Cambridge: At the University Press.

DAVID, M. D. 1975. John Wilson: portrait of a missionary. ICHR 9.128—46.

DE, LAL BIHARI. 1896. Vedāntaparīkṣā. Allahabad: North India Christian Tract and Book Society.

— 1904. Vālmīkīyarāmāyaṇaparīkṣā. Trinidad: Canadian Mission Press.

DE, SUSHIL KUMAR. 1962. Bengali literature in the nineteenth century 1757—1857 (2nd ed.) Calcutta: Firma K. L. Mukhopadhyay.

DERRETT, J. DUNCAN. 1968a. A juridical fabrication of early British India: the Mahānirvāṇa-Tantra. Zeitschrift für Vergleichende Rechtswissenschaft 69.138—83.

— 1968b. Religion, law and the state in India. London: Faber and Faber.

DESHPANDE, P. Y. 1971. Genesis: a Hindu reflection on the Bible. JES 8.575—80.

DE SMET, R. V. 1963. Categories of Indian philosophy and communication of the gospel. RS 10.20—26.

— 1964. Sin and its removal in India. IA (3rd series) 1.163—73.

— 1965. Materials for an Indian Christology. RS 12.6—15.

DEUSSEN, PAUL. 1906. Allgemeine Geschichte der Philosophie, 1, 1. Leipzig: F. A. Brockhaus.

— (ed. and trans.) 1963. Sechzig Upanishads des Veda. Darmstadt: Wissenschaftliche Buchgesellschaft. (1st pub. 1897.)

— 1973. The system of the Vedanta. (Charles Johnston, trans.) New York: Dover Publications, Inc. (1st pub. 1912.)

DEVA SASTRI, BAPU (trans.) 1860—62. Sūryasiddhānta [with the Siddhāntaśiromaṇi translated by L. Wilkinson.] (BI, 32.) Calcutta: The Asiatic Society.

DEVADUTT, V. E. 1960. The incarnation and Hindu thought. Canadian Journal of Theology 6.81—91.

DEVASSIA, P. C. 1977. Kristubhagavatam: a mahakavya in Sanskrit based on the life of Jesus Christ. Trivandrum: Jayabharatam.

Dharmādharmaparīkṣāpatra: discussions on Christianity with Hindu pandits. 1861. London: n. pub.

Dictionary of national biography. 1917. London: Oxford University Press.

DIMOCK, EDWARD C. 1976. Hinduism and Islam in medieval Bengal. Aspects of Bengali History and Society, ed. Rachel Van M. Baumer, 1—12. New Delhi: Vikas.

EDGERTON, FRANKLIN (trans.) 1972. The Bhagavad Gītā. Cambridge: Harvard University Press. (1st pub. 1944.)

ELIADE, MIRCEA. 1959. The sacred and the profane. New York: Harcourt, Brace, Jovanovich.

ELLIS, FRANCIS. 1822. Account of a discovery of a modern imitation of the Vedas with remarks on the genuine works. AR 14.1—59.

FARQUHAR, JAMES N. 1913. The crown of Hinduism. Oxford: Oxford University Press.

FILLIOZAT, JEAN. 1941. Bibliothèque nationale. Départment des manuscrits. Catalogue du fonds sanscrit, 1. Paris: Adriene-Maisonneuve.

FRYKENBERG, ROBERT. 1976. The impact of conversion and social reform upon society in South India during the late company period: questions concerning Hindu-Christian encounters, with special reference to Tinnevelly. Indian Society and the Beginnings of Modernization, c. 1830—1850, eds. C. H. Philips and M. D. Wainwright, 187—243. London: School of Oriental and African Studies.

GAIL, ADALBERT. 1969. Buddha als Avatāra Viṣṇus im Spiegel der Purāṇas. Zeitschrift der Deutschen Morgenländischen Gesellschaft, Supplementa 1, Vorträge, Teil 3, 917—23.

GARBE, RICHARD (ed.) 1895. The Sāṃkhya-pravacana-bhāṣya: or commentary on the exposition of the Sānkhya philosophy by Vijñānabhikṣu. (Harvard Oriental Series, 2.) Cambridge: Harvard University.

GARDNER, CHARLES E. 1900. Life of Father Goreh. London: Longmans, Green and Company.

GENSICHEN, HANS WERNER. 1967. 'Abominable heathenism' a rediscovered tract by Bartholomaeus Ziegenbalg. ICHR 1.29—40.

GHOSE, JOGENDRA CHUNDER and ESHAM CHUNDER BOSE (eds.) 1978. The English works of Raja Rammohun Roy. New York: AMS Press, Inc. (1st ed. 1906.)

GISPERT-SAUCH, G. 1972. The Sanskrit hymns of Brahmabandhav Upadhyay. RS 19.60—77.

GLASENAPP, HELMUT von. 1960. Toleranz und Fanatismus in Indien. Jahrbuch der Schopenhauer-Gesellschaft 41.44—51.

GOLDSTÜCKER, THEODORE. 1862. The religious difficulties of India. Westminster Review 20.245—63.

GONDA, JAN. 1966. Loka: world and heaven in the Veda. (Verhandelingen der Koninklijke Nederlandse Akademie van Wetenschappen, Afd. Letterkunde, New Series, Deel 73, no. 1.) Amsterdam: n. v. Noord-Hollandsche Uitgevers Maatschappij.

— 1970. Viṣṇuism and Śivaism: a comparison. London: Athlone Press.

GOPAL, SAMUEL. 1896. Some reminiscences of the late Father Goreh, S. S. J. E. ICQR 9.52—60.

GOREH, NĪLAKAṆṬHA (Nehemiah). 1860. Ṣaḍdarśanadarpaṇa: Hindu philosophy examined by a Benares pandit. Calcutta: Calcutta Christian Tract and Book Society. (6th ed., 1950, Allahabad: North India Christian Tract and Book Society.)

— 1884. Do I honestly believe in the doctrines of the Church of England which I have solemnly professed to believe by subscribing to her prayer book and articles? Poona: Panch Howds Mission Press.

— 1888. SSJE ms. Goreh to Father Page, 28 Sept., Allahabad.

— 1889. The existence of Brahmoism itself a proof of the divine origin of Christianity. (2nd ed.) Allahabad: North India Christian Tract and Book Society.

— 1891. The philosophical systems of the Hindus. ICQR 4.139—170.

— 1893. God's foreknowledge and man's free will. ICQR 6.193—221.

— 1897. A rational refutation of the Hindu philosophical systems (Fitz-Edward Hall, trans.) (2nd ed.) Madras: Christian Literature Society for India. (1st ed. 1861.)

— 1898a. Original sin: an answer to theistic objections. ICQR 11.35—43.

— 1898b. The supposed and real doctrines of Hinduism, as held by educated Hindus; with the true source of the former. (Papers for Thoughtful Hindus, 2.) London and Madras: Christian Literature Society for India.
— 1900. Father Goreh on the holy trinity. etc. ICQR 13.184—92.
— 1904. Vedantism and the essence of Christianity: Vedāntmat kā bicār aur khriṣṭīyamat kā sār. Allahabad: North India Christian Tract and Book Society. (1st pub. 1853.)
— 1951. Śāstratattvavinirṇayaḥ, ed. S. L. Katre. (Scindia Oriental Institute Series, 3.) Ujjain: Scindia Oriental Institute.
GOSH, RAMACHANDRA. 1893. Biographical sketch of the Rev. K. M. Banerjea. Calcutta: n. pub.
GRAFE, H. 1972. Hindu apologetics at the beginning of the Protestant mission era in India. ICHR 6.43—69.
GRIERSON, GEORGE A. 1916. Mādhvas, Madhvāchārīs. Encyclopedia of Religion and Ethics, ed. James Hastings, 8.232—35. New York: Charles Scribner's Sons.
GUPTA, ŚRĪ MUNILĀL (ed.) 1964. Śrīmadbhāgavatamahāpurāṇam. 2 vols. Gorakhpur: Gītā Press.
HACKER, PAUL. 1957. Religiöse Toleranz und Intoleranz im Hinduismus. Saeculum 8.167—79.
— 1958. Der Dharmabegriff des Neuhinduismus. ZMR 42.1—15.
— 1964. Zur Geschichte und Beurteilung des Hinduismus. Kritik einiger verbreiteter Ansichten. Orientalistische Literaturzeitung 59.231—45.
— 1978. Aspects of neo-Hinduism as contrasted with surviving traditional Hinduism. Kleine Schriften, ed. Lambert Schmithausen, 580—607. Wiesbaden: Franz Steiner Verlag.
— 1980. The situation of the Church in India. Theological Foundations of Evangelization, ed., Johannes Dörmann, 79—100. Veröffentlichungen des Instituts für Missionswissenschaft der Westfälischen Wilhelms-Universität, Münster. St. Augustin: Steyler Verlag.
HALBFASS, WILHELM. 1975. Zur Theorie der Kastenordnung in der indischen Philosophie. Nachrichten der Akademie der Wissenschaften in Göttingen, Philologisch-Historische Klasse, 277—316.
— 1977. Anthropological problems in classical Indian philosophy, Beiträge zur Indienforschung: Ernst Waldschmidt zum 80. Geburtstag gewidmet. (Veröffentlichungen des Museums für indische Kunst, 4). 225—36. Berlin: Museum für indische Kunst.
— 1981. Indien und Europa: Perspektiven ihrer geistigen Begegnung. Basel: Schwabe and Co.
HANDIQUI, KRISHNA KANTA (trans.) N. d. Naiṣadhacarita of Śrīharṣa. (Deccan College Building Centenary and Silver Jubilee Series, 33.) Poona: Deccan College.
— 1949. Yaśastilaka and Indian culture: on Somadeva's Yaśastilaka and aspects of Jainism and Indian thought and culture in the tenth century. (Jīvarāja Jaina Granthamālā, 2) Sholapur: Jaina Saṃskṛti Saṃrakshaka Sangha.
HAUER, J. W. 1961. Toleranz und Intoleranz in den nichtchristlichen Religionen: Beitrag zu einer weltgeschichtlichen Betrachtung der Religion. Stuttgart: W. Kohlhammer Verlag.
HAZRA, R. C. 1975. Studies in the puranic records on Hindu rites and customs. (2nd ed.) Delhi: Motilal Banarsidass.
HERAS, H. 1952. The devil in Indian scriptures. Journal of the Bombay Branch of the Royal Asiatic Society 27.214—41.
Hinduism and Christianity [review of K. M. Banerjea's Truth defended, error exposed.] 1841. CCO 11.311—15.
HOHENBERGER, ADAM. 1967. Das Bhaviṣyapurāṇa. Wiesbaden: Otto Harrasowitz.
HOOPER, JOHN S. M. 1957. Greek New Testament terms in Indian languages. Bangalore: Bible Society of India and Ceylon.

HUART, ALBERT. 1956. Hindouisme et tolérance religieuse. Nouvelle Revue Theologique 78.834—52.

HUME, DAVID. 1975. Enquiries concerning human understanding and concerning the principles of morals. (3rd ed. revised by L. A. Selby-Bigge.) Oxford: Clarendon Press. (1st ed. 1777.)

HUSAIN, SYED SAJJAD. 1960. A descriptive catalogue of Bengali manuscripts in Munshi Abdul Karim's collection. (Asiatic Society of Pakistan Publication, 3.) Dacca: Asiatic Society of Pakistan.

India Correspondence. 1890. Cowley St. John Evangelist (Oxford) (Jan. 1.) 35—36.

JAGADĪŚALĀLAŚĀSTRĪ, Paṇḍita (ed.) 1970. Kathāsaritsāgaraḥ. Delhi: Motilal Banarsidass.

JAMBUVIJAYAJI (ed.) 1961. Vaiśeṣikasūtra of Kaṇāda with the commentary of Candrānanda. (Gaekwad's Oriental Series, 136.) Baroda: Oriental Institute.

JAMES, EDWARD. 1830. Brief memoirs of the late... John Thomas James,... Lord Bishop of Calcutta. London: J. Hatchard and Son.

JHAḶAKĪKARA, BHĪMĀCĀRYA. 1893. Nyāyakośa: or, dictionary of the technical terms of the Nyāya philosophy. (Bombay Sanskrit [and Prakrit] Series, 49.) Bombay: Department of Public Instruction.

JOHNSON, W. F. 1876. Śivaparīkṣā. Calcutta: Christian Tract and Book Society.

JONES, KENNETH W. 1976. Arya dharm: Hindu consciousness in 19th-century Punjab. New Dehlhi: Manohar.

JOSHI, LAXMAN SHASTRI (ed.) 1937. Dharmakośa, 1, Vyavahārakāṇḍa, 1. Wai: Prajña Pāṭhasālā Maṇḍala.

KANE, PANDURANG VAMAN. 1941. History of Dharmaśāstra, 2, 1. Poona: Bhandarkar Oriental Research Institute.

— 1946. History of Dharmaśāstra, 3. Poona: Bhandarkar Oriental Research Institute.

— 1953. History of Dharmaśāstra, 4. Poona: Bhandarkar Oriental Research Institute.

— 1958. History of Dharmaśāstra, 5, 1. Poona: Bhandarkar Oriental Research Institute.

— 1962. History of Dharmaśāstra, 5, 2. Poona: Bhandarkar Oriental Research Institute.

— 1968. History of Dharmaśāstra, 1, 1. (2nd ed.) Poona: Bhandarkar Oriental Research Institute.

KATRE, SADASHIVA L. 1942. Śāstratattvavinirṇaya: the work and its author. New Indian Antiquary 4.397—413.

KEITH, A. B. 1887. Catalogue of the Sanskrit (and Prākrit) manuscripts in the library of the India Office, 2, 1. London.

KELLY, J. N. D. 1972. Early Christian creeds. (3rd ed.) London: Longmans.

KENNEDY, VANS. 1831a. Oriental translations of the scriptures. AJ, n. s., 4.169—80.

— 1831b. Remarks on Dr. Mill's Sanscrit renderings of scripture terms. OCS 2.200—07.

KEUNEN, ABRAHAM. 1877. Prophets and prophecy in Israel, with an introduction by John Muir. London: Longmans, Green, and Co.

KEVALĀNANDASARASWATĪ (ed.) 1954. Mīmāṃsākoṣaḥ, 3. (PPMGM.) Wai: V. G. Joshi, for Prājña Pāṭhashālā Maṇḍala.

KHAN, SIDDIQ. 1961. William Carey and the Serampore books (1800—1834). Libri 11.197—280.

KHONDKAR, ABDUR RAHIM. 1976. The Portuguese contribution to Bengali prose, grammar and lexicography. Dacca: Bangla Academy.

Khrīṣṭīyānerder mat ki. 1805. Serampore: Mission Press.

KITTEL, GERHARD (ed.) 1964—72. Theological dictionary of the New Testament, 2. Grand Rapids, Mich.: Wm. B. Eerdmans Co.

KLIMKEIT, HANS-JOACHIM. 1978. Zur Ordnungskonception des politischen Hinduismus der Neuzeit. Zeitschrift für Religions- und Geistesgeschichte 30.306—27.

KÖHLER, HANS-WERBIN. 1973. Śrad-dhā in der vedischen und altbuddhistischen Literatur. (Glasenapp-Stiftung, 9.) Wiesbaden: Franz Steiner Verlag.

KOPF, DAVID. 1969. British orientalism and the Bengal renaissance: the dynamics of Indian modernization 1773—1835. Berkeley and Los Angeles: University of California Press.

— 1979. The Brahmo Samaj and the shaping of the modern Indian mind. Princeton: Princeton University Press.

KRÄMER, ADELHEID. 1958. Christus und Christentum im Denken des modernen Hinduismus. Bonn: Röhrscheid.

KULANDRAN, SABAPATHY. 1958. The tentative version of the Bible or the "Navalar Version". Tamil Culture 7.229—50.

KUPPUSWAMI SASTRI, S. S. 1929. Rāvaṇa-bhāṣya. Journal of Oriental Research (Madras) 3.1—5.

LACH, DONALD F. 1965. Asia in the making of Europe, 1. Chicago: University of Chicago Press.

LAIRD, M. A. 1972. Missionaries and education in Bengal 1793—1837. Oxford: Oxford University Press.

LAVAN, S. 1977. Unitarians and India: a study in encounter and response. Boston: Beacon Press.

LE MAHIEU, D. L. 1976. The mind of William Paley: a philosopher and his age. Lincoln and London: University of Nebraska Press.

LE SAUX, HENRI. 1965. Sagesse Hindoue mystique Chretiénne: du Védanta à la Trinité. Paris: Éditions du Centurion.

Life and letters of the Right Honorable Friedrich Max Müller, 1. 1902. (ed. by his wife.) London and Bombay: Longmans, Green and Co.

LIPNER, J. J. 1978. The Christian and vedantic theories of originative causality: a study in transcendence and immanence. PEW 28.53—68.

LOGIN, E. DALHOUSIE. 1970. Lady Login's recollections: court life and camp life 1820—1904. Patiala: Punjab Languages Dept.

LORENZEN, DAVID N. 1972. The Kāpālikas and Kālāmukhas: two lost Śaivite sects. Berkeley and Los Angeles: University of California Press.

MAHADEVAN, T. M. P. 1969. Philosophical trends v. history of sciences of India — orthodox systems. Indian Journal of History of Science 4.27—39.

MAṆḌALĪKA, VIŚVANĀTHA NĀRĀYAṆA (ed.) Padmapurāṇam. (ĀSS, Extra 1.) 4 vols. 1893—94. Poona: Ānandāśrama Press.

MASSON, JOSEPH. 1966. Die Religionsfreiheit aus hinduistischer Sicht. Concilium 2.55—58.

MATTHEWS, N. and M. D. WAINWRIGHT. 1965. A guide to Western manuscripts and documents in the British Isles relating to South and Southeast Asia. London: Oxford University Press.

MAZOOMDAR, P. C. 1883. The Oriental Christ. Boston: George H. Ellis.

MEHTA, VED. 1976. Mahatma Gandhi and his apostles. Harmondsworth: Penguin Books Ltd.

MENSCHING, GUSTAV. 1971. Tolerance and truth in religion. (H.-J. Klimkeit, trans.) University, Ala.: University of Alabama Press.

MILL, WILLIAM HODGE. N.d. Bodleian ms., Mill 205.

— 1822a. SPG ms., C.Ind.I 9(1)3. Mill to Anthony Hamilton. 27 July, Ajmer.

— (trans.) 1822b. Decalogus. [SPG Archives, C.Ind.I (6)33.] N. p.

— (trans.) 1823. Pratītivākyatrayam: Fidei christianae, Symbola tria... Sacro Vatum Indicorum Idiomate nunc primum expressa. [SPG Archives C.Ind.I (6)33a.] N. p.

— [1828.] Proposed version of theological terms, with a view to uniformity in translations of the holy scriptures, etc., into the various languages of India. Part the first — Sanscrit. With remarks upon the rendering proposed by Dr. Mill by Horace Hayman Wilson, Esq. Calcutta: Bishop's College Press.

— 1831—37. Śrīkhrṣṭasaṃgītā: Christa-Sangita, or the sacred history of our Lord Jesus Christ in Sanscrit verse. Calcutta: Bishop's College Press. (2nd ed. 1842.)
— 1833. SPG ms., C.Ind.I 9(1)85. Mill to SPG. 1 May, Bishop's College, Calcutta.
— 1837. Dr. Mill's reply to the Asiatic Society. Calcutta Monthly Journal, n. s., 3.721.
— 1842. SPG ms. (Bishop's College Papers, unreferenced.) Mill to Bishop's College.
MITRA, VIHARI LALA (trans.) 1978. The Yoga-Vāsishtha Mahārāmāyana of Valmiki, 2, 1. Benares: Bharatiya Publishing House.
MOFFITT, JOHN. 1977. Incarnation and avatara: an imaginary conversation. JES 14.260—87.
MONIER-WILLIAMS, MONIER. 1861. The study of Sanskrit in relation to missionary work in India. London: Oxford University Press.
— 1891. Brāhmanism and Hinduism; or, religious thought and life in India... (4th ed.) New York: Macmillan and Co.
— 1962. Indian wisdom. (Chowkhamba Sanskrit Studies, 36.) Benares: Chowkhamba Sanskrit Series Office. (1st ed. 1875.)
— 1976. A Sanskṛit—English dictionary... new edition. Delhi: Motilal Banarsidass. (1st pub. 1899.)
MORTON, WILLIAM (trans.) 1846. Vajra Suchi, the needle of adamant; or the original divine institution of caste examined and refuted by the Buddhist pandit Ashwa Gosha. MS 6.152, 161, 169—70, 177.
MUIR, JOHN. N. d. Itihāsatamomaṇi. N. p.
— N. d. Nistāramārgadīpikā. N. p.
— N. d. Śrīvidyācamatkārikā. N. p.
— 1833. Passages, ancient and modern, from the story of India. Calcutta: Church Mission Press.
— 1836. India's resurrection. CCO 5.360—61.
— 1837a. Rough notes of an essay on Christianity, Mohammedanism, and Hindooism. FI (weekly) 3.387—88.
— 1837b. School-book society for the Western Provinces. CCO 6.184—85.
— 1837c. The claims of Sungskrit, etc. on the attention of the friends of education. FI (weekly) 3.188.
— 1837d. To the editors of the Friend of India. FI (weekly) 3.228.
— 1838a. Dr. Mill's Christa Sangita — book IV. CI 8.180—82.
— 1838b. On the use to which the pseudo Vedas written by the Roman Catholic missionaries, might be turned for the refutation of Hindu errors. CCO 7.506—08.
— 1838c. St. Paul a model for the missionary. CCO 7.63—73.
— 1838d. The Baconian philosophy applicable to the mental regeneration of India. CCO 7.123—26.
— 1838e. The importance of missionaries studying the higher branches of Hindu literature and the Sanskrit language. CI 8.376—77.
— 1838f. The importance of the study of Sanskrit. CCO 7.372—73.
— 1839a. Mataparīkṣā: a sketch of the argument for Christianity and against Hinduism. Calcutta: Bishop's College Press.
— 1839b. Nūtnodantodotsaḥ: the fountain of the water of fresh intelligence. A description of England. Calcutta: Bishop's College Press.
— 1840a. Itihāsadīpikā: a sketch of the history of England. Calcutta: n. pub.
— 1840b. Mānasadharmadīpikā. N. p.
— 1840c. Mataparīkṣā: a sketch of the argument for Christianity and against Hinduism. (2nd ed.) Calcutta: Bishop's College Press.
— 1840d. On the arguments by which the alleged eternity of the Vedas may be refuted. CI 10.341—47.
— 1840e. Pāpamocanayathārthopāyapradarśanam: the inefficiency of the Ganges to wash away sin, with a statement of the true atonement. Calcutta: Baptist Mission Press. (Reviewed in CCO, 1840, 9.14—18.)
— 1840f. Rough notes on the Ganges and Hindu places of worship. CI 10.245—52.

— 1841. Śarma-paddhati: the way of happiness. A sketch of the true theory of human life. London: Richard Watts.
— 1842. Considerations on religion, its nature, effects, the steps of its progress, and the obstacles to its practice; addressed to the cultivated classes of society. Edinburg: R. Grant.
— 1843. Conciliation in matters of religion. Church of England Quarterly Review 24.86—112.
— 1844. LGPGD (April—June) Range 214.63, no. 59.
— 1845a. LGPGD (May) Range 214.68, nos. 62—91.
— 1845b. LGPGD (April—July) Range 214.68, no. 124.
— 1845c. On the best mode of reasoning on the subject of religion with educated Hindus and Mohamedans; and the qualifications necessary for that purpose. CI 15.363—73, 403—410.
— 1845d. Vyavahārālokaḥ: brief lectures on mental philosophy and other subjects delivered in Sanskrit to the students of the Benares Sanskrit College. Allahabad: Presbyterian Mission Press.
— 1846. Īśvaroktaśāstradhārā: the course of divine revelation. Calcutta: Bishop's College Press.
— 1847. Vedantism. CI 17.125—30.
— 1848a. The prospects of India — religious and intellectual. BM 1.344—74.
— 1848b. Śrīyeṣukhṛṣṭamāhātmya: the glory of Jesus Christ. Calcutta: Ostell and Lepage, British Library. (Reviewed in BM, 1849, 2.402—06.)
— 1848c. Śrīyeṣukhṛṣṭapreritapaulacaritra: a short life of the apostle Paul. Calcutta: Encyclopedia Press.
— 1849. An essay on conciliation in matters of religion: the proper adaptation of instruction to the character of the people taught... by a Bengal civilian. Calcutta: R. C. Lepage and Co.
— 1851. The Benares Sanskrit College. BM 4.94—108.
— 1852a. Hints on missions in India. CI 22.89—93.
— 1852b. On learned missionaries. TM 2.155—56.
— 1852c. Remarks on the conduct of missionary operations in northern India: and on the training of missionary agents. Cape Town: Saul Solomon and Co. (Reviewed in TM, 1853, 3.15—19.)
— 1852—54. Mataparīkṣā. (3rd ed.) 2 vols. 1, A consideration of the Hindu sastras. Calcutta: Bishop's College Press. 2, An exposition of the evidences of Christianity for Hindus. Mirzapore: R. C. Mather.
— 1853a. Are all the heathen damned? CI 23.121—25.
— 1853b. On certain unguarded statements. TM 3.359—62.
— 1853c. Paramātmastava: a Christian hymn in Sanskrit verse and Hindee prose. Allahabad: Allahabad Mission Press.
— 1856. Indian literature. North British Review (American edition) 20.109—24.
— 1861. A brief examination of prevalent opinions on the inspiration of the scriptures of the Old and New Testaments, ... with an introduction by Henry Bristow Wilson. London: Longman, Greene, Longman, and Roberts.
— 1868a. Original Sanskrit texts on the origin and history of the people of India, their religion and institutions, 1. (2nd ed.) London: Trübner and Co.
— 1868b. Original Sanskrit texts, ... 3. (2nd ed.) London: Trübner and Co.
— 1870. Original Sanskrit texts, ... 5. (2nd ed.) London: Trübner and Co.
— 1871. Original Sanskrit texts, ... 2. (2nd ed.) London: Trübner and Co.
— 1873. Original Sanskrit texts, ... 4. (2nd ed.) London: Trübner and Co.
— 1875. On Dr. Lorinser's Bhagavad Gītā and Christian writings. IA 4.77—81.
— 1877. Notes on the lax observance of caste rules and other features of social and religious life in ancient India. IA 6.251—64.
— 1878. Asita and Buddha, or the Indian Simeon. IA 7.232—34.
— 1879. Metrical translations from Sanskrit writers with an introduction, many prose versions, parallel passages from classical authors. London: Trübner and Co.

— 1910. Mataparīkṣā: an examination of religions. Allahabad: North India Christian Tract and Book Society. (reprint of 3rd ed.)

MUKHERJEE, SUJIT KUMAR. 1949. The Vajrasūcī of Aśvaghosa. Crit. ed. with notes and translation. Visva-Bharati Annals 2.125—84.

MUKHOPADHYAYA, BRAJALAL. 1894. Khristadharmakaumudisamalocana: a critical review of Dr. J. Ballantyne's Khristadharmakaumudi. Calcutta: People's Press.

MÜLLER, F. MAX. 1860. History of ancient Sanskrit literature. (2nd ed.) London: Longmans and Co.

— 1899a. Auld Lang Syne, 2. New York: Charles Scribner's Sons.

— 1899b. The six systems of Indian philosophy. London: Longmans and Co.

MUNDY, GEORGE. 1834. Christianity and Hindooism contrasted; or, a comparative view of the evidence by which the respective claims to divine authority of the Bible and Hindoo shastrus are supported. (2nd ed.) 2 vols. Serampore: Serampore Press.

MUNI, VIJAYA (ed.) 1944. Dhūrtākhyāna of Haribhadra Sūri: with a critical essay by Dr. A. N. Upādhye. (SJS, 19.) Bombay: Bharatiya Vidya Bhavan.

MURDOCH, JOHN. 1968. Classified catalogue of Tamil printed books with introductory notes. Madras: Tamil Development and Research Council. (1st pub. 1865.)

MUTTUCUMARASWAMY, V. 1965. Arumuga Navalar: the champion reformer of the Hindus. (1822—1879). Colombo: n. pub.

NAIPAUL, V. S. 1977. India: a wounded civilization. Harmondsworth: Penguin Books Ltd.

NAKAMURA, HAJIME. 1961. Indian heterodoxies in comparative light. Adyar Library Bulletin 25.550—81.

— 1975. Parallel delopments: a comparative history of ideas. Tokyo and New York: Kodansha.

NAMBIAR, SITA K. 1971. Prabodhacandrodaya of Kṛṣṇa Miśra. Delhi: Motilal Banarsidass.

NATH, RAI BAHADUR LALA BAIJ (trans.) 1913. Adhyatma Ramayana. (SBH, extra vol. 1.) Allahabad: Pāṇini Office.

NEMESHEGYI, PETER. 1960. The problem of transposing the Judeo-Christian idea of God into Greek and Oriental terms. Proceedings of the IX International Congress for History of Religions, 161—71. Tokyo: Maruzen.

NEWTON, J. 1867. Rāmaparīkṣā. Ludhiana: n. pub.

NICHOLLS, GEORGE. 1907. Sketch of the rise and progress of the Benares Patshalla or Sanskrit College, now forming the Sanskrit department of the Benares College. Allahabad: Government Press. (1st pub. 1848.)

OBERHAMMER, GERHARD. 1966. Die Begegnung Indiens mit dem Christentum. Kairos 1.33—44.

O'CONNELL, JOSEPH. 1973. The word 'Hindu' in Gauḍīya Vaiṣṇava texts. JAOS 93.340—44.

O.FLAHERTY, WENDY DONINGER. 1971. The origin of heresy in Hindu mythology. History of Religions 10.271—333.

— (ed. and trans.) 1975. Hindu myths. A sourcebook translated from the Sanskrit. Harmondsworth: Penguin Books, Ltd.

— 1976. The origins of evil in Hindu mythology. (Hermeneutics: Studies in the History of Religions, 6.) Berkeley and Los Angeles: University of California Press.

OLIVELLE, PATRICK. 1978. Ritual suicide and the rite of renunciation. WZKS 22.19—44.

PALEY, WILLIAM. 1838. The works of William Paley, D.D. (new ed.) London: William Smith.

PĀṆḌEYA, RĀMĀTEJA (ed.) 1962. Śrīmadbhāgavatam, with the Sanskrit commentary of Śrīdhara. Benares: Paṇḍita Pustakālaya.

PARADKAR, BALWANT A. M. (ed.) 1969. The theology of Nehemiah Goreh. (Confessing the Faith in India Series, 3.) Bangalore: Christian Institute for the Study of Religion and Society.

PENNER, PETER. 1970. The James Thomason school in Northern India, 1822—1853. Ph.D. diss., McMaster University.

PENZER, N. M. (ed.) 1925. The ocean of story: being C. H. Tawney's translation of Somadeva's Kathā Sarit Sāgara, 4. London: Charles J. Sawyer, Ltd.

PHRA, KHANTIPALO. 1964. Tolerance: a study from Buddhist sources. London: Rider and Co.

Physical Errors of Hinduism. 1849. CR 11.397—444.

POŘIZKA, VINCENC. 1940. The Bhagavadgītā and the New Testament: some notes on the presumed parallelism. Archiv Orientální 11.210—41.

POTTS, ELI DANIEL. 1967. British Baptist missionaries in India, 1793—1837: the history of Serampore and its missionaries. London: Cambridge University Press.

POULLAIN, CHARLES. 1951. L'Hindouisme agressif. Doctor Communis 4.139—59.

POWELL, A. A. 1976. Maulānā Raḥmat Allāh Kairānawī and Muslim-Christian controversy in India in the mid-19th century. Journal of the Royal Asiatic Society, 42—63.

PRABHUPĀDA, SWAMI A. C. BHAKTIVEDANTA (trans.) 1975. Śrī Caitanyacaritāmṛta of Kṛṣṇadāsa Kavirāja Gosvāmī, 6. New York: Bhaktivedanta Book Trust.

Proceedings of the Asiatic Society. 1837. JASB 6.401—02, 616.

PUHAKKA, KAISA. 1976. The roots of religious tolerance in Hinduism and Buddhism. Temenos 12.50—61.

PULIGANDLA, R. 1971. Could there be an essential unity of religions? International Journal for Philosophy of Religion 2.14—27.

QUÉGUINER, MAURICE. 1956. Intolérance hindoue et tolérance indienne. Études 290.161—76.

RAGHAVAN, V. 1956. Modern Sanskrit writings. (Adyar Library Series, P. 31.) Adyar: Adyar Library and Research Center.

— 1957. Contemporary Indian literature. New Delhi: Sahitya Akademi.

RAJAMANICKAM, SAVARIMUTHU. 1972. The first oriental scholar. Tirunelveli: De Nobili Research Institute, St. Xavier's College.

RAJAN, H. N. 1972. Mankind through manvantaras — sixth manvantara. Hindu Vishva 8 (no. 4.) 29—31.

RAO, K. L. SESHAGIRI. 1969. Mahatma Gandhi and C. F. Andrews: a study in Hindu-Christian dialogue. Patiala: Punjab University Press.

— 1972. Hindu attitudes to other religious traditions. Japanese Religions 7.38—49.

RICHTER, JULIUS. 1902. Eine literarische Fehde wider das Christentum im Indien. Allgemeine Missions-Zeitschrift 29.343—48.

— 1908. A history of missions in India. (Sydney H. Moore, trans.) Edinburgh: Oliphant, Anderson and Ferrier.

ROCHER, LUDO. 1978. Hindu conceptions of law. The Hastings Law Journal 29.1283—1305.

ROY, RAMMOHUN. N. d. Remarks on the Proposed Version of Theological Terms. SPG ms., C.Ind.I 9(1)55.

ROY, S. N. 1965. Date of Viṣṇu-Purāṇa's chapters on Māyāmoha-legend. Purāṇa 7.276—87.

RUBEN, WALTER. 1966. Bible and Purāṇa. Indian Studies: Past and Present 7.137—51, 337—48.

SAINT-HILAIRE, BARTHÉLEMY. 1864. De l'Etat actuel de la philosophie Hindoue dans ses rapports avec le Christianisme. Journal des Savants 49.173—88.

SALDANHA, JOSEPH L. (ed.) 1907. The Christian Puranna of Father Thomas Stephens. Mangalore: Simon Alvarez.

SANYAL, J. M. (trans.) 1970. The Srimad-Bhagavatam of Krishna-Dwaipayana Vyasa, 2. New Delhi: Munshiram Manoharlal.

SARADANANDA (Swami). 1953. Sri Ramakrishna the great master. (Swami Jagadananda, trans.) Madras: Sri Ramkrishna Math.
SARASVATĪ, DAYĀNANDA. 1970. Light of truth (Durga Prasad, trans.) (reprint of 2nd ed.) New Delhi: Jan Gyan Prakashan. (1st pub. 1875; 1st pub. of 2nd ed. 1882.)
ŚĀSTRĪ, HṚṢĪKEŚA (ed.) 1886—1891. Vṛhannāradīyapurāṇa. (BI, 107). Calcutta: The Asiatic Society.
Satyadharmaniścayārthapatra: letters discussing the evidences of the Christian and Hindu religions. 1850. Callcutta: Calcutta Christian Tract and Book Society.
SAVARKAR, VINAYAK DAMODAR. 1942. Hindutva. Poona: V. G. Ketkar (1st pub. 1923.)
SAVERIMUTTU, NICHOLAPILLAI MARIA. 1978. Relations between Roman Catholics and Hindus in Jaffna, Ceylon, 1900—1926: a study of religious encounter. Ph.D. diss., University of London (School of Oriental and African Studies).
SEN GUPTA, KANTI PRASONNA. 1970. The results of the Christian missionary activities in Bengal (1793—1833). BPP 89.74—95.
SHARMA, ARVIND. 1978. Some misunderstandings of the Hindu approach to religious plurality. Religion 8.133—54.
— 1979. All religions are — equal? one? true? same?: a critical examination of some formulations of the neo-Hindu position. PEW 29.59—72.
SHARMA, B. N. 1970. Religious tolerance and intolerance as reflected in Indian sculptures. Umesha Mishra Commemoration Volume, 657—68. Allahabad: Ganganatha Jha Research Institute.
— 1971. Purāṇic message of religious tolerance and its limitations. Purāṇa 13.4—25.
SHARPE, ERIC. 1965. Not to destroy but to fulfill: the contribution of J. N. Farquhar to Protestant missionary thought in India before 1914. (Studia Missionalia Upsaliensia, 5.) Uppsala: Almqvist and Wiksell.
— 1977. Faith meets faith: some Christian attitudes to Hinduism in the nineteenth and twentieth centuries. London: SCM Press Ltd.
SHASTRI, HARI PRASAD (trans.) 1959. The Ramayana of Valmiki, 3. London: Shanti Sadan.
SHASTRI, DHARMENDRA NATH. 1964. Critique of Indian realism: a study of the conflict between the Nyāya-Vaiśeṣika and the Buddhist Dignāga school. Agra: Agra University.
SHASTRI, SURENDRANATH (ed.) 1963. Viśvaguṇādarśacampū of Śrī Veṅkaṭādhvarī. Vidyabhawan Sanskrit Granthamala, 98. Benares: Chowkhamba Vidya Bhawan.
SHERRING, M. A. 1879. The missionary life and labors of the Rev. William Smith. Benares: Medical Hall Press.
SIAUVE, SUZANNE. 1968. La Doctrine de Madhva. Pondichéry: Institut français d'Indologie.
SINGH, IQBAL. 1958. Rammohun Roy, 1. London.
SIRCAR, D. C. 1971. Studies in the religious life of ancient and medieval India. Delhi: Motilal Banarsidass.
SLEEMAN, W. H. 1844. Rambles and recollections of an Indian official, 2. London: Hatchard and Son.
SMITH, DONALD EUGENE. 1963. India as a secular state. Princeton: Princeton University Press.
— (ed.) 1966. South Asian politics and religion. Princeton: Princeton University Press.
SMITH, GEORGE. 1878. The life of John Wilson, D. D., F. R. S. London: John Murray.
SMITH, WILLIAM. 1847. CMS ms., 0.265. Report of the Reverend William Smith, March to Oct., Allahabad.
— 1848. Sat-mat-nirūpaṇa: an inquiry into the true religion. Allahabad: Presbyterian Mission Press.
— 1850a. Dwij: the conversion of a brahman to the faith of Christ. London: James Nisbet and Co.

— 1850b. Din i haqq ki tahqiq: an investigation of the true religion. (2nd ed.) Calcutta: Church Missionary Society.

SOMANATHA [Subājī Bapu]. 1839 Mataparīkṣāśikṣā. IOLR ms. 5992.

SPEAR, PERCIVAL. 1970. The early days of Bishop's College, Calcutta. BPP 89: 177—88.

SRINIVASAN, THOMAS. 1936. Missionaries of the Carnatic. New Review (Calcutta) 4.127—39.

STAAL, JOHAN F. 1959. Über die Idee der Toleranz im Hinduismus. Kairos 1.215—18.

STAFFNER, HANS. 1953. Antireligiöse und antichristliche Tendenzen in Indien. Christen und Antichristen, ed. Laurenz Kilger, 69—81. Münster: Jesu-Missionshaus.

STARK, A. L. 1974. Sri Ramakrishna's approach to the dilemma of religious plurality. Ph.D. diss., Boston University.

STERNBACH, LUDWIK. 1971. Similar thoughts in the Mahābhārata, the literature of "greater India" and in the Christian gospels. JAOS 91.438—42.

STOCK, EUGENE. 1899. History of the Church Missionary Society. London: Church Missionary Society.

STREIKER, LOWELL D. 1966—67. The Hindu attitude toward other religions. Journal of Religious Thought 23.75—90.

Subodhasaṃskṛtaślokāḥ saṭīkāḥ. 1868. Calcutta: Calcutta Christian Tract and Book Society.

SUBRAMANIAN, N. 1965. The Hindu tripod: an essay on Hinduism and Western values. Madras: Institute of Traditional Cultures.

Suggestion to translators on the mode of expressing the term "trinity". 1837. CCO 6.458—60.

SUKTHANKAR, VISHNU S., S. K. BELVALKAR, et. al. (eds.) 1927—59. The Mahābhārata. 19 vols. Poona: Bhandarkar Oriental Research Institute.

SUNDARARAJAN, K. R. 1979. The Hindu understanding of the Christian doctrine of trinity. Insight 3.34—47.

SURYANARYANA SASTRI, S. S. (ed. and trans.) 1973. The Sāṃkhyakārikā of Īśvara Kṛṣṇa. (Madras University Philosophical Series, 3.) (2nd rev. ed.) Madras: University of Madras.

TARKAPAÑCĀNANA, HARACANDRA. 1840. Mataparīkṣottaram: or an answer to a sketch of the argument for Christianity and against Hinduism. Calcutta: Sumachurn Chundrica.

THIBAUT, GEORGE (trans.) 1890. The Vedānta Sūtras of Bādarāyana with the commentary of Śaṅkara, 1. (SBE, 34.) Oxford: Clarendon Press.

— (trans.) 1896. The Vedānta Sūtras of Bādarāyana with the commentary by Śaṅkara, 2. (SBE, 38.) Oxford: Clarendon Press.

THITE, GANESH. 1976. A note on Pāñcarātra and heresy. Purāṇa. 18.84—87.

TILIANDER, BROR. 1974. Christian and Hindu terminology: a study in their mutual relations with special reference to the Tamil area. Uppsala: Almqvist and Wiksell.

Tribute of the pandits to the Rev. W. H. Mill, D. D. 1837. JASB 6.710—11.

TRIPATHI, RAMA SHANKAR. 1939. Religious toleration under the imperial Guptas. Indian Historical Quarterly 15.1—12.

UPADHYE, A. N. 1942. Hariṣeṇa's Dharmaparīkṣā in Apabhraṃśa. ABORI 23.592—608.

— (ed.) 1970. Uddyotana-Sūri's Kuvalayamālā, 2, Ratnaprabha-Sūri's Kuvalayamālā Kathā. (SJS, 46.) Bombay: Bharatiya Vidyā Bhavan.

VAN BUITENEN, J. A. B. 1973. The Mahābhārata, 1, The book of the beginning. Chicago: University of Chicago Press.

— 1975. The Mahābhārata, 2, The book of the assembly hall; 3, The book of the forest. Chicago: University of Chicago Press.

— 1978. The Mahābhārata, 4, The book of Virāṭa; 5, The book of the effort. Chicago: University of Chicago Press.

VARADACHARYA, K. S. (ed.) 1969. Nyāya-Mañjarī of Jayantabhatta with tippaṇi-nyāyasaurabha by the editor. (Oriental Research Institute Series, 116.) Mysore: Oriental Research Institute.

VĀSU, CANDRANĀTHA. 1892. Hindutva. Calcutta: Vālmīki Press.

VENKATARAMANIAH, N. 1924. Religious persecutions in mediaeval south India. Madras Christian College Magazine (quarterly series) 4.42—49.

VIDYĀLAṄKĀRA, MṚTYUÑJAYA. 1817. The Vedānta Chandrikā: an apology for the present system of Hindu worship. Calcutta: Government Gazette Press.

WEBER, ALBRECHT. 1850. Madhusūdana-Sarasvatī's encyclopädische Uebersicht der orthodoxen brahmanischen Literatur. Indische Studien 1.1—24.

— 1859. Über die Vajrasūchī (Demantnadel) des Açvaghosha. Abhandlungen der Königlichen Akademie der Wissenschaften zu Berlin, Philologisch-historische Klasse, 203—64.

WEITBRECHT, J. J. (Mrs.) 1858. Missionary sketches in north India. London: James Nisbet and Co.

WEZLER, ALBRECHT. 1976. Zur Proklamation religiös-weltanschaulicher Toleranz bei dem indischen Philosophen Jayantabhaṭṭa. Saeculum 27.329—47.

WHATELY, RICHARD. 1822. The use and abuse of party feeling in matters of religion. (Bampton Lectures, 1822.) Oxford: Clarendon Press.

WICKI, JOSEF. 1955. Die ältere katholische Mission in der Begegnung mit Indien. Saeculum 6.345—67.

WILKINSON, LANCELOT. 1834. On the use of the siddhāntas in the work of native education. JASB 3.504—19.

— (ed.) 1839. The Wujra Soochi: or refulation [sic] of the arguments upon which the brahmanical institution of caste is founded. Also the Tunku by Soobajee Bapoo, being a reply to the Wujra Soochi. N. p. (Reviewed in CCO, 1840, 9.161—68; CI, 1842, 12.28—33.)

— 1841. Introduction to an essay on the second marriages of widows, by a learned brahman of Nagpore. N. p.

WILLIAMS, ROWLAND. 1856. Paramēswara-jnyāna-gōshthī: a dialogue of the knowledge of the supreme lord, in which are compared the claims of Christianity and Hinduism. Cambridge: Deighton, Bell and Co.

WILSON, HORACE HAYMAN. 1840. The Vishnu Purāna, a system of Hindu mythology and tradition. London: Oriental Translation Fund.

— 1976. Essays and lectures on the religions of the Hindus, ed. Reinhold Rost. New Delhi: Asian Publication Services. (1st pub. in AR, 1828, 16.1—136 and 1832, 17.169—314.)

WILSON, JOHN. 1830. Translation of a Murat, hee [sic] tract. OCS 1.359—64.

— 1830—31. On the Sunskrit and Murat, hee [sic] renderings of theological terms. OCS 1.356—58, 2.50—55.

— 1831. On the Sanscrit renderings of scripture terms. OCS 2.318—20.

— 1832. An exposure of the Hindu religion: in reply to Mora Bhatta Dandekara, to which is prefixed a translation of the Bhatta's tract. Bombay: American Press. (1832 lithographed Marathi edition, Hindudharma prasiddhīkaraṇa.)

— 1834. A second exposure of the Hindu religion: in reply to Narāyana Rao of Satārā, including strictures on the Vedanta. Bombay: American Press. (1835 Marathi edition, Dusreṃ hindudharmaprasiddhīkaraṇa.)

WINDISCH, ERNST. 1917—20. Geschichte der Sanskrit-philologie und indischen Altertumskunde. Grundriss der indo-arischen Philologie und Altertumskunde, 1, 1B, 1—22. Strassburg: K. J. Trübner.

WINTERNITZ, MAURICE. 1967. History of Indian literature, 3, 2, Scientific literature. (Subhadra Jhā, trans.) Delhi: Motilal Banarsidass.

— 1972. A history of Indian literature, 1 and 2. (Trans. by S. Ketkar and rev. by the author.) New Delhi: Oriental Books Reprint Corp. (1st pub. 1927, 1933.)

WOODROFFE, SIR JOHN (trans.) 1971. The great liberation (Mahānirvāṇa Tantra). (5th ed.) Madras: Ganesh and Co., (Madras) Private Ltd.

WYLIE, MACLEOD (Mrs.) 1854. Contributions towards a history of biblical translations in India. Calcutta: Auxilliary Bible Society.

YANDELL, KEITH E. 1976. On the alleged unity of all religions. Christian Scholars Review 6.140—55.

YATES, WILLIAM and JOHN WENGER (trans.) 1962. Dharmapustakasya śeṣāṃśaḥ. Bangalore: Bible Society of India and Ceylon (1st pub. 1840—52.)

YOUNG, RICHARD F. 1979. Church Sanskrit: an approach of Christian scholars to Hinduism in the nineteenth century. WZKS 23.205—31.

ZAEHNER, ROBERT C. (trans.) 1969. The Bhagavad-Gītā. London: Oxford University Press.

ZEITLER, E. 1965. Der Papstbesuch in Indien — interpretiert von Hindu-Extremisten. ZMR 49.115—20.

ZIEGENBALG, BARTHOLOMAEUS. 1719. Thirty four conferences between the Danish missionaries and the Malabarian bramans (or heathen priests) in the East Indies, concerning the truth of the Christian religion: together with some letters written by the heathens to the said missionaries. (Jenkin Thomas Philipps, trans.) London: n. pub.

ZIMMER, HEINRICH. 1951. Philosophies of India. (Joseph Campbell, ed.) (Bollingen Series, 26.) New York: Pantheon Books.

WORD INDEX

(Sanskrit translations of, or equivalents to Christian terminology)

GENERAL INDEX